D1465807

THE LEGEND OF HEREWARD

It is the reign of William the Conqueror, a king determined to hold on to his rich new kingdom with an iron fist. It is not long before his greedy eyes stray to wealthy religious buildings in his land, but the Abbey of Ely, almost hidden in the flooded mysterious Fens, finds itself an unlikely champion in the brave but unpredictable Hereward. Yet who was this Hereward whose resistance to the Norman invaders soon leads to murder, deceit, robbery, rebellion and finally open war?

THE LEGEND OF HEREWARD

THE LEGEND OF HEREWARD

by

Mike Ripley

Magna Large Print Books
Long Preston, North Yorkshire,
BD23 4ND, England.

British Library Cataloguing in Publication Data.

Ripley, Mike
    The legend of Hereward.

    A catalogue record of this book is
    available from the British Library

    ISBN   978-0-7505-3821-3

First published in Great Britain in 2007 by
Severn House Publishers Ltd.

Copyright © 2007 by Mike Ripley

Cover illustration © Collaboration JS by arrangement with
Arcangel Images

The moral right of the author has been asserted

Published in Large Print 2013 by arrangement with
Mike Ripley

Magna Large Print is an imprint of Library Magna Books Ltd.

Printed and bound in Great Britain by
T.J. (International) Ltd., Cornwall, PL28 8RW

Except where actual historical events and characters are being described for the storyline of this novel, all situations in this publication are fictitious and any resemblance to living persons is purely coincidental.

In fond memory of
ELIZABETH WALTER
1927–2006

Historical Note

At the height of Hereward's activities, the King of England was William I (also known as the Conqueror or the Bastard) following the Norman invasion of 1066. Thomas of Ely would have been writing during the reign of Henry I [1100–1135]. Gerald of Wales, a century later, had been a notable churchman, scholar and traveller, under kings Henry II [1154–1189], Richard I (the Lionheart) [1189–1199] and (Prince) John [1199–1216].

Gerald of Wales (Giraldus Cambrensis) really did exist and was the author of twelfth-century bestsellers such as *The Journey through Wales* and *The Topography of Ireland*. He died in obscurity, possibly in Lincoln, around 1223.

Hereward also existed, though whether he was ever called 'the Wake' by his contemporaries is unlikely. The famous novel, *Hereward the Wake, the Last of the English,* was written by Charles Kingsley in 1866, though the author is far better known for *The Water Babies*. The best modern accounts are without doubt *Hereward: The Last Englishman* and *The English Resistance: The Underground War Against the Normans* both by Peter Rex and published by Tempus in 2005 and 2004 respectively. I am also indebted to the magisterial translation of the *Liber Eliensis* by

Janet Fairweather (Boydell Press, 2005).

I was taught about Hereward the Wake many years ago at primary school. It struck me then that this was far too interesting and exciting a slice of history to be left to proper historians.

MR
East Anglia, 2006.

Geographical Note

In the eleventh century, the Isle of Ely (the 'isle of eels') really was an island, said to be seven miles long and four wide. It was accessible from the sea via Wisbech ('capital of the Fens') and the Wash, but otherwise protected by the flooded wetlands and marshes which made up the Fens, sadly little of which survives today. Ely itself was the most important settlement on the isle, and though its famous and staggeringly beautiful cathedral dates officially from 1109, its natural defences had already made it the ideal refuge for monks and outlaws alike for 400 years.

ENGLAND

90 MILES

Danish Raids
1069-1070 AD

Lincoln

Bourne Wisbech
Peterborough Lynne
Ely

Cambridge

Scaldermariland

FRIESIA

Ipswich

THE FENS

LONDON

Guines
Calais
St Omer

FLANDERS

St Valery

Rouen
Jumieges
Caen

NORMANDY

THE FENS

Lynne

Ouse Magna

"The Wellstream"

Littleport

Little Ouse

Bromdun

Grunty Fen

Ely

Witchford

Stuntney

Theoford

Aldreth

Soegham

R. Ouse

Burwell

Reach

Cottenham

R. Cam

Cambridge

One

Giraldus

Lincoln, 1205 AD

This is not fit work for a man who should be the Archbishop of Wales.

This is not – may God pardon my vanity – fit work for one who has studied law, philosophy and theology in Paris (albeit in Paris); for one who was an archdeacon by the age of twenty-nine, one who has tutored princes and served kings. For one whose mother was the daughter of a king, or at least a king's mistress.

This is hardly fit work for the most humble of copyists, let alone one who has written seventeen books, and therefore cannot be humble, which scholars and even bishops have favourably reviewed for their elegance of style and copies of which have been sold by almost the dozen.

And yet, here am I, such a man entering, by the grace of God, his sixty-first year and forced into retirement in this draughty cell in Lincoln where the wind cuts from the east like a knife and it is said that the mortal sin of suicide is more common than the sin of bestiality in my native Wales, if such a thing can be countenanced. Only on Judgement Day will the blessed Saint Peter know if this is true.

19

I am Giraldus Cambrensis, or Gerald of Wales, for although three-quarters of my blood is Norman, I am most proud of the one quarter which is Welsh.

I have been commissioned to write, which is what I do and do well, but now I write neither history nor philosophy, nor the topography of an unknown land (the writing I am most famous for).

I write a family tree.

Even worse, I am expected to lie about it, which is shameful. I am also expected to steal from the work of a brother in Christ, one Thomas of Ely, of blessed memory.

However inferior the work to be plundered, that, to the true scholar, is surely sinful, but by God's good grace, Brother Thomas's book is a little known work. It is possible that the first eyes to examine its pages since it was confined to the priory scriptorium are mine.

I have searched in vain to find even a poor copy of *The True History of Hereward the Outlaw* by Thomas of Ely in any other church or convent library. It is even unknown here in the cathedral library at Lincoln, which takes much pride (too much, perhaps) in its collection of books and rolls.

But while the book may be unknown, its subject is anything but forgotten.

Alewives, fishwives, travelling players, every villain, cottar and serf, every orphan, all know the story of Hereward, the last Saxon nobleman to defy the Normans. The ballads and songs abound, not just here in Lincoln and in the Fenlands to the east, but throughout all England. They tell of how the noble Hereward, returning from the wars

20

(though which war is never specified) found his manor house and his lands around the parish of Bourne sequestered by Norman overlords following the victory of King William at Hastings. Of how Hereward disputed with the new owners of Bourne to the point of violent rebellion and how Hereward was declared to be *silvaticus* – banished to the woods, or outlawed, and how he gathered followers around him and defied even King William himself in the watery island fortress that he made of the Isle of Ely.

From that siege come all the famous stories of Hereward as a leader of men, who resisted for many months the best stratagems of the Normans, which included the use of witches and female sorcerers to throw spells and curses down upon the defenders of Ely.

Such is the stuff of drunken tavern talk and tales told around the fires and hearths on long winter nights. It is the base metal from which I must forge my history and were it not for the book of Brother Thomas, it would be my only source.

But Brother Thomas did write his book, though to what purpose I do not know. Thomas was a monk of some small learning, which can be seen from the style of his prose even in Old English, but his book must be taken seriously as he could have talked with men who lived when Hereward did and may even have claimed kinship with the great hero. Thomas, as a churchman, may even have spoken with Hereward's own parish priest and confessor.

Still, my task is not merely to write a recension of Thomas's history of Hereward, although I am no stranger to the art of recension – revising and expanding a manuscript. My own, much-praised book *The Topography of Ireland* has gone through four recensions by my hand and today exists at more than double the length it was when first dedicated to his Excellency Henry the Second, invincible King of the English, Duke of Normandy, Count of Anjou and Aquitaine, and his beloved son John, then Prince but now King, if only of the English.

No, my task is far more delicate.

I must take the history recorded by Thomas of Ely and mould it into a correctness politically and diplomatically acceptable not only to the Bishop (God preserve!) who provides my living here at Lincoln, but also to the Lords of the estates of Bourne, for they are now a family of some importance as well as great wealth, here in Lincolnshire. It need not be recorded here that their generosity to the Church knows few bounds.

The new Lord of Bourne, and my benefactor, is the noble Baldwin, whose grandfather on his mother's side was Baldwin Fitzgilbert, the founder of the small priory there, which is the only reason why anyone in this world or the next will remember the name of Bourne.

Fitzgilbert is, however, a name already enshrined within the ranks of nobility, for Baldwin Fitzgilbert, as his name imparts, can trace a noble Norman ancestry which includes his great uncle Richard, the Abbot of Ely and Count Gilbert of Brionne, whose own father Godfrey was tutor to none other than William Duke of Normandy, the conqueror himself, and (it is rumoured) his illegitimate half-brother.

With such a lineage, the good Norman name of Fitzgilbert should, in all humility, be good enough for this new Baldwin, whose inheritance has been nurtured and protected by the noble Norman knights who brought order and a strong Church to this land.

But no; for this Baldwin, although a Fitzgilbert on his mother Emma's side, has chosen instead to name himself after his father, one Hugh Wac, a knight and gentleman-at-arms of no significant lineage or particular fame, save for the fact that he married Emma Fitzgilbert and sired young Baldwin.

Thus the new Lord of Bourne, rejecting his Norman heritage, chooses to style himself Baldwin Wac, or Wake, favouring an uncertain and unrecorded English lineage above a true and noble Norman one.

Such is the folly of youth spurred on by fashion.

In the time of the second King Henry, who spoke Latin and French but not a word of English, the spurning of a good Norman name for a quaint but unrecognizable English one, would have been unthinkable. Some may even have called it treason.

Good King Henry, though, has been with God these past sixteen years and times, and fashions, have changed. England has been ruled by Richard, generally regarded (where men keep private council) to have been a bad king but, fortunately, an absent one. And now we have King John, whom I served loyally enough as Prince, but who is proving a great disappointment to right-thinking

23

men who mutter (increasingly not in private) that he is a king not absent enough.

Small wonder then that the heroes of popular ballads and the sagas declaimed by travelling players (at the slightest suggestion of a mug of free ale), concern those who would defy royal authority and ignore their duty to it these days. Most popular of all, for the uneducated, are the tales seeping down, like poison in a wound, from the north, in particular Nottingham and Yorkshire, a land which if God has not abandoned, then He surely ignores. From there come fantastical tales of outlaws and rogues who have taken to wearing woodsman's hoods on their jackets and travelling in gangs. Even if not legally outlawed, they live by robbing innocent travellers passing through the dark forests over which they claim lordship with impunity and by some mystery the common people think of them as heroes.

Such a fashion is not new in folklore and ballad, and it is a foolish nobleman who fails to recognize the potency of cheap ballads. But now even the nobility appear to be caught up in the fashion.

If fashion follows events, then none other than King John himself is to blame. Within the last year, this once proud Norman prince has become a king without lands in Normandy! Defeated at arms by the smaller and almost insignificant Kingdom of France, John has been forced to abandon his dukedom, land and other titles which have been the basis of Norman power for two hundred years.

Norman barons, whose ancestors came over with William, now have to choose whether to be

English or whether to be Norman, which is to say French. Brothers have divided family estates, one taking the lands in England, the other preferring to pay homage and taxes to the French king. It is usually the younger sibling who retains custody of the family seat back in Normandy for, as in the time of William and his great book of reckoning called Domesday, England is still a far richer land than Normandy. Why else would William the Bastard have come here in the first place?

So new loyalties must be sworn, to France (and Normandy) or to England, where the royal household speaks nothing but French, but does not mention the war which lost them Normandy.

With a pledge for England has come a fondness for all things English rather than Norman and to be truthful, things Norman and Normans themselves are regarded as foreign and foreigners. The Normans who came to these islands as invading foreigners have now turned their backs on the land which bore them and those families which have intermarried with the old Saxon lineages (if proved) find themselves much in favour.

Such noble Saxon lines as are left are those where the blood flows thin indeed and always on the female side for it is uncontested by historians that when William defeated Harold Godwinson, sometimes known as Harold the Usurper or Harold Break-Word, on the hill near Hastings, he killed not only the last English king, but all the English nobility almost at a stroke.

And so it is that our current nobility often scramble in vain to find a forgotten Saxon in their family trees though of course they do not do the searching themselves. All over this land an army of scholars, clerks and lawyers are employed searching parish records and the court rolls and scribes and humble writers such as myself can command decent fees for once, if they understand the Old English of the Saxon chronicles, though in truth, few can.

Indeed, I am one of the last generation of churchmen to be taught to read and write in Old English – taught in my youth by the Benedictines at Gloucester – but taught what is now a lost art. Since the year of Our Lord 1154, when good King Henry II ascended the throne, no church, monastery or court has recorded matters in anything except Latin, and bad Latin at that. It is said the monks of Peterborough were the last chroniclers to write in English.

Fifty years on, all things English, that is to say Saxon, are highly prized and it seems that the more disreputable the provenance, the better. The street ballads proclaim that the outlaws who now wear hoods and roam the forests of the north robbing innocent people, all come from a Saxon nobility dispossessed and oppressed by the Normans. So it seems that not only must every noble have an English ancestor, but he must also be an outlaw!

Thus it is that my most noble benefactor Baldwin Wac, lord of the manor of Bourne, requires a family history which incorporates a suitably fashionable Saxon lineage and who better than that other famous resident of Bourne (the only other resident of Bourne known to anyone outside the parish boundary), the legendary Hereward, a

Saxon and an outlaw to boot. Even better, Hereward was the last, perhaps the only, Saxon to successfully resist William of Normandy, the Conqueror.

Or so the legend says.

I shall go through Brother Thomas's writings with great care to learn more of this hero.

Two

Thomas

Ely, 1107 AD

It is fitting that I, Thomas of Ely, should have been chosen by God and my abbot, to write down this tale so that the truth will be known in preference to the songs and tales of the balladeers and alewives.

It is fitting not because I have been blessed with any particular skill or talent but only that I was born and have lived my life here on the isle or island of Ely where much of this history took place and where there are still men alive who remember those days of fire and destruction almost two score years ago.

Such men have I talked with. Men who remember the coming of Guillame, Duke of Normandy, known as William but also called King of the English, the Conqueror and also, but only since his death, the Bastard.

And of how William, father to our noble King Henry, came to our watery fens with the pride of his knights to crush the last resistance to his rule and the man called Hereward, who was known as Hereward the Twice-Outlawed, but also Hereward the Hard Man, Hereward the Witch-killer, Hereward the Plunderer, Hereward the Berserker and Hereward the Firestarter.

Already legends and ballads abound about this Hereward.

But I will write the truth, however much it disappoints the fishwives and gossipmongers and minstrels.

Three

Giraldus

My dear brother Thomas, of blessed memory, has set me a problem from his very prologue. I now have many names for this Hereward, yet none are suitable, even if they are true.

Not suitable at all for a family history even in these times when the deeds of outlaws who have taken to the woods are praised in song.

My patron, Baldwin le Wac, may well be flattered to find he has a hooded man as an ancestor especially if I were to suggest he robbed only the rich and distributed alms to the poor, or some such fanciful flummery. And legend does indeed say that Hereward was declared Outlaw after his attempts to reclaim his lands at Bourne, by the Norman nobles the Conqueror had placed there.

But Brother Thomas refers to Hereward the Twice-Outlawed. Twice?

This is a tale I have not been told before now.

I will double my request for candles and continue to read Thomas's book through the night, for now I am curious.

Four

Thomas

Men say that Hereward is descended from Earl Leofric of Mercia, an important Saxon Lord or 'King's Thegn', who held lands in Bourne in Lincolnshire and was married to the Lady Godiva. But she herself is the subject of so many ballads and alehouse sagas in her own right that it seems unlikely that she could have been the mother of Hereward without the minstrels recording the fact in song.

In any case, Leofric was *thegn* to the old King Edward, called the Confessor, and his legitimate son and heir is well-known to have been Aelfgar, the Earl of East Anglia. Now Aelfgar was legally outlawed during the reign of the Confessor as was Hereward, and may explain the confusion. But where Aelfgar, son of Leofric, was outlawed for his loud and constant opposition to the influence of the Godwins – which many would say now was the act of a true hero – Hereward was outlawed for far less noble reasons. The truth is that Hereward is descended from a house of noble standing, but not that of Leofric.

The noble house in question is that of Toki, the lord of extensive lands and thirty or more churches in Lincolnshire and Nottingham, who also held claims to property around Bourne and Spalding. This is the same Toki who kept his hall in Lincoln and it was on the site of that very hall that the blessed Bishop Remigius oversaw the building of our beautiful cathedral.

Before the arrival of William of Normandy, Toki of Lincoln was a man of substance and influence, generous to both the Church and to the people who worked his lands. He had six sons, of which the two eldest and the youngest are known to history.

The eldest of Toki's children, was Brand, who was to become Abbot of Peterborough. Then came his brother Aschil, sometimes written Asketil and sometimes called Asketil Tokisson, and sixthly arrived Godric, a pious and devoted monk here in Ely. Of the intervening three brothers, little is known, but it is said that any one of the six could have been Hereward's father, although Brother Godric, God preserve, would have been an infant himself when Hereward was born.

Those who remember Hereward in his youth all attest that he was almost certainly born in the house of Aschil, in Bourne, Lincolnshire, and born to the wife of Aschil. Yet none can recall him referring to Aschil as his father, only as the lord to whom he owed service. Much fonder was he of

Abbot Brand, whom he called 'uncle' and to whom he would turn whenever his soul or person was in danger.

Whatever his parentage, Hereward the boy was brought up within Aschil's household as it moved around the family estates. He also spent many months in Toki's hall in Lincoln and what little education he received was at the hands of his uncle Brand and his fellow brothers at Peterborough. Suffice it to say that under the care of his grandfather, Hereward learned the shield, the sword, the axe, the bow and the spear. Under the tutelage of Brother Brand, he learned nothing of history or theology, but much of the strengths and weaknesses of Peterborough Abbey, something which would stand him in good stead in the future.

By the time the boy Hereward was twelve years old, he stood among the ranks of Toki's most trusted men-at-arms and had no less skill at the martial arts, or at least those traditionally practised by the English. Being a good judge of men, old Toki saw that Hereward's future lay most profitably in the field of arms as a *vir strenuus* – a hard man – and perhaps the old man had dreams of Hereward rising to the ranks of the King's House Carls, the royal bodyguard first raised by Canute. If he proved unsuited to royal service, there was always ample opportunity for a man to make a living as a mercenary, however short that life may be.

But warfare, as so much else, was changing in those days, and in Flanders and France and Normandy no army was complete without squadrons

31

of armoured cavalry, although the English were the last fighting men to realize this and only discovered the error of their ways when it was too late to save their country. Hereward's grandfather saw this, though, and insisted that Hereward take a squire who could teach him all there was to know about horses and horsemanship.

The squire Toki appointed was a foundling from one of the villages in the wet and mysterious Fenlands near the Isle of Ely who had been baptized with the name Martin but was known as Lightfoot from his speed as a runner. As a child he had lived in Toki's hall and acted as a messenger but was soon noticed for his skill at befriending horses, sometimes befriending them away from their lawful owners.

Hereward and Martin Lightfoot were to become inseparable, to the despair of all who encountered them, for everything Martin taught Hereward about horses, Hereward repaid by sharing his already extensive knowledge of wine, ale and games of chance.

No village fayre, no market, no alehouse and few churches were safe from this roistering pair when they were with drink taken, which was often. As youths under the protection of Toki's name, such behaviour went unpunished but not unnoticed and Toki, who was wise even in his grey years, sent both boys to live in one of his son Aschil's houses in Bourne, more than thirty miles from Lincoln on the edge of Deeping Fen.

Now the tenure and holdings of Bourne, a village of some wealth thanks to wool and weaving, had long been claimed by Toki's family despite the estates being in the gift of Peterborough Abbey in law, custom and memory. The dispute had been the subject of court hearings for some ten years without any indication that Toki's claims would ever be upheld, yet this did not prevent the twelve-year-old Hereward from boasting to any who would listen that the manor of Bourne was his by right of family and that he would, one day, be Lord of Bourne and that day would be the day his 'uncle' Brand became the Abbot of Peterborough.

In the Year of Christ 1067, Brand was indeed elected Abbot of Peterborough but it was by then too late to save the Lordship of Bourne for anyone but a Norman. It was too late to save England and as for Hereward, even at that young age, it was too late to save anything of Hereward.

Not even his soul.

Five

Giraldus

I take back all I have said about Brother Thomas's style. The man has a gift for story-telling. Admittedly, a small gift, but there is a spark there.

If his account is to be believed, then Hereward is not the 'Saxon' hero of song and ballad, but clearly of Danish stock.

That should not surprise me, for in the days of the Conqueror, England was a land not of two peoples, but of three: Saxons, Normans and

Danes, descended from the Viking pirates of old who had settled and farmed here rather than raped or pillaged. Or rather settled on stolen farm land here after they had raped and pillaged, some having settled here as far back as in the days of King Alfred, and later suffering themselves from the raids of their Viking kin from Norway.

And certainly the existence of Toki and his hall here in Lincoln is beyond doubt. Records in this very library prove the fact that our blessed cathedral was built on the site of the hall of a Danish lord, just as the burghers of the city have recorded that no fewer than 166 houses were demolished to make way for the building of King William's castle here.

Even when men forget their Danish and Viking forebears, the value of lost or stolen property stays long in their minds.

So Brother Thomas has set the scene: a young hero skilled in arms, a faithful companion, a disputed birthright and a warning of lost souls.

And all this before the arrival of William and the Normans! Indeed, a legend in the making.

Six

Thomas

Hereward the Outlaw

On mid-summer's eve in the year 1063, just before noon, two young men, heavily armed, rode into Bourne looking for a fight. The instant the priest saw them he knew they were trouble, but only suspected he knew who they were.

The priest pulled at the bridle of the ageing nag he was leading so that the men could have the path into the village. The two riders fixed him with their eyes as they approached and he met their gaze unflinching. He did not know to be frightened of them. Yet.

They were of much the same age, the priest thought, perhaps eighteen, no more; but different in appearance. One was tall and thin, deathly pale of complexion with short black hair which was slick with grease; the other much shorter, a head shorter than the priest, and stout, but broad with muscle not fat. His hair was long and golden, falling over his shoulders. This one wore a sleeveless leather hauberk covered with flat iron rings and long leather trousers bound around the calves and feet with leather thongs dyed blood red. Both had short hunting bows and quivers of arrows slung across their backs and knives in their belts.

35

The golden-haired one carried a longsword in a wooden scabbard across his lap and the tall, thin one had a long handled axe hanging from his saddle, the edge of its blade embedded in a strip of softwood to protect the flanks of the horse.

The priest had seen such a trick before, among the reed-men and wildfowlers who plied their trade in the Fens in small, fragile boats often regarded as more valuable than horses and equally vulnerable to a sharp, misplaced blade.

When his old, broken-winded horse caught the scent of the men and their much younger, finer mounts, it whinnied softly and pawed the ground, though without much strength.

'Steady, old friend,' said the priest, touching the nag on its muzzle. 'Let them pass.'

But he knew that men like those could never pass by an unarmed man on foot, with an overloaded pack horse on a lonely road, especially one who did not drop his eyes to avoid their superior gaze.

'Ho there, priest!' shouted the golden-haired one with a smile. (The priest knew it always began with a smile.) 'What business do you have in Bourne today?'

'I have no business, only God's and that of Abbot Leofric, and their business in Bourne is concluded,' answered the priest firmly.

The riders pulled up their horses, blocking the track way, their muzzles so close that the priest could feel their breath, but they made no move to dismount.

'Then we are both men of Peterborough,' said the swordsman, still smiling. 'For I have pledged my fealty to Abbot Leofric and the brothers there, so you could say that I am about the Abbot's business too. Did you visit with the Lord of Bourne whilst you were there, priest?'

'I stayed in the hall of Asketil Tokisson, true enough, but the lord is absent, believed to be touring his estates in Northamptonshire,' the priest answered, noticing now that there was something wrong with Golden Hair's eyes.

'Then you were well looked after by the lady of the manor?'

'I was not.'

The smile slid away from the young rider's face.

'Was the Lady Aedina not present?'

The priest planted his feet firmly apart, as if bracing himself for a blow.

'The body of Aedina is still in Bourne, but her spirit is with God.'

'My mother is dead?'

The horseman shouted his question to the sky but it was the priest on earth who had to answer.

'She was taken two weeks ago, suddenly and without pain. Her last act was to send word to the Abbey of Peterborough.'

'Does her husband know?'

'Word will not yet have reached Lord Asketil,' said the priest, thinking it was a question he had not expected.

The golden-haired youth turned in his saddle to face his companion.

'The hall is ours!' he shouted joyously.

As the riders spurred their horses, the priest caught sight of a broad smile splitting that oval-shaped face and a flash in those peculiar eyes and then men and horses were flying down the track.

The priest was left listening to the drumming of hooves and breathing the dust from the summer-dry path.

'Hereward...' he said; though if it was a warning, there was no one to heed it but himself.

They caught up with the priest in the dead of night. Not even his horse heard them coming.

The first he knew of their presence in his make-shift camp was the sound of more wood being piled upon the fire he had lit, more for companionship than for warmth in the mild summer night. The priest struggled awake and he felt the heat as the dry sticks caught and the fire crackled, flames shooting into the night sky, turning the surrounding trees into weaving, dancing shadows of themselves.

'Only a man at ease with his God can sleep so soundly,' said a voice.

'Or a man about to meet with his God,' came another.

The warrior with the long golden hair had spoken first. He was crouched on his haunches a few feet from the priest, as if he had been studying him while he slept. Across his knees he had balanced the long sword in its wooden sheath. His taller, spindlier companion was moving around the fire, loading it with more wood and dry bracken, the flames licking higher into the night.

'The fire is not your friend, priest. We saw it a mile away. Without it we might not have found you.'

'I was not hiding,' said the priest, finding his

voice, 'but neither was I expecting to be sought out by Hereward of Bourne.'

'So you know who I am?'

'The Lady Aedina spoke of you.'

As indeed she had in previous months, bemoaning the fate of her wayward son and what she claimed was his relationship with his squire, the foundling Martin Lightfoot.

'Then you know I am Aedina's son, and the grandson of Toki of Lincoln, and their heir to the lordship of Bourne?'

The priest began to unwrap himself from the blanket which covered him as tight as a shroud.

'She said you were her son, Hereward, but any claims on the estates of Bourne are a matter for Abbot Leofric and the courts at Peterborough.'

'What is your name, priest?'

'Oswulf of Ely.'

For the first time, the priest felt fear on the back of his tongue as Hereward shuffled closer, still crouched on his haunches, like a crab circling its prey. Behind him, his companion stoked the flames of what was now a bonfire, spitting sparks into the still air.

'You are a Fen Man?' Hereward smiled sweetly.

'I was born a Fen Man, now I am a Man of God, going wherever I am needed,' replied the priest.

'Yes, yes, of course you are, but being from the Fens could explain why the priest is really a thief at heart.'

'I am no thief!'

Oswulf struggled clumsily to his feet but Hereward did not move, remaining crouched, not even bothering to turn his face upwards towards the priest as he spoke.

'Then what will my faithful squire find in the bags which weigh down your horse? Martin!'

His companion was already slitting the cords of the packhorse sacks where Oswulf had unloaded them to allow his ancient nag to sleep easier.

'There's coin here, and jewellery and plate, some silks and books – fucking books!'

Oswulf groaned inwardly. The serf known as Martin Lightfoot had no conception of the value of books among the monastic communities, who read everything and jealously hid their libraries, or the nobility, who read nothing but liked to show off their collections.

'Those were the goods of the Lady Aedina,' said Oswulf.

'So you admit to being a thief?' Hereward's voice was calm and soft, as if he was reasoning with the grass at his feet.

'I am no thief! It was the wish of Aedina that her worldly goods should pass to the Abbey at Peterborough on her death. I am merely carrying them to Abbot Leofric.'

Oswulf saw Hereward's golden mane move from side to side as he slowly shook his head and feared that a storm was building within the lad.

'Leofric ... Leofric.... Has not that bastard opposed my grandfather's rightful claim to the manor of Bourne these past ten years? What right does he have to also steal from my mother, a noble woman who owned property in her own right?'

'Lady Aedina made her penitence at Peterborough on Shrove Tuesday and left instructions concerning her property with Brother Brand ... your uncle, I believe?'

The priest knew he had said too much. Transfixed, he watched Hereward slowly straighten to his feet and in the light from the roaring fire could make out the muscles flex in his arms and see the sinews strain in his neck. Despite the warmth from the fire, Oswulf shivered as Hereward turned to him and smiled.

'Brother Brand is indeed my uncle. I am sworn to him as I am sworn to protect the abbey, its holy men and all its property. You say these goods from Bourne Manor are now the property of the abbey, therefore it is my obligation to protect them. Martin, get our horses.'

'What about the priest's nag?'

'Leave it. The priest can ride into Peterborough to give the abbey the news that its property is safe in the lands of the Lord of Bourne.'

'I cannot allow that,' said Oswulf, his mouth dry. Hereward laughed as he looked up into the face of the much taller man.

'*Cannot allow?* Who are you to allow me anything, priest?'

'Lord Hereward is his own man,' shouted Martin Lightfoot from the shadows and the trees.

'A man sworn to defend the Abbey of Peterborough,' retorted Oswulf bravely.

'The abbey and its monks, but not some thieving country priest sneaking through the night.'

Those eyes, thought Oswulf, there was something about those eyes.

'I am no thief! My business in Bourne was legal by the law of the land and the law of God.'

'This is my land by right and here I am the law!' Hereward screamed, so close into Oswulf's face that the priest could smell sour wine on his breath. 'As for God's law; I leave it to Brother Brand to plead my case there. For now, you are on my land, you have my mother's property and you are a thief.'

'You call me thief, you defy the Church. You cannot do that.'

'Do *not* tell me what I cannot do!'

The smaller man moved so quickly, the priest never saw the blows coming. Hereward struck with the scabbard of his sword, a scabbard made of hard box wood and hooped with iron rings, jabbing first into Oswulf's stomach and then swinging upwards, as if with a club, to take him in the throat.

The priest landed on his back on the ground, the breath driven from his body, so close to the fire that he could see the hairs on his arm singe, but then Hereward's foot was on his shoulder, pinning his right arm to the ground and he could hear the terrible sound of the sword being drawn.

'This is how we deal with thieves in the Manor of Bourne.'

In the firelight, the blade of the longsword flashed above his head and then Hereward struck downwards and severed the right hand of Oswulf the priest at the wrist, jumping backwards as he did to avoid the spray of blood.

Oswulf looked in horror at the bloody stump which was now his forearm and his last conscious act was to thrust that arm into the heart of the fire.

'I've said it before, Brother Brand, you should have been stricter with him when he was a boy.'

'He was always headstrong, Brother Abbot, and his grandfather believed that you should give a strong horse its head, not the whip.'

Abbot Leofric buried his face, and much of his beard, in a wide mug of ale. It was the last of the abbey's winter brews, a thick stock ale heavily flavoured with bog-myrtle, just the way he liked it, even in summer. The lay brothers would only taste it mixed with one of the weaker spring brews, which had suffered that year – again – from salty, sour water as the wells had been breached in the winter floods.

'His grandfather, Toki of Lincoln, was a Viking pirate! And it sounds as if this Hereward takes after him! He is supposed to be sworn as a man of the abbey, sworn to protect the abbey and its property, and yet he accuses one of our brethren of being a thief, judges him without trial and carries out the appropriate punishment as if he has a right to do so.'

'I would remind my Lord Abbot, that Toki of Lincoln has been a generous supporter of the church and this order,' said the monk called Brand.

'As well as the biggest money-lender in Lincoln and probably the biggest horse thief in the eastern wetlands, not to mention your father, Brand! Perhaps he should have been stricter with you when you were a child.'

Brother Brand bowed his head and remained standing as Abbot Leofric finished his morning ale, seated at the end of the long refectory table. The two were alone in the echoing stone room, which was pleasantly cool now summer was here, as the rest of Peterborough's monks tended the herb gardens, fish ponds, eel ponds and beehives or managed the extensive livestock of grazing cattle and sheep, or checked the thousands of reed traps in the outlying marshes for the daily, and bountiful, harvest of wild fowl.

It was not the first time the two men had discussed the problem of young Hereward, but they had always managed to skirt around the subject of Hereward's parentage. That he was born of the Lady Aedina in the manor house at Bourne was not in doubt, but few, including Hereward himself, recognized her husband Lord Asketil as the boy's father. In so many ways, except perhaps wisdom, the boy clearly reflected the features of Asketil's elder brother, the monk Brand, to whom the boy was truly and loyally devoted. But such kinship could not be recognized, not because of the illegitimacy (it was said that the rich and influential Toki of Lincoln had no idea who his father had been) or because of Brand's position within the abbey, for it was not uncommon for churchmen to have wives and children. The charge of incest, however, of lying with his sister-in-law, was not one which Brand could survive, and one which Abbot Leofric did not wish to have brought.

So Hereward had been raised in Toki's hall in Lincoln where he was taught all the skills of a man-at-arms and seemed destined to serve in Toki's household, protecting his grandfather's estates which spread north into Yorkshire and across the Humber river. But just as every freeman should have a lord, by custom and law, so every freeman can choose which lord to serve.

When Hereward chose to pledge his loyalty to the Abbey of Peterborough and swore to defend with his life the holy relic of St Oswald's arm, the abbey's most treasured possession, all knew that in truth he was swearing himself to Brother Brand. Yet Brand, for all his learning, could not control the wild spirits within Hereward, for whom loyalty did not mean obedience, and the monk had to call on every bond of kinship and church duty to keep the boy and his odious squire, Martin Lightfoot, as far away from Peterborough and Bourne as possible.

Old Toki had filled the boy's head with dreams of inheriting the lordship of Bourne and its estates one day, although Toki's claim to those lands had been disputed within the ecclesiastical courts for more than ten years. Brand knew that the abbey, whilst happy for Toki's family to lease the estates as tenants, would never agree to Toki's claims of ownership and he also knew that he was the most likely successor to Abbot Leofric and therefore could not be seen to intervene in the dispute.

So Hereward had been sent north to serve the Earls of Northumberland and then south and west into Wessex to offer his skills to the religious houses at Winchcombe and Westbury before finally lodging at Glastonbury itself, the richest abbey in England. His sojourn in any one hall or house was never very long. In Northumbria, the

45

Earl's favourite hunting dog, a huge white mastiff with fur as thick as a polar bear's, went missing. At Winchcombe there were mysterious fires which destroyed stables and barns and at Westbury, the custodian of the library there was nailed into a half-empty barrel of ale and rolled down a nearby hill for the amusement of the serfs working in the abbey's fields. At holy Glastonbury, the fourteen-year-old daughter of an Irish nobleman on pilgrimage there, was deflowered by a blond-haired boy claiming to be the son of the King of Cornwall. It was even whispered that this spurious royal son of Cornwall, where there are no kings, was aided in his assault on the maidenhead by his groom.

That he was, in name at least, the son of Asketil Tokisson probably saved Hereward from the attention of numerous shire-reeves as he and his unworthy companion Lightfoot journeyed back to Bourne that summer, although the pair tactfully avoided entering Asketil's lands until almost home in Lincolnshire.

'When we sent this young good-for-nothing away I thought we might have heard the last of him,' said Abbot Leofric, 'I prayed that he might acquire some learning, some charity and above all, some humility. But God has chosen not to bestow these favours on Hereward. Not a three-month has gone by without a report reaching me of mindless acts of lewdness, drunkenness, debauchery and arson; always arson. The boy is possessed with the urge to destroy with fire wherever he goes. I have received remonstrations not only from our brothers in Hampshire, but from Bishop

Ethelwine of Durham and even Archbishop Eald-red of York himself. It is only by God's grace that the madman has not killed anyone yet. Perhaps...' Leofric paused for thought, then drank more ale before continuing. 'Perhaps we should send him somewhere where he can.'

'My Lord Abbot is thinking of Flanders?' suggested Brand. 'The noble houses of Flanders are forever at war with each other and are constantly in need of men who have skill with the weapons of war and who fight out of love of money as well as loyalty.'

'Flanders is certainly a land of opportunity for a man of Hereward's talents,' mused Leofric, 'but Normandy would be good too. The Duke of Normandy, it is said, is building quite an army of hard men. Hereward would fit in well.'

'I will suggest it to him most strongly,' said Brand, fingering the cruciform hanging around his neck from a leather braid.

'We must do more than suggest, Brand,' snapped the abbot. 'Hereward cannot rob and maim a brother of this order with impunity.'

'With respect, Abbot, the incident on the road to Bourne involved only a country priest, a confessor, not a monk.'

Leofric took his beard in one hand and squeezed it, as though wringing out the ale he dribbled over it.

'He is still a brother in Christ, Brand. What was his name?'

'He is called Oswulf and he comes from the island of Ely.'

'Where is he now?'

'In the infirmary. He showed courage and quick thinking. If he had not used fire to seal his wound, he would have bled out by the time he arrived here. Our physicians say they can find no pus around the stump and he has no fever.'

'What are we to do with him?'

'It seems he has – had – some small skill at reading and writing and was being tutored, in the name of charity, by Abbot Thurston, that most pious of our brothers at Ely. This Oswulf's father was a sokeman, a paid farm labourer, of the Ely estate, so the family was known there.'

'Would Thurston be willing to take him in, crippled as he is?'

'Thurston is a good and kindly monk famed for his charity.'

'Thurston can afford it,' growled Leofric. 'Ely is almost as rich a house as Glastonbury, though it is true that Thurston himself is a man of few worldly pleasures. What of the goods at the heart of this dispute?'

'The Lady Aedina, whom God preserve, wanted her valuables deposited in the abbey after her death. (In the days before banks, valuables were regularly deposited within monasteries for safe keeping.) This she told me herself at her Shrove Tuesday penance. They were her personal property to dispose of as she pleased and she bequeathed her books to our library and the coin and jewels to be used in the glory of God and the veneration of St Oswald.'

'She left nothing to Hereward?'

'Nothing. She felt that Hereward's future was best served by a donation to God.'

48

'The woman showed wisdom,' said the abbot, then added slyly: 'In some things.'

Brother Brand shuffled uncomfortably.

'Hereward did not know of his mother's bequests – he had not seen her for two years – and it was by pure chance that he was returning to Bourne just as Oswulf was carrying out Aedina's last wishes.'

'But he did not stop to ask before he acted, did he? From what I am told, this man of Belial, this ne'er-do-well, did not even visit his mother's grave. When he and this Lightfoot creature found the manor empty, they pillaged the larder, drained the brewhouse and then sacked the house itself seeking Aedina's goods. When they discovered nothing, they set out to run down poor Oswulf.'

'Be assured that my sister-in-law's bequest is now safe in our treasury,' pleaded Brand. 'Hereward handed everything over once he realized the error of his ways.'

'You and I will be with God for eternity before that boy admits the error of his ways, Brand. You know that, I know that, and most certainly God knows it. You have sheltered and protected him all you could, my brother. Let him seek his fortune and his salvation in some other place – some very *foreign* place.'

'But Hereward believes he will inherit the estates at Bourne,' said Brand softly.

'And why should he expect that?'

The monk shrugged his broad shoulders.

'His mother filled his head with tales of noble warriors doing noble deeds. Such warriors must have titles and estates.'

49

The abbot shook his head.

'Mothers can be forgiven for talking nonsense to their children, for that is what mothers do, but Hereward is a man now, not a child. Has his father – his legal father – ever given him cause to think he will inherit Bourne?'

'No. My younger brother would never encourage the boy to have such dreams. Asketil is well aware that our father's claims on Bourne are unlikely to be recognized by the ecclesiastical courts.'

'And Asketil will not grieve if Hereward ... follows a career abroad?'

'He has just lost a wife, although the news may not yet have reached him. To lose a son as well...'

'Brand,' said Leofric sternly, 'this is your superior speaking. Would Asketil grieve if he did not see Hereward again?'

'No, he would not,' conceded Brand.

'And you accept that I have every right to try, and punish, Hereward under the *infangentheof* law?' (Old English – The right to try a thief caught on an estate and confiscate the stolen goods.)

'Of course, but Hereward has handed over all Aedina's property.'

'There is still the offence and the assault on Brother Oswulf, as I suppose we must now call him. That is the alternative, Brand: trial or exile. Perhaps the choice should be yours.'

'What if Hereward does not accept exile? He is his own man now.'

'On that there will be no debate; no choice. The abbey will declare Hereward *silvaticus*. (Latin – Literally, someone who lives 'in the woods'.) He will be outlawed.'

'An outlaw? Hereward is not some common brigand.'

'No, he is not!' thundered Leofric with a fury which stunned the monk in front of him. 'He is a most un-common brigand and a very dangerous one. It is only by God's mercy that he has not murdered someone already. He does not respect this abbey or its laws.'

'He is sworn to defend this abbey unto death,' pleaded Brand.

'Thanks to God and our pious King Edward, this abbey is not at war with anyone. If we were, I admit, I would want a hundred Herewards to defend us. Let him go where there are wars, where his talents can be best employed.'

'Or he can be killed.'

'That is in God's hands, my brother, but I do fear that Hereward will not die in his bed. Where is he now?'

'He is camped with his squire outside the Bolhithe Gate. I thought it best for him to stay outside the abbey precincts until we had held our council,' said Brand with quiet defeat.

'Let him stay outside these walls. Go to him and tell him he is outlawed and so is the squire Martin Lightfoot if he intends to remain as Hereward's man.'

'Lightfoot will stay with Hereward, that is sure,' said Brand, 'and however far away they travel and whatever their fate, Hereward will, one day, return to Bourne.'

'May God prove you wrong, Brother Brand,' said Leofric, 'for I fear you may be right.'

51

And so it was that Brother Brand, that wise and gentle monk, made his way to the eastern gate of the Abbey of Peterborough carrying the news that Hereward was to be outlawed for the first time.

From a narrow window slit in the infirmary, the priest known as Oswulf nursed the leather-bound stump of his right arm and watched as Brand crossed the hythe, the landing place busy with unloading boats, to where Hereward and Martin Lightfoot were seated on wooden casks, drinking wine intended for the abbot's cellar and eating smoked eels intended for the abbot's table.

And Oswulf saw that sad, kindly monk give Hereward a purse of coins, place a hand on that blond head in blessing and tell him he was outlawed, in the twenty-second year of the reign of Edward, the last of the Old English kings.

Seven

Giraldus

This book by Brother Thomas is really rather good. What is more, it seems to be mostly true, though truth is rarely a requirement of history. Certainly Thomas's chronology is accurate. The twenty-second year of Edward's reign was indeed the Year of Our Lord 1063, although few today would call the blessed Edward (canonized during my lifetime, not Thomas's) the last of the English kings. Perhaps it was safer for Thomas to do so, but now we scholars tend to acknowledge that Harold Godwinson who died at Hastings was the last English king (and he, despite his Danish name, was a true Saxon, or at least a West Saxon).

There are finer points of fact which can be confirmed. I have had the rolls of the parish of Bourne scoured and for sure, the Lady Aedina did die in the year 1063, although I can find no record of her husband Asketil's demise. Perhaps he never returned to Bourne.

Of Abbot Leofric, much is known, from chronicles both here in Lincoln and at Peterborough itself. A respected leader of his community, Leofric's sin, if it be a sin, was to stray from his religious life into the world political.

For reasons known only to himself and God, Leofric became allied to the claims of Harold Godwinson, the Earl of Wessex, who stole the throne of England in 1066. It is said that Leofric was present on the eve of the battle at Hastings, carousing with the house carls of Harold's bodyguard and some sources suggest he was wounded in the battle itself. Many other sources suggest that whilst Harold's army spent the eve of battle drinking, William and his Norman cavalry, along with his Flemish mercenaries, spent the night in prayer; which is why William became king and the flower of Saxon nobility lay slaughtered on the hill.

Some time after the battle, Leofric returned to Peterborough Abbey where he promptly died, possibly of his wounds. The order of brothers there wasted no time in electing Brand as their new abbot, though I presume Thomas's book will eventually mention this fact.

Of the priest Oswulf, so cruelly treated by Hereward, I can discover nothing here in the library at Lincoln or in Peterborough. Thomas's book maintains that he was sent to Ely to enter the monastery there under the mentorship of Abbot Thurston, so I will send word to Ely to see if anything is known of him there. Such work is slow, and often fruitless, but is one of the burdens we serious historians must bear.

This brings me to the family history I must write for my patron, Baldwin le Wac, the current and undisputed owner of the lordship of Bourne.

What Thomas has told me so far simply will not do, not do at all.

Even a writer of my talents cannot make a distinguished ancestor out of a brigand and assaulter-of-priests such as the Hereward portrayed here. It would be like spinning the truth upon its head, though I fear that is exactly what my Lord Baldwin expects of me.

Yet Thomas's text has much to commend it. Not only is it a pleasure for a scholar such as I to read in the Old English when so many have lost the skill, but it is joyful to read of some of the old attitudes which prevailed before the coming of the Normans.

For example, Hereward's mutilation of poor Oswulf, although undoubtedly a crime, was not regarded as seriously as it would be today, as Oswulf was 'only' (as Brand describes him) a country priest and not a monk. In the days of good King Edward, who may himself have been a pure and pious man, country priests were often regarded as

54

objects of scorn because of their veniality, sloth and ignorance. If William of Normandy did nothing else for this island (which he most certainly did), he greatly strengthened the Church by imposing on it the rigours and discipline he imposed on his armies – rigours and disciplines which came naturally to the monastic orders – and today monks and priests are both regarded with equal honour.

Many today would also be amused to read of the Lady Aedina's bequests to Peterborough Abbey, which Hereward so disputed. Yet it is true. In the days when England was ruled by the Saxons and the Danes, women were indeed entitled to own property and dispose of it as they saw fit, incredible as that may sound today. As is the natural order of things, the law only applied to women of a certain rank, but nonetheless, Saxon women could and did accrue large estates and influence. The Normans soon put a stop to all that, though.

Yet some things are still recognizable. The shire-reeves who took an interest in Hereward's misdeeds, we would now call 'sheriffs' and they remain much exercised by the lawlessness of those who choose to rob and roister among the greenwood trees. The current incumbent of the post in Nottingham, it is said, has been almost driven to madness by the activities of the outlaws in his shire.

The true scholar reading Thomas's history can also hear the music of many a folk ballad and saga, for surely this is the basis for some of the wild tales which have sprung up about Hereward. Thomas mentions the disappearance of the

55

Earl of Northumbria's favourite white hunting dog; and is there not a ballad still sung about how Hereward went to the north and made a pet of a polar bear? And does not every child know the saga of how Hereward helped to steal away the daughter of the King of Cornwall so that she may marry an Irish prince?

Brother Thomas knew that there was never a King of Cornwall and that the Irish prince of the story was no more than a subterfuge for Hereward's own lust.

Such points of logic may well impress the historian, but they will not interest my patron Baldwin, and neither will the account of Hereward being declared outlaw for so ignoble a reason. Perhaps it will be better not to mention any of that.

In fact, all I can take from this early chapter for my recension of Thomas's book, is the fact that Hereward's ancestral home (I shall say no more than that) was indeed at Bourne in Lincolnshire, although the manor house he would have known has long since faded and decayed, replaced by Baldwin's sumptuous and expensive new residence.

I must hope for more useful facts in the next chapter.

Eight

Thomas

Hereward the Hard Man

Little of substance is known of Hereward's departure from England that autumn.

Some say he and Martin Lightfoot set off along the old Roman road towards London, but never reached that city, disappearing instead into the woods near Godmanchester, from whence came stories of a merchant being robbed in his own home and a church pillaged as it prepared for the harvest festival. Within a month, Hereward was said to have attracted a dozen or more *silvaticii* to his side, but the Shire-reeve of Cambridge was quick to act and Hereward and his squire were captured in ambush.

Claiming to be a sworn man of Peterborough Abbey, word was sent to Brother Brand who intervened on behalf of the miscreants with a plea of clemency which was granted on condition that they proceeded to London with all haste.

Another version of the tale is that the new outlaws left Peterborough by river and made their way across the rivers and flooded lands of that region to Wisbech, which is known as the capital of the Fenlands. From there they spent Brand's purse on a passage for themselves and their horses, on a hulk bound for Rouen in Normandy.

But in this version too, they failed to reach their destination, for the hulk on which they sailed floundered during a storm and was wrecked among the sand dunes of the Flemish coast.

There were tales of how the shipwreck was not completely the fault of sudden storm, but that it was in no small part due to the bulk of the crew being unable to respond to their captain's commands after an all-day drinking bout started by Hereward's discovery in the ship's hold of a consignment of strong mead bound for the Abbey at St Valery. Despite the fact that the finest English mead was worth more than double in weight than the best German wine, and that it was not his property, Hereward had no hesitation in broaching the casks. (Mead, made from honey, would have been the equivalent of modern day alcoholic spirits and at this time, the most sought after wine in Europe would have been German, not French).

Other tales told of how Hereward struck a crewman across the face with his sheathed sword in its wooden scabbard, breaking the sailor's nose, over a game of dice. The ensuing melee resulted in a fire breaking out on the deck of the hulk and the captain, fearing for his cargo, beaching the ship on the nearest point of the coast, and then expelling Hereward and his groom Lightfoot.

But such tales – and even wilder ones – are regular currency among the seamen who work the hulks and the keels which cross the waters between England and Flanders, or Normandy, or even France, though there is little worth trading with that insignificant, self-styled kingdom. And as such, these stories cannot be said to be certainly true, but what is not in doubt is that Hereward and his companion Martin Lightfoot found themselves wandering the sea-shore on foot until accosted by armed and mounted men sworn to the Count of Flanders, who escorted them to the Count's household currently situated within the precincts of the Abbey of St Bertin near the town of St Omer.

'I am Robert, son of the Count of Flanders and a sworn advocate and defender of the Abbey of St Bertin and all the lands claimed by my father.'

'I am Hereward, Lord or *thegn* as we would say – of the manor of Bourne in Lincolnshire in England, and a sworn man of the Holy Abbey of Peterborough. My squire and I thank your noble lord for his hospitality, which we will look to repay in the future in England, for we cannot here, destitute as we are by reason of a shipwreck which has claimed the lives of my bodyguard and all the valuables in my portage.'

It should be pointed out here that while Brother Brand of Peterborough could take much credit for young Hereward's small skill in diplomacy and manners, he bears no blame for Hereward the Outlaw's talent for lying.

'Most noble Hereward, if you are sworn to Abbot Leofric, who is known even here as a dedicated servant of God, then my house is yours,' said Robert of Flanders, and by saying it in front of the assembled dignitaries of his court, he

59

made it so.

Viscount Robert's house was strange to Hereward; larger than Bourne Manor, larger even than Toki's hall in Lincoln. His was a fortified house built mainly of stone, though not yet on the scale of the stone castle in the Norman style which were then unknown in England. In Sir Robert's great hall was a huge stone fireplace the like of which Hereward had never seen and his eyes became transfixed on the roaring fire there. So much so that he had to be called thrice to Sir Robert's table where his knights had gathered to take their evening meal sitting alongside the monks of St Bertin, as was customary.

In borrowed clothes, Hereward took his place among the company and Sir Robert, in the absence of his father, acted as host, introducing his other guests.

Among them was a tall German knight by the name of Hoibrict, the Norman aristocrat Sir William de Warenne and his brother-in-law, the Flemish knight Sir Frederick Oosterlese-Scheldwindere. All three were strong young men of military bearing with close-cropped hair in the Norman fashion and all three made great play of Hereward's long, blond hair, suggesting in ribald tones that English warriors were 'beautiful like girls'.

'English enemies do not notice our hair once they see our blades,' responded Hereward.

'And English warriors seem most reluctant to be parted from their longswords,' said Sir Robert. 'For was it not the only possession you managed to rescue from your shipwreck?'

'Shipwreck? What shipwreck?' snapped the tall German by the name of Hoibrict. 'Why was I not informed of this?'

Hoibrict's question was perfectly legitimate, for he was the nephew of the Count of Guines, whose estates bordered those of the Count of Flanders and who held authority over shipwrecks on the Flemish coast.

'My men found only the young Lord Hereward,' said Sir Robert, 'and his groom. The only things of value they carried were their souls and one finely decorated sword.'

'That I would like to see,' said Sir William de Warenne, who prided himself on his expertise of all military things.

'So you shall,' said Hereward and he called for Martin Lightfoot, dining in the servants' quarters with the gluttons – the serving boys of the abbey.

'Where exactly was this shipwreck?' persisted Hoibrict.

'On the coast, where they usually are,' said Sir Robert and the entire company, except for Hoibrict, laughed at his wit.

'It is the law that my uncle the Count of Guines be informed of all shipwrecks on this coast,' he said sternly.

'The law has not been broken,' said Sir Robert, who knew just how far he could torment Hoibrict before tempers flared. 'Had my men seen a ship-wreck, they would have reported it to the noble Count, but they did not. Nothing was left of the ship which foundered on our shores and stranded our English guests.'

'Nothing? No bodies? No timber? No salvage?'

'Not a trace. It was almost as if the noble Hereward and his groom descended from heaven into our sand dunes.'

At this, many of the monks at table frowned, but Sir Robert was known for his wit and his father, the Count of Flanders was a generous benefactor of the abbey. Hoibrict, though, was a *vir strenuus,* a hard man, a man of action, unaware of such niceties.

'There was no salvage at all? No spars or sails or casks? Truly, a mysterious shipwreck,' he said haughtily.

'Come, come, my dear Hoibrict, you know as well as I do that the tides and winds of our coast are treacherous. What is washed up on one tide can be spirited away on the next. There are many riddles in the sands hereabouts.'

'I cannot believe your men saw nothing,' growled Hoibrict.

'Either there was nothing to see,' said Hereward with a broad smile, looking directly into Hoibrict's face, 'or Sir Robert's men are lying to him. Or it could be that Sir Robert is lying to you, or even that I am lying to Sir Robert.'

'No one has suggested anyone is lying,' soothed Sir Robert, realizing that his military guests had fallen silent and the silence was spreading amongst the eating monks the length of the table.

'This English "girl" has some spirit,' Sir Frederick whispered to his brother-in-law, 'staring down a knight almost twice his size.'

'He is a dangerous man,' said William de Warenne, after washing down a mouthful of bread with a draught of the renowned St Omer cider.

'That's what makes Hoibrict such a useful warrior,' agreed Frederick.

'I didn't mean him,' said Sir William. 'I meant the English one.'

Hereward and Hoibrict continued to look each other in the face until Martin Lightfoot appeared in front of their table bearing Hereward's longsword in its wooden scabbard.

'My Lord Hereward...' Martin addressed him with a courteous bow, as he had been instructed to do so, and offered the sword.

His smile even broader, Hereward gestured to his groom to present the sword to the German giant.

'Please,' he said politely, 'allow me to present my only treasure for your inspection. It is the only wealth I have, but the only wealth I need.'

Hoibrict seemed to have to tear his gaze away from Hereward's face and he was heard to mutter, almost to himself 'Those eyes...' as he stood and then he shook his head as if to clear it after a bout of heavy drinking and took the offered sword, pulling it half way from its scabbard.

Sir Robert intervened.

'My lords, we do not draw arms in this hall unless it is to defend this house from outside attack.'

It was the custom at St Omer, as in all holy houses, for the defenders of such religious orders to leave their weapons ranged against the walls of the hall. At table, nothing more dangerous than an eating knife was carried even by the Viscount himself.

'My German friend is merely examining some fine English steel,' said Hereward standing, almost dwarfed by the tall Hoibrict. 'And from the scars he carries, he has some judgement in these matters.'

'My scars were not made by English blades, even ones forged in the Danish style, like this,' grunted Hoibrict examining the herringbone pattern of decoration on the sword blade. 'This is what they call "firesteel", where the metal is twisted during forging.'

He showed the partly exposed blade to the two Norman knights still seated, still eating, to his right.

'See the pretty pattern? That's all it is. Firesteel is no stronger than ordinary steel, just fancier.' He pushed the blade back into its scabbard and then began to examine the scabbard itself. 'The English obviously think highly of their blades to protect them so. This scabbard weighs more than the sword! What is it lined with? Iron?'

The German was correct in that, for Hereward's scabbard was made from strips of oak lashed over a frame of iron rods, the whole thing bound tightly with sewn leather.

'We English protect our most valuable possessions,' said Hereward with a wide grin.

'When you have so little, you must protect it as well as you are able,' said the German, which brought a snort of laughter from Sir Frederick.

Distracted for that split second, the German took his eyes from Hereward's face and in that moment, Hereward took the scabbard from him with both hands. Holding the still-sheathed blade by the hilt with a double-handed grip, Hereward pointed the sword at the floor and then jerked the

64

scabbard with all his strength, bringing it up sharply between Hoibrict's legs.

The giant warrior roared in pain and collapsed across the table, clutching his groin, sending dishes of food and jugs of cider flying into the air.

Sir William de Warenne turned to his brother-in-law and said: 'I told you he was dangerous.'

It is said that the old pagan gods of the north always favoured the recklessly brave. If that is true, they would have smiled on Hereward, just as Hereward smiled at the shocked faces of the knights and monks in that refectory in St Omer.

Sir William and Sir Frederick were immediately prepared to avenge what they saw as an assault on the honour of a fellow noble fighting man, even as Hoibrict, still writhing in pain, was carried to the infirmary by no less than six of the lay brothers. But Sir Robert intervened, as was his right, and said that Hereward, although impetuous and foolish, was doing no more than avenging what he saw, albeit mistakenly, as a slight on his honour; and in any case, Hereward had not legally broken the custom of the abbey, as he had not drawn the firesteel blade whilst at table, Hoibrict had. Reluctantly, the Norman knights held their tongues and deferred to their host.

Thus, on his first day of his exile in Flanders, Hereward made three enemies and one friend, Sir Robert.

Hereward was not to know it, but Sir Robert and his father, the Count, had long feared the growing power of Normandy and its fearsome Duke

William, to the south and west, although the traditional enemies of Flanders lay to the north on the islands and coast of Friesia. A strong and military-minded Flanders would suit Normandy, for Duke William was constantly in search of fresh troops, but no longer would he accept mere levies or outlaw mercenaries. William was creating a new model of an army in Normandy, a hard and well-disciplined force, the cutting edge provided by squadrons of armoured cavalry responding to flag signals. And so William had recommended that Hoibrict, a warrior schooled in the new warfare, be appointed *Magister Militum,* or master of the knights, to the Count of Flanders to oversee the training of his army.

Now Sir Robert, who would himself one day be Count, had the chance to create his own *Magister Militum* and who better than the young Hereward who had so rudely unmanned Duke William's champion?

Sir William de Warenne made no secret of the fact that he thought this choice unwise and insulting, but the bounds of hospitality and rank prevented him from pressing his protest. As the De Warenne clansmen made to leave St Omer, Sir William was heard to say that the sooner Flanders went to war with somebody the better, for the sooner the upstart English vagabond met his end in battle, the better.

At once Hereward rose to the challenge and suggested that Sir William or his brother-in-law Sir Frederick, or both, might wish to try and make an end of Hereward there and then.

'We do not fight beautiful girls,' said Sir Fred-

66

erick haughtily as the Norman entourage turned their horses to the road from St Omer, 'or deign to fight with those beneath us.'

'What does the fat bastard mean by that?' Hereward had raged.

Sir Robert, once Hereward was securely restrained by Martin Lightfoot, had explained.

'Those Normans are of noble birth and have chosen to follow the codes of behaviour which Duke William has introduced in Normandy. To meet them in open warfare, where it is their duty to *fight*, is one thing, but a challenge to single combat can only be met when the knights are of equal rank. The Normans are rigid in this code. They are like an army of monks, such is their faith in their code.'

'Then make me a knight,' pleaded Hereward, 'so I may challenge them.'

'That I cannot do,' Sir Robert said with a laugh, 'for it is not within my power. Nor would it be wise. Do not look to make enemies of the Normans, Hereward, it may well be that they come looking for you.'

The advice Sir Robert gave young Hereward, though he was only one year older himself, was good and true and in those early months in Flanders Hereward could have learned much, had he listened. But Hereward had no head for politics and ignored the speculations of Flemish nobles and the monks of St Bertin who all saw the Duke of Normandy exerting his influence over the pious, but weak and, importantly, childless, Edward, King of England. (Later to be known as Edward the Confessor.)

Such matters did not concern Hereward for he was busy and happy leading the life of a military master, responsible for the equipping and training of the small army of the Count of Flanders. In this he had a natural talent as well as a deep interest in weapons, armour and the use of heavy horses in battle. He remembered much he had been told by his grandfather Toki and realized that the old Saxon custom of fighting on foot with long axes sometimes as tall as a man would no longer hold against an attack by organized cavalry protected by archers on the flanks. In Martin Lightfoot he had the perfect finder of horses and many were the freemen of Flanders who complained in vain to the Count that their best horseflesh was disappearing, usually at night. As a skilled bowman himself, Hereward personally undertook the training of a company of Flemish archers including the shooting of fire arrows by both day and night.

Within six months, Flanders had an army which had successfully bloodied itself against French outlaws and Friesian pirates and which had come to the attention of Normandy.

Once again, Sir William de Warenne and Sir Frederick Oosterlese were received at St Omer, this time on a mission from the Duke of Normandy himself, in order to secure Flanders as an ally.

What was proposed to the Count of Flanders, a man no longer of an age to wish to quarrel with the more powerful Duke of Normandy, was that if Flanders wished to increase its lands and revenues to the north, then Normandy would not stand in its way provided that Flanders was always willing to support Normandy in its own territorial claims.

The old Count had long cast greedy eyes on the estates of his neighbour, the Count of Guines, and was quick to agree to the Norman proposal and the alliance was sealed by a Mass in the Abbey of St Bertin, followed by a feast and, on the next day, a display of horsemanship, archery and the throwing of lances by the best squadrons trained by Hereward.

De Warenne was impressed with the skill displayed on the St Omer tournament fields and complimented Sir Robert on the discipline of his troops, adding his admiration for the longhaired English master-at-arms.

'I had thought you would have had to hang that Viking vagabond by now,' said Sir William, indicating that he wished to speak to Sir Robert alone. 'You know he is declared outlaw in England, by the abbey he claims to be sworn to protect?'

'I have not heard that story,' admitted Sir Robert with a smile, 'though I have heard many stories these past months about my young captain. How does such news come to Normandy?'

'The monastery at Jumieges recently played host to a party of monks from England on a pilgrimage to Rome. They were led by an abbot of the name Thurstan from the Benedictine house at Ely. This Thurstan has a reputation for being a charitable and humble man, who does much for the sick and the poor and who has no interest in worldly things. Among his company was one monk that he especially treated with compassion and was teaching the monk to write *sinister* – with his left hand – in the hope that he will become in time a skilled copyist. The abbot was doing this out of charity for the monk, a certain Brother Oswulf, had lost his right hand to that shiny blade your captain carries.'

'Hereward? Hereward marked a holy brother as a common thief?'

'I understand that this Oswulf was not a monk at the time, but has since been admitted to holy orders. Therefore, he cannot have been a thief and your captain must have acted unjustly, for he was outlawed.'

'But the laws of England do not hold sway in Flanders,' said Sir Robert with some guile.

'Nor in Normandy,' agreed Sir William, 'and Normandy will not judge him. If he is useful to Flanders, then Flanders must keep him close; keep him on a tight reign.'

'That will not be easy, but a small war with the city of Guines may keep him busy.'

'Keep him even busier,' said Sir William. 'Give him a wife.'

'A wife? He takes women when he has to, but he has shown no interest in having a wife,' answered Sir Robert, who was taken by surprise at the suggestion.

'There is someone suitable in St Valery,' said Sir William as if the thought had just been visited upon him. 'A maid called Turfrida who comes of a wealthy merchant family and who has some skill with embroidery or so I am told.'

'I know of this maid,' said Sir Robert, 'and I am told she has some skill with witchcraft.' (Witchcraft at this time would have been regarded as mysticism and 'white' magic. The connotations of demonic possession and 'black' magic came later.)

'Perhaps not enough skill,' Sir William said, laughing, 'for she remains unmarried at twenty-five.'

'And is she not betrothed to the noble Hoibrict?' asked Sir Robert, trying hard not to smile.

'Indeed she was, but Hoibrict no longer has any interest in women and as that is mainly due to the actions of your English hard man, it seems only fitting that Hereward should take his place in the marriage bed, just as he has taken Hoibrict's place as your captain.'

'I will choose the moment carefully when I give Hereward the good news.'

'Do not take too long, Sir Robert. The Count of Guines will not give up his lands willingly and I would hate for Turfrida to be a widow before she is a wife.'

'I do not think Guines holds any fears for Hereward, but a witch for a wife may just do so.'

'Good. That young man needs something to be frightened of, for he seems not to fear man or God.' Sir William grasped Sir Robert's arm and pulled him close. 'Do not, I beg you, become too fond of that man.'

And so, within a year of arriving horseless, penniless and outlawed on a foreign coast, Hereward had found shelter in a noble house, a position of trust, a career at arms and a wife.

The campaign against the Count of Guines was short and brutal. Short, because the city of Guines was not expecting an attack and brutal because Hereward showed the inhabitants no mercy, laying about them with fire and sword. Especially fire.

Viscount Robert's Master-At-Arms returned in triumph to St Omer with his spoils and was told that he had also won a wife.

'Is she rich?' was all he asked Sir Robert.

That winter was a winter of stories about Hereward the Hard Man, at least in Flanders. Almost all were scandalous and immoral in the re-telling; but many were true.

There was the tale of Hereward's first visit to the port of St Valery to view his future bride and how he insisted on 'tasting the goods before he bought them', something which Turfrida herself never complained about or denied. An even more outrageous version of this story had Hereward offering the same privilege to his groom Martin, though few truly believed this.

There was no doubt that Hereward did demand a dowry of Turfrida in the form of a shipload of high quality whetstones from southern Norway, enough to equip the army of Flanders. And everyone believed that Hereward's wedding gift to his bride was a cheap pewter brooch which he won in a game of dice with the sea captain trading goods between St Omer and Cheapside in London, where such trinkets are made.

Whether Hereward ever truly loved Turfrida, or she him, only God will ever know, but married they were in the chapel of the Abbey of St Bertin and the wedding feast resulted, for the first time that any of the monks could remember, in the cellars of the abbey running dry of ale, cider and wine. This in turn gave rise to the tale that Turfrida had to use all her powers as a witch to enable Hereward to perform the duties of a husband on his wedding night.

She also used all her skill as a seamstress to make fine tunics with gold embroidery for him to wear, something which, along with Hereward's refusal to cut his hair short at the back and the sides in the Norman fashion, brought many a sly comment about the 'girlish warrior' who fought for the Count of Flanders. None of these comments, if heard, went unchallenged by Hereward or the loyal Lightfoot and many a bone was broken and head cracked among the troops of Flanders.

For the next year Hereward learned from the example being set by Duke William of Normandy, adopting Norman discipline, weapons and tactics in his campaigns as *Magister Militum* under the patronage of Viscount Robert. Yet he never appointed Flemish officers, preferring instead to send word to England with one of the monks of St Bertin, to recruit his kinsmen, the two cousins called Siward and distinguished by the titles Siward the Red and Siward the White, to serve as his lieutenants and bodyguards.

When the two Siwards arrived at St Omer, they brought with them a ship's cargo of goods as wedding presents, including fine bone combs with carved animal head handles from Sweden, ornaments of the best walrus tusk ivory from Norway, much woollen cloth of the closest English weave and a wealth of silks, wines, olive oil, bronze jewellery and Syrian glass, all bought at London's main

73

trading wharf known as the Billingsgate.

The gifts surprised Hereward and delighted Turfrida, who immediately began a two-day inventory
on the dockside while her husband and the two
cousins went on a three-day drinking spree. Un-
beknownst to Hereward, news of his military exploits and marriage had been reported in England
by the messengers who regularly travelled between
the monastic houses. Nowhere was the news of
Hereward's success greeted more favourably than
in the abbeys at Peterborough and Ely and in the
halls of Lincoln, where the men of the east of
England took pride in the growing reputation of
one of their own kin and showed their appreciation in their generous wedding presents.

There were rumours, as there always were
among monks, that many of the gifts were raised
and paid for by none other than Brother Brand,
partly out of a sense of guilt at Hereward's out-
lawing and exile without property or hope of inheritance. But again, these rumours were spread
quietly and well out of earshot of Hereward and
the growing number of men (for Hereward was
always generous with the spoils of his campaigns)
who were beginning to give their loyalty more to
their captain than their liege lord.

The ageing Count of Flanders, deferring to the
wise advice of his son Robert, decided that a
well-armed and well-trained army was most
usefully employed in what it did best, which was
war. Therefore Sir Robert, Hereward, the cousins
Siward and much of the force of Flanders were
despatched in a fleet of some forty shallow-
draught ships to Scaldermariland off the coast of

Friesia (The Zeeland area of modem Holland, at the mouth of the River Schelde.) to collect unpaid tribute from the island farmers and fishermen there.

The expedition sailed shortly after Easter when a bright, long-haired shooting star was seen trailing the skies for a week, which many thought to be a portent of doom. (It was Halley's Comet, visible in late April, 1066.)

And so it seemed to be, for the Scaldermariland campaign did not go well for the pride of Flanders. The resistance of the local population was fierce and they used their flooded island territory to the best of their advantage. Whenever Hereward did record a victory, the spoils were poor and Hereward's temper became short and his actions more cruel. When one Friesian village sent two priests as peace envoys to discuss the unpaid tributes, Hereward soaked their robes in oil and put a torch to them. By jumping into a seawater drainage ditch, the priests saved their lives if not their skins.

Whilst his courage in battle could not be doubted, the loyalty of the men he had trained began to falter as he became as harsh with them as with his enemies. By the end of that summer, the tributes from Scaldermariland remained unpaid and Hereward's laying waste of the land ensured that they would not be paid for several years.

Two months before Christmas, Viscount Robert, who had been sick with salt-marsh fever, called off the campaign and ordered a withdrawal to St Omer, where they were greeted with the news of momentous events.

The old Count of Flanders had died, leaving Sir Robert to succeed him and Sir Robert, despite the recent campaign, had no doubt of the worth of Hereward as a hard man to stand by his side. As the Count, Sir Robert was now in a position to raise Hereward in rank, an offer which his wife Turfrida was anxious for him to accept, but the monks of St Bertin had other, more tempting, news.

William Duke of Normandy, who had for so long cast a covetous eye on the riches of England, had spent the year constructing a fleet at Dives-sur-Mer and then had assembled his forces, including Breton, Flemish and even French mercenaries, at St Valery and sailed for England in September. Landing unopposed, he engaged the army of Harold Godwinson of Wessex near Hastings and God granted him victory over the usurper king. William would himself be crowned the true King of England by Christmas.

Yet the news of most interest to Hereward was that which concerned Abbot Leofric of Peterborough, who had sided with Harold Godwinson and had been fatally wounded at the battle near Hastings. It was feared that Leofric was not long for this world and may even already be in the next, so the monks of Peterborough were looking to elect his successor and the most likely candidate was the honourable and worthy Brother Brand.

What need had Hereward of honours in Flanders when he felt sure he could now return to Peterborough and claim the manor of Bourne, which was his by right and which now no man would deny him?

Nine

Giraldus

God's truth, but Brother Thomas has an exciting
tale and knows how to tell it!

I have read few chronicles in Old English which
include so much fine detail and even the actual
words of the men whose deeds are listed. And it
all rings true. A dowry of Norwegian whetstones
is exactly the dowry a fighting man of Danish
heritage would demand! And the accounts of
Hereward's love of drink are surely echoes of his
upbringing in Toki's hall in Lincoln, where feasting would have been to excess or not at all.

In his narrative, Thomas tells us how Hereward
came to be a man of some military skill; his ex-
periences in Flanders serving him well in later
years. He also tells us how Hereward gained a
wife, though that fact alone is of dubious historical
merit, for she does not feature in the legends and
ballads of our hero.

Perhaps she died in childbirth, as women are
wont to do.

Most importantly, Thomas gives us facts which
can be checked against accounts already published and known. It is true that Abbot Thurstan
of Ely did visit Rome in the year of Our Lord
1065, and would have taken the hospitality of
religious houses, such as Jumieges in Normandy,

77

along the way. Similarly it is well known that Abbot Leofric of Peterborough sided with Harold Godwinson of Wessex in 1066, that year of three battles (Fulford Gate near York, Stamford Bridge and Hastings.) and three kings in England, all presaged by the flaming star in the sky that Easter. Whether Leofric actually fought at Harold's side at Hastings has never been proved, but it is known that by Christmas he was dying 'of wounds' and early in the new year, the brothers of Peterborough did indeed elect Brand as their abbot.

But what of this can I fit into an honourable family tree for my patron Baldwin Wac? There is precious little, so far, which is suitable.

Hereward the Outlaw or Hereward the Mercenary in Flanders, there seems to be nothing noble in either of these careers. Indeed in both it seems that Hereward cannot control his temper and, wherever he goes, he shows disrespect to priests, assaulting poor Oswulf in England and then setting fire to two more in Scaldermariland.

His military career in Flanders may have been a useful one, but it was hardly glorious, and he deserted his lord, the generous Sir Robert, and spurned the offer of rank and prestige in Flanders in order to return to England to pursue his dubious claim to the estates of Bourne. Estates to which, according to the old legal rolls, he never held legal title under Saxon, Danish or Church law.

Yet Bourne seems to have magical powers for Hereward, drawing him as a moth is drawn to a candle flame and, according to legend, it is in

78

Bourne where Hereward's personal war against the Normans begins.

No doubt Brother Thomas's account will lead me there. Perhaps I will encounter poor crippled Oswulf again, for he has featured in Hereward's story twice already. If he did become a Brother at Ely and was adopted by Abbot Thurstan then perhaps there is some record of the one-handed monk who visited Rome in that last summer before the Normans came.

I have written to Ely to seek out what is known of Brother Thomas. I shall write again in search of Brother Oswulf. Should I receive an answer it is not likely to help me in my history of the noble Wac family, but it may satisfy my idle curiosity.

There is one other question in my mind which Brother Thomas's account may yet answer. Dear Brother Oswulf and the unfortunate German warrior Hoibrict were both strangely fixed by Hereward's eyes in the moments before he struck at them.

What was it about his eyes?

Ten

Thomas

Hereward the Berserker

Leaving his wife Turfrida in St Omer under the protection of the cousins Siward the Red and Siward the White, Hereward and Martin Light-foot bought passage on a hulk bound for London. When they landed it was the first time they had stepped on English soil in over three years.

The Normans had been in England for only five months but already the country and the capital were changing fast. Duke William had been crowned King of England on Christmas Day in St Peter's Abbey, built by Edward the Pious as the west monastery (or Westminster) more than a mile from the city of London, on a marshy island where the river Tyburn flowed into the greater Thames.

Not that Hereward or Lightfoot were interested in seeing the new abbey. Nor is there any sign that they attended the famous church of St Paul's in the city itself, or the fine church of All Hallows known as the Grass Church for its thatched roof or the old wooden church of St Andrew in Holborn.

Perhaps, as a military man, Hereward did notice that King William (as he must now be called) had already begun the construction of two castles in the city, in the south-west and south-east corners. The south-eastern fortress defended the approach from the sea while the south-western castle would protect the outlying villages such as Stephenhede and Chenistun (Stepney and Kensington) with their rich farming lands and Fuleham (Fulham), which had long enjoyed fishing rights on the Thames; all three being important suppliers of food to William's new capital, where there were more than ten thousand mouths to feed even without William's army. Each day the Billingsgate wharves creaked with the unloading of cut and trimmed stone from Caen in Normandy to provide the foundations of the new fortifications. And if this were not enough to ensure that the English never forgot their defeat, the King's brother, Bishop Odo, had commissioned the famous school of embroiderers at Canterbury to begin work stitching the history of the Normans' conquest on to canvas, on a scroll said to measure more than two hundred paces of a tall man.

Although amply supplied with coin from his wife's purse, Hereward chose rude lodgings in Cheapside near the old West Cheap market, from where, each day, he would venture to seek out news from the Fenlands and Martin Lightfoot would scour the stables of London for horses which could be borrowed, stolen or, as a last resort, bought for a fair price.

Neither task was simple. News from the east of England was sparse for King William was progressing northwards, through Cambridge and Huntingdon with his army, imposing Norman authority on the land. To do this required horses and few were available for those who did not carry the writ of a Norman noble.

In a city crowded with troops, two more armed men were not unusual, though their long hair and preference for stout leather jerkins rather than shirts of chain mail singled them out from the King's Norman guards and their speech proved they were not Breton levies. It was assumed that they must be Flemish mercenaries and could have claimed safe passage anywhere by declaring their allegiance to Count Robert of Flanders. But Hereward could never pass unnoticed and now in England saw no reason to, for he was in his home country and about to claim his rightful inheritance, or so he thought.

It was a dispute in the West Cheap market which drew Hereward to the attention of the Portreeve's men, who were responsible for maintaining the King's law and order in the city. (The Portreeve was in effect the Governor of London, who in 1067 was Geoffrey de Mandeville, one of William's leading supporters.) It was not, as many would have predicted, a dispute with other military men in one of the hundreds of seedy taverns of the area, nor an altercation over the value of his Flemish coins with one of the many goldsmiths or silversmiths who worked there. It was rather an argument with a herbalist over the price of the root of the Christmas rose, a medication which Hereward firmly believed in; some say on the advice of his wife Turfrida who was known to have some skill in witchcraft, which is an art if not a skill much akin to being a herbalist or apothecary.

Whatever the rights and wrongs of the argument, the end result was a street brawl in which Hereward laid about him with his sword fortunately still in its sheath. It was still sufficient a weapon to break heads and forearms but at least no one was killed. The herbalist, who sold his plants and potions on behalf of the Benedictine houses near London (for monastic houses and witches had a monopoly on such items), petitioned for assault and damage to his stock of goods and Hereward and Martin were summoned to account for their actions at the Portreeve's house in the east of the city. Yet as they entered the mansion, armed and with their heads held high, they were greeted not by the Portreeve but by one of his trusted lieutenants.

'I thought it must be you, my Viking berserker friend, as soon I heard of the trick of smashing a man's arm, not to mention his balls, with a sword still in its scabbard,' said Sir William de Warenne. 'I shall fine you six silver pennies: two to the herbalist you assaulted and four to the King.'

'You can not be serious!'

'I am very serious. King William will not tolerate brawling in the streets and daylight robbery by any of his sworn subjects.'

'I am sworn to Robert, Count of Flanders, not William of Normandy,' shouted Hereward foolishly.

'We are not in Flanders,' said Sir William as though talking to a child. 'We are in England.'

'Where I am a sworn man of Peterborough Abbey!'

Hereward's voice, raised in anger, caused Sir

William's crossbow men (for he rarely travelled with less than twelve armed men at his side in those days) to finger their weapons.

'Then you are a liege man of Abbot Leofric, who gave counsel and support to the Usurper Harold Godwinson?' asked Sir William quietly, setting the trap.

'Leofric is dead,' answered Hereward, 'and I shed no tears for him. My uncle, Brand, is now the abbot and it is my intention to journey to Peterborough to pledge myself to him. There, I will be knighted in the English manner and claim the manor and estates of Bourne which are held for me by the abbey.'

If Sir William was surprised by Hereward's outburst, he concealed it well.

'You seem very sure of your future, my young captain – for that is all you are, a captain in a foreign army. Whilst you have been in Flanders, things have changed in this land.'

'What is changed is that I am now Lord of Bourne,' said Hereward defiantly.

'That,' replied De Warenne softly, 'remains to be seen. You are sure this Abbot Brand will speak for you?'

'There are ties of kinship and blood which bind us. Brand is loyal to me.'

'The question is whether Brand is loyal to King William, nothing else matters. For the present, the King is willing to accept Brand's election as abbot, for he has much business to attend to elsewhere. Swear to me here and now that your business in this country does not challenge the King's law or authority.'

Hereward shrugged his shoulders at that, as if the question were beyond his understanding.

'My business is in Peterborough and it is mine alone.'

'Then pay your fine, keep the King's peace and be on your way. Just remember, Hereward, this is not the land you left for Flanders. Things have changed and men must change with them.'

De Warenne dismissed the pair with a flick of his gloved fingers and Hereward gave a curt bow in the Norman fashion, his long blond hair falling over his face.

'One thing in particular has changed, Hereward,' added Sir William with a smile. 'No longer can a fighting man be taken seriously if he wears his hair longer than a maiden does, as many a Saxon widow will testify.'

Hereward's right hand twitched towards the hilt of the sword hanging from his belt but before he could reach it he felt another hand, Martin's, restraining him.

'I look forward to proving you wrong on that count, Sir William,' he said, staring at the Norman, 'after I am knighted and have claimed my lands in Lincolnshire.'

'I wish you well in your quest for a noble name, Hereward, for I could not possibly soil my blade on a mere outlaw.'

As soon as Hereward and Lightfoot had left his presence, Sir William beckoned one of his clerks to approach.

'Bring me the monk who reported them,' he ordered. 'The monk with one hand. There is something I must ask of him.'

'This man Hereward, he is known to you?'

'Well enough, my Lord,' said Oswulf, nursing the leather-bound stump on his right arm. 'Though with God's mercy, he no longer remembers me.'

Sir William tugged at his beard then acknowledged a serving boy who approached bearing a tray on which were a jug, pottery beakers and a plate of bread chunks soaked in olive oil and cold roast parsnips.

'Will you take some apple wine, Brother Oswulf? Or would you prefer English ale?'

'Neither, my Lord, but I will take a morsel of bread if I may.'

The monk chewed daintily, holding the stump of his right arm across his chest with no attempt to conceal it. There was little need, as de Warenne was a professional soldier who had seen many amputations and cruel disfigurements in battle.

'My clerks tell me you are becoming a fair copyist with your unnatural hand,' said the Norman.

'Such skill I have is down to God's grace and the patience of Abbot Thurstan who tutors me in scripting as well as teaching me Latin and Greek.'

'You are becoming quite the scholar,' said Sir William, not unkindly. 'How long have you been with Thurston at Ely?'

'Four years this Michaelmas.'

'Since Hereward took your hand?'

'Yes, my Lord.'

'Things have changed much in four years, Brother Oswulf, for both you and this country.'

'It can only be God's will.'

'Indeed it is, yet this Hereward seems not to care or even notice that there is a new power in the land. What are these manors and lands he thinks he has a right to?'

'He claims lordship over the manor of Bourne, a small place of little significance in the gift of the Abbey of Peterborough. For many years the tenant was one Toki of Lincoln, a landowner and money-lender whose allegiance was always to the Danish kings of old. This Toki always claimed the manor of Bourne as his by right of tenancy but his claim was rejected by the Church courts.'

'So why does Hereward cherish hopes of inheritance?'

'It is a childish dream he has, encouraged in his youth by his grandfather Toki in whose hall he was raised, and later by a foolish mother, who wished the best for her only son.'

'So in law, Hereward has no case?'

'None at all; title to the estates of Bourne was never granted to Toki of Lincoln.'

'And what of Hereward's father?'

Sir William stared at Oswulf, sensing the monk's discomfort.

'Asketil of Bourne was the husband of Hereward's mother,' Oswulf said carefully, 'and he died of a fever two years ago. Hereward's adopted father is his uncle, Abbot Brand.'

If Sir William was surprised at that he hid it well.

'And possibly his true father?' he said, sipping on a cup of cider.

'So some would say.'

'Is Abbot Brand likely to indulge Hereward's fantasies of becoming the new Lord of Bourne?'

Oswulf shook his head.

'Not Abbot Brand. He is an honourable man of God and upholder of church law. He would not be tempted to dispose of church property, whatever ties of kinship are strained.'

'Well put, Brother Monk. Your loyalty to your house is commendable, but it is not a temptation likely to be put before your Abbot Brand.'

'My Lord...?'

'The estates of Bourne have already been allocated to a new owner, a certain Ogier, a Breton and friend of the King. If Hereward goes there, he will find a new master sitting at the hearth of Bourne Manor and a new shire-reeve in town.'

'He *will* go there, my Lord, nothing is more certain.'

'And I cannot stop him. He is a Captain of Flanders and Flanders is an ally of Normandy. He is not yet our enemy, though I fear it is only a matter of time before he is, and for the present we have enemies enough to deal with. Is your business in London done, Brother Oswulf?'

'It is, my Lord. I start my return to Ely in the morning.'

'Take the east road out of the Bishopsgate, for Hereward and his companion will surely take the north road.'

'I am not frightened of Hereward.'

'You of all men should be,' said Sir William with a harsh laugh.

'I am already forgotten by Hereward. I was delivering herbs and medicines to the West Cheap market from my abbey's gardens when he attacked the herbalist there. I was close enough to touch him but he never saw me. I mean nothing to him.'

'But I think he means something to you, Brother Monk, for he still owes you a hand.'

Hereward used almost all the money he had taken from Turfrida's purse to buy two horses at prices which made him blaze with anger, settle the account at their Cheapside lodgings (which resulted in a brief fist fight with the landlord) and pay his sixpenny fine to the Portreeve's clerk. Then he and Martin Lightfoot took the road north at speed, hurrying to where they felt sure that property, rank and wealth awaited them, determined not to be diverted from a prize they felt sure was there for the taking.

So intensely did they keep their eyes on what lay ahead in Bourne, that they failed to notice almost everything about them.

In Cambridge, if they saw the building work on the castle there, they did not comment on it. At an inn in Huntingdon, the talk was all about the rising in Wales by the outlaw Eadric known as 'the Wild', but Hereward and Martin showed utter disinterest. On the approaches to Peterborough, they failed to notice that the Norman soldiers they saw on the road, or stopped them at gatehouses and asked their business, wore the livery of the house of Sir Frederick Oosterlese-Scheldwindere, the brother-in-law of Sir William de Warenne, though the colours should have been familiar enough to them from their time in Flanders.

The journeying pair rode to the west of Peterborough, avoiding the town itself, the quicker to get to Bourne. Had they visited the abbey there and met with Abbot Brand before arriving in Bourne, then the story of Hereward could have been so different.

Perhaps a few sokemen and villeins working the Lincolnshire fields or tending the cattle or sheep in their care saw Hereward and Martin Lightfoot ride into Bourne as if accepting a Roman triumph. If any recognized them, none spoke their names aloud as they followed the same road upon which, four years previously, they had fatefully met Oswulf the country priest.

Hereward's return to the manor house of Bourne was equally fateful, though not in the manner he had expected.

With his military experience, Hereward would have noticed the changes already made to the manor: the strengthening of the main doors with stout timbers, the newly cut slit windows just wide enough to fire crossbow bolts, the diversion of a stream into newly dug ditches running between house and stables to provide water should anyone fire the thatch. But if Hereward noticed these changes – changes which were happening to many large English houses that year – they did not deter him from marching straight into the main hall, scattering servant girls and scullery boys before him with blows from the flat of his sword's scabbard.

Such commotion – the screams of young girls, especially when under the attention of Martin

90

Lightfoot, the crashing of furniture and voices raised in anger in three or more languages – quickly brought forward the new master of the house, a portly man twice as old as Hereward and though he carried no weapon of his own or had any armed men to hand, he showed no fear of the two intruders.

'What is the meaning of this intrusion?' growled the older man in a thick Breton accent. 'Who are you to appear unannounced and uninvited?'

For an instant it seemed as if time had stopped and then Hereward sprang into the face of his accuser, so close to him that his spittle soaked the older man's beard.

'I am Hereward of Bourne!' he shouted. 'And this is my fucking house!'

He continued to shout this, over and over, as he clubbed Ogier the Breton to the floor and it was only when their boots were slipping in the blood spilled on the packed dirt floor, did Martin Lightfoot throw his arms around his master and pull him away.

'By a miracle of God, Ogier the Breton still lives,' said Sir Frederick.

'He is a merciful God,' replied Abbot Brand.

'Mercy does not seem to be a quality your ... nephew ... understands for he attacked, unprovoked, an unarmed man twice his age.'

'I hear that no sword was drawn,' argued Brand, though his heart was not in the sentiment.

'I have seen the tricks your Hereward can do whilst his sword is still sheathed and is not murder with a wooden club just as much murder as with a blade?'

'There can be no charge of murder for Ogier still lives.'

'Spoken like a true lawyer, Brother Abbot! Ogier lives inasmuch as he breathes, but the wounds to his head are beyond the skill of any physician in or out of Holy Orders. Ogier cannot walk or talk and has to be fed from a bowl like a baby. He empties his bowels where he sits and does not know his own children. For a knight who has fought shoulder-to-shoulder with kings is that not murder?'

Abbot Brand hung his head and clasped his hands as if in prayer.

'If Hereward had come to see me here in the abbey, I could have counselled him about the new Lord of Bourne.'

Sir Frederick slapped his gloves against his thigh.

'God's face, Abbot! How long will you protect this madman? This Hereward has no legitimate claim to the estate of Bourne and never had, except in his own mind's eye. He should have been disabused of the notion when he was a boy, but he was not. Now he attacks the man King William has made the legal owner. If he is a sworn man of Peterborough, then the King holds the abbey responsible for his actions. As the King's agent in the eastern shires, I must see the King's will carried out.'

'And what is the King's will in this matter?' asked Brand softly.

'The King's will is that his authority be respected and his laws obeyed, and you will see it done. Hereward is to be outlawed.'

'Again?' said Brand.

'The world has changed, Abbot. Under Norman law, when a man is outlawed, he stays an outlaw until the Day of Judgement – or until he dangles from a gibbet; whichever comes first.'

Brand watched from the library window as Sir Frederick assembled his retinue in the courtyard of the abbey. In all his dealings with his new overlord, as he must now think of him, Brand had never seen Sir Frederick travel with less than six soldiers at his side. They were mounted troops, dressed austerely in long leather jerkins over chain mail, each crowned with a conical metal helmet with a long, broad nose guard which obscured the face. Four of Sir Frederick's troop carried lances and long shields the shape of an upturned tear, two were armed with crossbows. The broadswords hanging from their belts slapped against the flanks of their large, powerful horses and their spurs jangled and clanged like bells against their iron stirrups.

How different, mused Brand, this army was from the Saxon levies or Danish raiders England had known of old. Save for Sir Frederick's family colours on their shields, it was impossible to tell these men apart. It was as if they were all part of a single fighting machine, which rode and turned and moved and fought as one; their horses bred and trained for the purpose as much as the men themselves. In an English army, no two knights would be dressed the same as a point of honour, in fact they would compete with each other for the most embroidered cloak or the brightest coloured leggings, and they would ride to the battle on scrawny but hardy ponies from which they would dismount to fight on foot, the easier and quicker to get to grips with their enemy, for an enemy not at close quarters was not a worthy fight.

Only when the abbey gates had shut behind Sir Frederick's troop and Brand felt sure they had reached the main road, did he send word for Hereward and Lightfoot, who had been hiding in the abbey brewhouse for two days, to join him in the scriptorium. At that time of day, the scribes and copyists would be at prayers so the scriptorium would be free from curious eyes and, Brand felt, the fewer who saw him with these dangerous young men the better. For that reason he gave instructions that the pair should be brought through the abbey cloaked and hooded.

They brought with them the sweet, earthy smell of malt from their nights sleeping on the brewhouse floor.

'Has that arrogant Norman bastard gone then?' was Hereward's coarse greeting to his uncle as his eyes roamed around the scriptorium, marvelling at the books and manuscripts being created there.

'Sir Frederick is a noble knight to whom we must show respect,' said Brand sternly.

'Respect? Respect a thief?'

'Be careful who you accuse, Hereward, and what you accuse them of. The Normans have taken this kingdom by force of arms and right of law.'

'Their law,' grunted Martin.

'I don't believe I asked you for a legal opinion, Master Lightfoot. You would do well to keep that tongue still if you want it to remain in your head. None of us can afford to offend Sir Frederick, not you, nor your master, nor I, nor this abbey. Sir Frederick is the brother-in-law of Sir William de Warenne...'

'He's the Norman bastard who ran us out of London,' snorted Hereward.

'And one of the richest Norman barons, who is himself married to Gunrada, the step-daughter of King William,' continued Brand. 'And like it or not, kinsman, King William rules this country and his word is law. He has allowed my election to stand and seems content to leave Peterborough in peace, for the moment.'

'He would not dare interfere with the sacred traditions of the monastery brotherhood!'

'Don't be a child, Hereward. He is the king. If he wants a Norman abbot in Peterborough, there will be a Norman abbot here by Christmas. For the moment, he seems content to allow me to continue to humbly serve our small community here. There is no secret of the fact that our brothers in Normandy have long regarded the Church in England as too soft and worldly in its ways. Bishop Odo of Bayeaux, who rules in the King's absence, is a hard master and a fierce churchman and will mould the Church to his will. There are many in the Church in England who would welcome that.'

'And many who would die rather than submit to Norman might.' Hereward's eyes flashed as he spoke and Brand found himself staring at them, unable to avert his gaze.

'Those who would die rather than submit to the Normans have done so, Hereward. They died at Hastings alongside Harold Godwinson. The Normans have won. William their Duke has been the anointed king for almost a year now. This is his country now and there are none to oppose him.'

'There is a revolt in Wales even as we speak,' said Martin Lightfoot, proving that he listened to the tavern gossip even if Hereward did not.

'There is always a revolt in Wales,' countered Brand, 'and there will be unrest in the north fuelled by the malcontent Scots no doubt; but they will not trouble King William unduly. Have you not seen the castles he is building? Have you not seen the discipline of his troops? The chroniclers are already comparing them to the Roman legions of ancient times, and William is likened to Julius Caesar himself.'

'Who?' asked Hereward, to Brand's eternal shame.

'A Roman general who was betrayed and killed by his own people,' said Martin, unable to stop himself from admitting to more scholarship than a mere groom should be entitled.

'Perhaps the same fate will befall King William,' said Hereward with a huge, childish grin.

'Unlikely,' said Brand dryly. 'King William is said to keep his friends near to his bosom, but his enemies even nearer.'

Hereward looked perplexed.

'There is simply no one left with the strength of purpose, or of men and arms, who could challenge William the Norman,' said Brand.

'Svein of Denmark could,' said Lightfoot, causing Hereward and the abbot to stare at him in surprise. 'King Svein is a friend to all men of the east of England. They would welcome him as a liberator from the iron fist of Normandy.'

Realizing he had perhaps said too much, Lightfoot's chin sank on to his chest and his face burned.

'My dear Hereward,' said Brand with much irony, 'you are fortunate indeed to have a groom and servant who is obviously schooled not only in history but in politics as well. Perhaps Master Lightfoot would like to check on the accuracy of our copyists whilst he is here in the scriptorium, or possibly we should remove ourselves to the library where he can read to us from the texts he knows so well?'

'I am a man of the Fenland,' hissed Martin, 'and I am not ashamed of my Danish kin. The same Danish blood ran in the veins of your father, Abbot, and Hereward's grandfather, did it not? Was Toki of Lincoln ashamed of his Viking blood? I think not.'

'Be quiet!' shouted Brand. 'You will not talk to me like that! You are foolish and headstrong, the pair of you, but God has not yet told me you are evil. If, however, you begin to spread treason by looking for an army of Danish Vikings to save England from the Normans, then King William will call you evil and he will crush you as he crushes all who oppose him.'

'He could try,' said Hereward, pushing out his chest.

'He would not have to try very hard,' observed

Brand, 'but he has left your present fate in the hands of Sir Frederick and Sir Frederick has decided on your punishment.'

'Punishment?' spluttered Hereward, starting to shake where he stood. 'For what? For claiming what is rightfully mine?'

'For the love of God and the Sweet Christ!' roared Abbot Brand with such force that Martin put his hand on Hereward's arm to restrain him. 'Can you not be told once and for all that you have no legal claim on Bourne Manor and estates? Your grandfather's claim was never upheld by the courts and now never will be. You have no say in what happens to the manor of Bourne and neither does this abbey. The King has given it to one of his most loyal followers, a companion who rode by his side at Hastings at a time, I would remind you, that you were abroad, fighting for Flanders, an ally of Normandy. You have no case in law and no challenge to the authority of the King or Sir Frederick.'

'I could challenge Sir Frederick to personal combat, then they would have to consider my claim to Bourne.'

Brand gripped the corners of a writing table, his hands like claws, straining as if trying to rip the wood in half.

'Did your mother soften what little wit God gave you, fool? Or has that wife of yours in Flanders put a spell on you?'

'It is true that Turfrida is well versed in witchery,' said Hereward reasonably, 'but she has no interest in my estates in Bourne. If she has cast a spell on me it is to protect me from Normans like Frederick and fat Breton thieves like that Ogier. But I have no fear of them with or without witchcraft.'

'That is your curse, Hereward,' said Brand sadly. 'You have no fear of anything.'

'And I will prove that by challenging Sir Frederick to a fair fight for my lands in Bourne.'

'By the holy relic of Saint Oswald's arm, you must be the biggest fool in England!' roared Brand. 'Do you not understand anything? Bourne is not yours, it is not mine, it is not this abbey's. It is not even Sir Frederick's to give, for the King has already given to another. And Sir Frederick would not agree to fight you for you are not of his rank.'

'Then make me a knight!' cried Hereward. 'Make me a knight in the Old English way, then Sir Frederick cannot refuse my challenge.'

'The fumes from the brewhouse must have clouded your dreams, Hereward, for I have no authority to make you a knight.'

'But you have!' Hereward shouted, then he sank to his knees before the abbot. 'My mother always told me you would make me a knight.'

'Your mother let her heart rule her head. She said much, much too much, of worldly things she did not understand. But I do not lie to you, I have no power to knight you or anyone else. To do so would bring down the wrath of King William on this abbey and his wrath would be terrible.'

'But she always told me...' Hereward's voice had diminished to that of a child's.

Martin placed a hand on his shoulder and said: 'Come, Hereward, do not beg.'

Brand glared at Lightfoot.

'And you, groom, remember your place! If you wish to serve your master well, take him from here now and find somewhere where he is not known and where the Normans will not look for him. You said you were a man of the Fens; take him into those swamps and hide there. No Norman will have a reason to go into the wet Fens in winter. When spring comes, take a ship back to Flanders or go to Denmark and drink with your friends at the court of King Svein. Do not come back to Peterborough and do not think of going back to Bourne unless you wish to die there.'

'And why, my Abbot, should we?' Hereward asked rising from his knees.

'Because Sir Frederick wants you outlawed.'

'Why?' Hereward asked, almost innocently.

'Because you have made a cripple of one of the King's favoured knights! Just be thankful Ogier the Breton still breathes otherwise there would be a price on your head. Go now, and stay gone. There is nothing here for you any more.'

'But I am a sworn man of the abbey...' Hereward began to protest.

'To keep you as such, even in name only, would be a slap in the face to Sir Frederick. I release you from your oath of loyalty to defend this abbey, now go. Take food from the kitchens, but nothing else, and may God guide you to a better life, for I cannot.'

And then Hereward stood straight-backed in front of Abbot Brand, fixed his uncle with his eyes and said: 'Twice I have come to Peterborough and twice I have left an outlaw. The next time I come, it will be different.'

Men have long argued what Hereward meant by that, or at least men of the Church or men of the east of England to whom it came to matter. Was Hereward speaking in hope or in threat? Did he really think he could reach some form of reconciliation with the Normans so that his misdeeds could be forgiven (if not forgotten) and he could return to Peterborough with a clean name or even a noble name? Or was he gifted with foresight – as it is said men who are married to witches can be – and he was predicting events over a year in the future when his return to Peterborough Abbey would set a flame to the eastern counties and the retribution of the Normans would be terrible indeed?

Whatever counsel he gave himself, or took from Martin Lightfoot (rarely far from his side in those days), it was not the counsel of caution or prudence.

Hooded and cloaked against the snows that were blowing in from the north-east, the two young men rode out of Peterborough and skirted the frosty waste of the Borough Fen until they came to Crowland Abbey, where they sought shelter, which was duly granted it being Christmas Eve. Fortune favoured them in that the season and the weather had conspired to delay the news of their sentence of outlaw reaching Crowland and they took care not to abuse the hospitality shown them.

Indeed they made a generous donation to the almoner of the abbey in return for their quartering and a large supply of powdered root of the

101

Christmas Rose from the master of the infirmary. More discretely, they purchased two sets of monks' robes of rough wool from the chamberlain, and from the loose-tongued cellarer (the monk in charge of meat and victuals) they learned not only of the quality of the wine stored in the abbey but also the location of the winter quarters in Norfolk of Sir Frederick Oosterlese-Scheldwindere.

And then, a week after Christmas, with frost on the ground each morning and the scent of snow on the air each afternoon, the two outlaws rode out of Crowland heading east, north of the Fens and south of the coast.

And there they disappeared.

Some said they spent the winter unmolested in the village of Littleport which lay on a small island to the north of the much larger Isle of Ely, bounded on three sides by flooded fenland and on one by the River Ouse, which ran all the way to the sea at Lynn (where it was known as the Ouse Magna or Great Ouse), forming the boundary with the shire of Norfolk.

This story gains in belief when it is remembered that Littleport was the birthplace of Martin Lightfoot and he had kin on the island. It is also true that travellers dressed in monks' robes were likely to go unnoticed in that region, so familiar were the comings and goings of the many monks of Ely, even in winter.

There are fenland tales from those days that this was when Hereward learned much of the craft of fen life which was to serve him well in the years of violence which lay ahead. Stories are still told of

Hereward's fascination with fire in the fens; of his delight on finding that certain beds of peat and webs of reeds would burn fiercely and at great length despite appearing to be surrounded if not covered by water. Hereward was also, like all unaccustomed to the fens, much taken with the will-o'-the-wisp lights, often known as 'fairy lights', which appeared as if by magic as small yellow flames in the most stagnant and stinking marshes where the fen waters never moved despite the season.

It is claimed that this was where Hereward discovered his appetite for lampreys, of which he was said never to have a surfeit, and smoked eel, a staple food of the Fenman in winter.

The stories also tell of a white wolf which Hereward tamed and used to lead him along the pathways and secret causeways across the fens, although it is well known that all Fenmen work closely with large dogs which were strong swimmers. But it is known for a fact that Hereward and Martin were taught the art of stilt-walking (a strange sight to folk who live on dry land, but a common enough sight on the Fens) at this time. It is even known that their teacher was a certain Hraga, a Norfolk man known as The Heron because of the long wooden stilts he strapped to his legs to allow him to cross the widest ditches and all but the deepest of flooded Fens with unnatural ease and speed.

However the pair spent their time that winter, it was mostly peaceful and they were not seen on the Isle of Ely nor anywhere near the precincts of the abbey there. Had they been, their presence there would surely have been reported to Abbot Thurston, who was known throughout England as the most humble of Christian men and the most honest of churchmen. A man who spoke and wrote passionately, condemning the corruption of the Church and in particular the practice of simony, yet one who would always quote the wisdom of Solomon that 'Love is the keeping of laws'. It is likely that had Hereward and Martin Lightfoot been brought before Thurston, the good abbot would have done his duty to the law and reported the outlaws to the King's officers.

But that was then, in the early part of the year of our Lord 1068. Such are the ways of men and the nature of events that another winter would freeze and thaw before Hereward would enter the holy precincts of Saint Etheldreda at Ely, but when he came he would be welcomed as a hero and a saviour.

Even though he would, by then, also be known to be a murderer.

The truth of the matter will never be proved, for there were no witnesses left alive and neither Hereward nor Martin Lightfoot ever confessed their part in the crime, but a crime it certainly was.

It is thought to have happened in the week before Lent.

Sir Frederick Oosterlese was staying at one of his properties in west Norfolk near the market town of Douneham where he had inherited not only an estate, but a family of hawkers and falconers with great knowledge in the training of birds of prey for sport and the table.

As everyone knows, the training of such birds is best done in the winter or early spring when there is less fresh game about to distract them from the falconers' lure and whistle.

And it was on such an occasion that Sir Frederick, accompanied only by his favourite clutch of hawks and a handful of servants, was riding the fields when his party must have been approached by the two hooded riders seen passing across Douneham Bridge that morning at dawn.

When the hawking party failed to return to Sir Frederick's manor house that afternoon, his bailiff called for all local sokemen, cottars and serfs to form search parties and it was by torchlight, as dusk fell, that they found the first of the bodies.

One of those sturdy Norfolk farmers, used to nature and by no means wary of the sight of blood, later described to his priest that the butchery of Sir Frederick's servants exceeded anything he had ever seen and could only be likened to the savagery of the berserker warriors of the Viking hordes. The slaughter had extended to the party's horses and dogs and it seemed that only Sir Frederick's hawks had escaped the massacre as there was no sign of them.

The worst had been reserved for Sir Frederick himself, for he had suffered deep slashes to his face and forearms in a vain attempt to ward off his attacker's blows, for his arms and fists had been his only weapon of defence as he had ridden out without armour or a weapon. But the greatest indignity was saved for when he must have been already dead or near death, for his body had been tied to a tree as if sitting down to rest there, and then a large fire had been built between his out-stretched legs.

It was said the charcoal was still glowing and the smell of roast meat thick in the air when his body was found.

When the news reached Sir William de Warenne, he flew into a rage and sent a troop of his most trusted cavalry into Norfolk to levy a fine of forty-six marks on the inhabitants of Douneham Market, a Norman custom that became known as the *murdrum* whereby the nearest town would be fined whenever a Norman was found dead by violence.

Sir William not only used his men to stake his claim to the estates of Sir Frederick as, being his brother-in-law, he was the rightful beneficiary, but also to ask far and wide who could have done this terrible deed?

His lieutenants did their job well, as Norman soldiers tend to, and before Lent was out, Sir William had received reports of how, weeks before, two travellers had caroused drunkenly in an ale-house in the port of Lynn and demanded that the alewife there cook them a pie from the dead birds slung from their saddle.

She had remembered this well, for the birds in question were three brace of fine hawks with their necks wrung and had told Sir William's investigators that she would not normally come across such fine birds for the pot, but simmered with a good handful of 'petersilie', which the more educated call parsley, they had proved tasty enough.

She described the travellers as young and strong and had paid her in Flemish coin and two suits of monks' robes, which she had in turn sold to a Lynn clothier who was grateful for the woollen cloth once the blood had been washed out of it.

The alewife was not prosecuted with any crime, but a monk from Ely was sent to Lynn to take a deposition from her. The monk pressed her to describe the men further but she would only add that one of them had long blond hair, matted in the Danish style, and eyes which seemed to fix the innocent so fiercely that it was only with the help of God did she herself manage to break their stare.

When the brother of Ely presented his report to Sir William, quartered in Cambridge, he uttered just one word.

'Hereward.'

Eleven

Giraldus

Oh, dear Jesu! This Hereward should be pruned from a family tree, not remembered in one.

An unworthy man; a sinner and a murderer. A hot-tempered man, no doubt, and a man given to deep and dark melancholies as witnessed by his fondness for the root of the Christmas Rose, a well-known remedy for the disease which attacks men's minds and withers them.

If, that is, the book of Brother Thomas is to be believed and I see no reason why it should not be.

Brother Thomas writes of those days – strangely innocent days – with the conviction of a man who saw events with his own eyes and heard men speak with his own ears. I can detect little recension of the books of other scribes in his work, or if there is, the work of those scholars is long forgotten, and best forgotten for the fewer books which tell this version of Hereward's life, the better.

I can forsee that I must write Hereward's story from the beginning if it is to satisfy my patron Baldwin le Wac, for the truth is simply not manageable. But there are some things I can use from Brother Thomas's account.

His mention, for example, of the building of the first Norman castles which must have seemed so strange to the English. Most were copied from the castles William had built across his Ducal lands in Normandy and many did indeed use stone imported from Caen. Today, of course, they are grander and stronger and more numerous than any seen by Hereward, and the cover the length and breadth of the country.

Soldiers with crossbows would also have been a rare sight for the Saxons, as the weapon was unknown in England before the year King William came, though well-known in more forward-thinking lands. Was it not his holiness Pope Urban II who banned the use of crossbows against fellow Christians, though not, of course, against Saracens (in 1097.)? And that prohibition, nobly meant and well-intentioned, lasted for several months before men conveniently forgot and the Church has yet to find the moment to remind them.

Thomas also refers to the great embroidery sewn for Bishop Odo by the craftsmen and seamstresses of Canterbury which depicted the coming of the Normans and the defeat of Harold Godwinson at Hastings. It is indeed a thing of wonder, as I have seen it in the church of Our Lady in Bayeux, to which Odo gave it and where it remains to this day, although in Normandy they call it Queen Matilda's Tapestry after William's wife, never mentioning the Kentish skill which created this wonder of the western world.

As for Thomas's descriptions of the places and habits of the Fenlands, all that he writes is confirmed by the chronicles and rolls of Peterborough, Ely and Crowland which I have read, save for the fact that the port of Lynn is called Bishop's Lynn (becoming King's Lynn in honour of Henry VIII.) since it fell into the gift of the Bishop of Norwich.

But I am not writing a topography of the eastern shires or a history of the monasteries of England. I must only consider what my mentor is likely to think worthy and noble when it comes to his lineage. I must take the facts which Thomas presents and, like a surgeon, remove those which are infected and diseased. Like a word doctor, I must nurse the ailing facts into better health. What we will be left will be presentable and palatable even if it is not the absolute truth, which only God knows and men rarely wish to hear.

From what Thomas calls Hereward in his 'Berserker' period I shall take the fact that he returned to England to find his house and home appropriated by unfeeling Norman landlords with whom he naturally disputed the title. After appealing to the Church (he did go and see Abbot Brand), he 'accepted' the title of outlaw (I will not mention this was the second time) and retired to the watery Fens where, as we all know, he was later to make his name.

As to the assault on Ogier the Breton (of whom history says nothing) and the murder of Sir Frederick in Norfolk (a case never proven in court), I think I will omit these facts from Baldwin's family tree.

It has been made clear to me that Baldwin is looking for brave and noble ancestors, not coarse thugs and murderers whose deeds have been softened by street songs and alehouse rhymes.

In my book, I will include only those acts of Hereward which can be regarded as just and valiant.

It could be a very short book.

Twelve

Thomas

Hereward the Plunderer

[i]

Hereward and Martin Lightfoot spent two weeks in Lynn skulking from tavern to tavern according to the testimony of the alewife who had cooked stewed hawk for them. No disturbances or incidents of riotous behaviour involving them were reported in this period, though it is quite possible they went unnoticed amidst the general disorder and lawlessness which is common to all working ports, but especially Lynne.

When their coin was exhausted on food, drink and stabling, they sold their horses for a pittance (for sailors who live in ports have little use for horses) and paid for passage on a hulk loaded down with wool, blocks of salt and malted barley, bound for Ipswich, then Dover and finally Calais, their ultimate destination being St Omer and the house of the Count of Flanders.

Their voyage around the eastern shires was a long and uncomfortable one, hugging the coast-line against the spring tides. More than once the look-outs on the hulk spied a lone Danish longship on the horizon and they stayed six days in Ipswich on hearing reports in the harbour that a flotilla of Danish ships was patrolling the mouth of the river Deben to the north, a well-known landfall for seaborne invaders throughout history.

The incident may be true or false, for it was a common enough saying in the shires of Norfolk and Suffolk that a man would have to be hiding from Vikings in order to feel the need to spend six days in Ipswich. But the tale is partly confirmed by the many references in shire and church chronicles for that year of our Lord 1068, to visitations by and sightings of Danish longships carrying the envoys and scouts of King Svein of Denmark, a ruler whom many in England, and especially in the eastern regions, looked towards as a liberator from the Norman yoke which was now clamped hard across the country.

For it is a fact that at this time, the true cost of the Norman invasion was being felt far and wide. Monasteries, for so long safe (safe and fat, some would say) under the rule of Saxon and English kings were now being made to give up much of their best farm land and historic grazing rights. They were also expected to surrender not only the deposits they held in care for noble families, but actual treasures of the church itself. Thus did many a fine tapestry and hanging decorated with gold or silver thread, find its way into a Norman castle.

And the very castles themselves, springing up across the land like mushrooms after a morning mist, required all the skilled and much of the unskilled labour there was as well as money. At times it seemed as if they needed as much money

112

as there was in the world and even then the final mason's bill would remain unpaid. For two years, no church or priory wall had been repaired, no roof mended. The building of William's castles seemed to consume all the stone, timber and nails in England and even then many hulks and keels were pressed into service to bring in further supplies from Normandy.

While villains and serfs laboured digging wells, ditches and carp and eel ponds (for what good is a castle if the garrison cannot be fed?) fields went untended. Harvests spoiled and the next year's crops went unsown.

There was hunger in English bellies, though not in Norman ones. They enjoyed all the spoils a victor can expect. King William was generous indeed in granting lands and rights to his Norman knights and his Breton and Flemish allies. Many gained more wealth and land by marrying the Saxon widows of warriors who had died at the battles in Yorkshire or at Hastings in the year of the Conquest, and there were many of them.

Rumblings there were aplenty, and not just in stomachs, for what William's barons did to the towns and lands, so did his brother Odo's priests and monks do to the Church, led by bishops and clergy schooled in the zealous Trinity Abbey of Fecamp in Normandy, where the Benedictines have a reputation for strict discipline only equalled by their reputation for making strong liquors from fruit.

The first stirrings of actual revolt against King William had come from Wales and the West but now there was growing discontent in the northern

113

shires, encouraged, as always, by the Scots. That such revolts were anticipated by the Normans was clear, for why else were they building castles and planting garrisons where there had been none needed since the legions of Rome left this island? But without a single strong leader to unite them, the rebellious English were surely doomed.

Of all these matters, Hereward was blissfully unaware, or if he was aware, he was unconcerned. His argument with the Normans was simply one of property. The Normans had stolen his manor and estate at Bourne, which he regarded (falsely) as his by right of inheritance; he cared not that the Normans had stolen England. That he had assaulted one of King William's knights and was strongly suspected of murdering another was, to him, a mere trick of fate. He had nothing against the Normans as such. Indeed he admired their skill in feats of arms and strategies in warfare, and had trained many a Norman solider or Norman ally during his time in Flanders. To them he imparted all the wisdom his grandfather Toki had given him about fighting on foot with longsword and axe. From them, he learned the power of the jabbing lance as wielded by a man mounted on a charging horse and also the use of unarmoured archers who could harry the strongest defensive line by running forward, firing and then retreating.

Apart from their military prowess, Hereward gave the Normans little thought. And although he himself would long nurse the memory of personal slights which he felt he had suffered, it never occurred to him that the memories of Normans were even longer.

[ii]

Hereward and Martin landed in Calais without a quarter-penny between them and debts to the master of the hulk they had sailed on; debts for gambling and a cask of ale which the pair had broached without permission. These were paid only by the surrender of their cloaks, daggers and sheepskin fleeces which the destitute outlaws had acquired during their winter in the Fens.

With their only possession Hereward's firesteel sword in its wooden scabbard, the pair set out on the road for St Omer and the villagers they passed along the way could have been forgiven for mistaking them for beggars. On more than one occasion they were rightly taken for thieves, as Hereward would call out to the women working the fields or foraging in the hedgerows, then approach them smiling his biggest smile and entrancing them with his eyes while Martin Lightfoot slipped behind them to where they had stored their midday meals of hard bread and straw-bound cheese for themselves and their children, or whatever fruits and roots they had gathered.

However paltry the results of their thievery, they laughed as they ran down the road to escape the howls and accurately thrown stones of their victims. At noon they rested in a hayrick and ate what they had foraged.

Hereward picked a morsel of soft cheese from his matted beard and then lay back in the hay, staring at the summer sun above.

'Be of good cheer, my faithful hound,' he said to Martin lying beside him, 'St Omer cannot be far and Sir Robert will make us welcome.'

Lightfoot sat up and began to examine the boots hanging by threads to his feet.

'I hope he will and that his generosity extends to his cobbler, for I am sorely in need of new shoes.'

'The Count will see us set right,' said Hereward with the confidence of a child. 'Did we not serve him well?'

'It is over a year since we served him and he is now the Count of all Flanders. He will have much to distract him and perhaps he has forgotten his faithful dogs of war,' observed Martin.

'How could he forget his English hard men? Did we not train the Count's army for him?'

'An army that now fights alongside the Normans and against the English.'

'Yes, yes, I know,' said Hereward irritably, 'but those Flemish troops which fought at Hastings with William against Harold, they were not Count Robert's men. And anyway, I never had any time for Harold Godwinson and his gang of West Saxon liars. My grandfather Toki also taught me never trust men from Wessex, for they would always betray you.'

'Old Toki may have given wise advice, but times have changed. William is King in England as well as Duke in Normandy. He is powerful. So powerful, there is none can stand against him.'

'Svein of Denmark could!' shouted Hereward. 'By God, he could! King Svein will not let his Christian English cousins be robbed and starved

116

by those arrogant Norman bastards. You keep a sharp eye on the east, Martin Lightfoot, and you will see the Danish fleet come to push the damn Normans out of England so that true men can reclaim their property.'

'Will King Svein bring a supply of shoes with him?' asked Martin, holding up his foot and waggling it until his threadbare boot fell off.

'Fool!' said Hereward, slapping him heartily across the chest.

Martin flung an arm around Hereward's neck and both roared with laughter as they wrestled and rolled until the hayrick collapsed under them.

A mile down the road they were still picking straws, seeds and insects from their hair and clothing, when Martin stopped in mid-stride and sniffed the air.

'Horses,' he said.

'Good,' said Hereward. 'We need walk no further.'

More prudent, God-fearing men would have left the road for a hiding place among the trees at the approach of unseen, unknown riders, especially two such ill-dressed and poorly armed strangers in a foreign land. But not Hereward and Martin.

Fearlessly, though some would say foolishly, they placed themselves in the middle of the road and faced the sound of oncoming hooves. Hereward stood, feet apart, legs braced, his sheathed sword resting on his right shoulder, both his hands entwined around the hilt, for he knew that men were less suspicious when they could see that a blade was still in its scabbard in plain sight.

Martin meanwhile collected a dozen stones

from the side of the road, none more than half the size of a man's fist, and laid them randomly at his feet, again in plain sight of anyone who would look, for who would think it strange to see stones on a road?

There were five riders and they were coming from the direction of Guines at a slow trot. Neither men nor horse wore armour or chain mail, but three of the riders hefted long lances and two had crossbows slung across their backs. The leading pair of horses were further burdened by a dead stag tied across the rump of one and a dead boar almost as big as the stag across the other.

'Hunting party,' said Hereward out of the corner of his mouth. 'Used to pig-sticking, not facing down men.'

'If they can stick a boar, they can stick us,' whispered Martin, weighing the stone concealed in his fist.

'Then we take the lance men first. The bowmen are no threat. Make no sudden movements and smile at them, make them feel at home.'

'They are at home,' observed Martin. 'We are the strangers.'

But he followed Hereward's instructions, seeing the sense of them. Two men on foot were no match for five mounted men coming at the charge, but horses which were not moving posed little threat to quick-witted men who could dodge between them, getting in close to the riders. Hereward had also rightly judged that the two riders with crossbows would not have time to load their weapons.

The riders in the hunting party drew their horses together as they approached the men on foot waiting in the middle of the road. Their leader, a young man of no more than sixteen years with no beard and his black hair cropped short, almost to the skin, was the rider whose horse carried the dead boar. He kept his lance pointed skywards, the butt resting on his stirrup, and reigned in his mount when only a few paces from the two men in the road. He addressed them in the Flemish tongue, which Hereward and Martin both understood well enough, but feigned confusion.

'Ho there, strangers, what business do you have on this road?'

Hereward and Martin muttered softly to each other and moved closer to the horsemen until they could feel the breath of the animals on their faces.

'Declare yourself! What men are you? What is your business?' the young huntsman said nervously.

'Our business is in St Omer, and it is our own,' answered Hereward. 'Who wishes to know?'

'I am Folcard, Captain of the Guard of Robert Count of Flanders. Any business you think you have in St Omer is therefore the business of the Count.'

'It is indeed, and you show wisdom for one so young,' said Hereward, although the difference in their ages was but five or six years.

'Then you will declare your business to me now before you give us the road.'

The young captain turned to his companions,

119

none much older than he, and they nodded in agreement with him.

'I will not share my business with a captain I have never heard of, however worthy he may be,' said Hereward with a smile. 'When I last had dealings with the Count, his captains were fine Englishmen called Siward. Cousins they were, and kinsmen of mine, called Siward the Red and Siward the White. I would share my business with them.'

Hereward said all this reasonably and with kindness in his voice, making no sudden moves though never did his eyes stray from the young captain's face.

'The fashion for English mercenaries has gone from these shores and the Siward cousins only exercise their sword arms by raising pots of ale in the whorehouses of St Omer these days.'

'That sounds like them,' said Hereward, his smile widening. 'We must hurry to their side, so we will be requiring your horses, young sir.'

'We do not have two horses to spare,' said Folcard, his brow furrowed at this odd request from the filthy stranger dressed in rags smiling up at him from below his horse's head.

'No,' said Hereward, 'you have five!'

And with that, he swung his sword with both hands so that the edge of the heavy wooden scabbard cracked Folcard's horse between the eyes.

As the animal's front legs began to buckle, Martin let fly with the stone he had been nursing, hitting the rider to Folcard's right in the middle of his forehead and scooped up more stones from his reserves on the road without waiting to admire his aim. Hereward jumped to his right and swung at the rider on Folcard's left flank, slashing his weapon at the boy's ankle as it rested in his stirrup. The crack of bone was heard above the whinnying of terrified horses and the rider screamed, for Hereward had no need of learning in ancient Greek history to know that a man's ankle is one of his most vulnerable spots.

Even before Folcard's horse had sunk to its knees, Martin had launched more stones at the fourth and fifth riders, who made no attempt to reach for their crossbows, scoring hits on both man and horse.

The skirmish ended as swiftly as it had begun, as Hereward grabbed Folcard's tunic and hauled him from his collapsing horse, flinging him into the dust. On Folcard's face was a look of pure disbelief; on Hereward's, a smile which had not moved and which remained as he smacked down his still-sheathed sword on the back of Folcard's neck.

One of the crossbowmen who had suffered the least from Martin's barrage of stones, attempted to turn his horse and ride away but the beast, weighed down with the carcase of the hunted stag and infected with the screams of the other animals, refused to answer the rein. Without hesitation, the young archer swung his leg over his saddle, jumped down into the road and began to run in the direction of Guines as fast as his legs could carry him.

Hereward laughed out loudly, revelling in the confusion all around him as he swung and chopped at unseated rider and prancing horse alike, while his more practical companion Martin began to gather loose bridle reins, making calming noises to the wide-eyed animals. So adept was he at his task, which he approached with all the skill of a natural-born horse thief, that only one horse bolted down the road and then only for a distance of some fifty paces before it too stood still, waiting to be captured.

Four young hard men of Flanders lay at Hereward's feet in the road; two of them dead to world, yet still breathing, one sitting cross-legged trying to rub his eyes clean of the blood pouring from the deep gash in his forehead and one writhing, clutching his broken ankle and crying for his mother, his priest and his God in that order.

Flushed, sweating and still with a smile fixed across his face, Hereward straddled the body of the inert Folcard and began to remove his leather boots.

'These should fit you, my old dog,' he shouted, throwing the boots at Martin. 'Then we can present ourselves to Sir Robert well-shod, well-mounted and with fresh meat for his table. That's what I call a good day's work!'

Beneath him, Folcard groaned and Hereward crouched down, grabbing a handful of the boy's hair and jerking his face out the dust.

'If you truly are a master of arms of Flanders,' Hereward said to him, 'then you should find yourself a new line of work, for you were not born to this one.'

Then he pushed the boy's face into the road.

As he swung himself into Folcard's saddle, he

stroked the dead boar strapped across the horse.

'You will make good eating tonight in St Omer, my friend,' he told the pig. 'And I give you fair warning that I have worked up a good appetite, as well as a mighty thirst. Hurry up, Lightfoot, the two Siwards await us in St Omer and a man need look no further for good drinking companions. I cannot wait to see the cousins again.'

Martin stomped his new boots until they fitted around his feet and just to make sure he kicked the man he had unhorsed with his first stone.

'And your wife,' he said.

'What?' Hereward looked puzzled.

'You left a wife in St Omer,' said Martin gently.

'Oh, yes,' said Hereward. 'We'll be seeing her too, I suppose.'

[iii]

Even Hereward could not fail to notice the changes to Count Robert's household in St Omer, most notably the fact that what had been a fortified house was now the centre of a castle being built on the Norman pattern. Whether its construction showed Sir Robert's admiration for the much vaunted strength of Normandy, or perhaps because he feared it, though, was a consideration beyond the wit of Hereward. For him, a return to St Omer was almost like coming home, for in all his short life, it had been the one place where he had been able to apply his talent for brawling and violence without recrimination and for profit.

In a courtyard crowded with labourers, masons

123

and hauliers, Hereward called out to the first armed guard wearing Sir Robert's colours that he saw.

'Where is Sir Robert? Tell him he has guests who have meat for his table and thirsts which will empty his cellars!'

The guard eyed the two riders with suspicion, distrusting their vagabond appearances and recognizing the five horses in their string. But the guard was a cautious man, with a wife and children, and had come across such wild men before.

'My Lord, the Count of Flanders is with the monks of St Bertin at the abbey,' he said carefully, 'where he rests until the castle walls are complete. The hospitality of the abbey is extended to all Christian travellers of pure heart.'

'A pretty speech,' said Hereward. 'The men of Flanders are now trained in the courtly arts, I see, as well as in skill at arms. Who is your captain here?'

'The man whose horse you ride,' said the guard, lowering his eyes.

'Ah, yes, the boy ... er...'

'Folcard,' whispered Martin Lightfoot.

'Yes, Folcard. We met him out hunting and he gave us the loan of these fine beasts. He will be along shortly. Do you not have a captain or even two captains called Siward? They are kin of mine and will vouch for us without hesitation.'

'The one they call Rufus, the red-beard, is here and can be found in the kitchens. Siward the White, as he is known, is with Count Robert at St Bertin,' the guard told them, looking nervously about him like a frightened animal.

124

'We have meat, so we shall take it to our kins-man in the kitchens to see how good a butcher he is!' Hereward cried jovially as he dismounted and began to pull Folcard's prize boar across his shoulders.

Hereward may have spoken in jest but in fact he spoke in truth for Siward the Red, naked to the waist and lathered in blood and sweat, was indeed performing the butcher's art on a pair of skinned and split sheep dangling by their hind legs from hooks in the kitchen ceiling. Siward was wielding a sharp flensing blade with one hand, the other plucking at loose entrails and offal and dropping them into a large bowl on the floor from which he was keeping two slavering dogs at bay with well-judged kicks.

Siward barely glanced at the two grimy figures as they entered the kitchens, each bearing a dead animal, wearing them as a man might wear a cloak.

'String them up,' he said, 'and they can wait their turn. And make sure that boar is dead. The last one almost took my fucking fingers off.'

'That would have been a loss to the ladies.'

'What do you...? Hereward! You little fucker! You're back! And so is that little sod Lightfoot!'

'That's right, Siward, the wild boys are back in town. Where do they keep the ale around here?'

Being in a manor house kitchen, the three companions had no shortage of ale or cider, or wine, once a pair of gluttons, as the serving boys were called, had been threatened with a sound beating unless they revealed the cellar's finest German vintages. Before dusk fell, the three companions became four when Siward the White arrived from St Bertin where runners had been sent by the house guards to report that Folcard's hunting party had not returned, but two English vagabonds had ridden in their horses and had laid siege to all the meat and drink in the house.

'I knew it had to be you two bastards!' Siward the White had roared as he embraced his old friends. 'What news of England?'

'None that cannot wait until we are drunk enough to tell it true,' roared Hereward. 'Before then, you tell me: how has Flanders survived without me this past year and more?'

And as the Englishmen began to settle into serious drinking, as only Englishmen can, around the kitchen's long table, the two Siwards told Hereward and Martin how much was unchanged in that Flanders continued to wage small wars against its Friesian neighbours, who were mostly pirates anyway, and quickly took to their boats rather than face a decent fight. Yet many things had changed in Hereward's absence.

The Count was not the carefree Sir Robert that Hereward had once known and loved. He was no longer a knight who would share the trials of warfare with his men, but rather one who commanded from afar. The Count was also much taken with the Norman way of things – was he not copying their fashion for castles here in St Omer? And if the Duchy asked, nay, demanded, more levies, did the Count not offer his best men, men that Hereward had trained himself?

To replace them, Flanders was prepared to take the basest of base recruits and even Frenchmen

126

could be seen in Flemish colours these days. Any serf, rogue or thief was welcome in the armed companies of Flanders; but not Englishmen.

No edict or official pronouncement had been made but it was clear to anyone with eyes to see that this policy was influenced by the need not to anger the Normans. Had not the two Siwards themselves suffered the indignity of being demoted from captains of men-at-arms? Siward the White now served as no more than a herald for Count Robert's entourage, and then only when heralding duties did not require knowledge of Latin or French or matters of etiquette. His cousin, Siward the Red, who had adopted the name Rufus, had fared even worse and had been dismissed from Sir Robert's armed company completely.

He did himself admit, amidst much laughter, that this was probably less to do with the fact that he was English, than the testimony – false, of course – that he had raped the daughters of a local weaver whilst they were in a state of grace on their way home from Mass in the church of Our Lady of Calais. The weaver's daughters had lied – all four of them – and so had the priest who had claimed to witness the rape; even claimed it had taken place *during* the Mass. Rufus himself could not remember the incident at all, his defence being that he must have been so drunk that the offence was possible only in the imagining of it, the deed itself being impossible. But who, in these troubled times, was willing to believe an English voice in a foreign land?

Siward the White defended the Count inasmuch

as Rufus had never stood trial for the alleged offences against the weaver's daughters, nor even, for that matter, the unexplained blinding of the priest of Our Lady of Calais some days later, and Sir Robert had (out of loyalty and charity) found him work as a butcher in his own kitchens.

When Martin Lightfoot had asked, with some difficulty due to the amount of ale he had allowed into his mouth to steal his tongue, 'Where did you learn the butcher's art?' Rufus replied that he never had been 'prenticed to a butcher, but he had done knife work on many a rogue and enemy in the past and the skills were much the same. Once the skin was sliced, all the innards which fell out looked much the same whether man or beast.

The four men agreed on this with a seriousness worthy of a great theological debate, then Hereward called for more wine and climbed unsteadily to his feet.

'I will have you reinstated as my captains, my friends, for we English must stick together.'

'That may not be an easy matter,' cautioned Siward the White.

'And why not? Will Sir Robert not welcome home the champion who led his men against the city of Guines and the Friesian scum who dwell on the outer islands? Will he not accept my sword if I offer it to him?'

'Sir Robert changed when he became the Count,' muttered Rufus. 'He no longer campaigns with his men, nor eats nor drinks with them. He moves in higher circles now.'

'A man does not forget his comrades so easily,' argued Hereward, 'and a lord – any lord – needs

128

hard men he can trust. Are you saying that the Count of Flanders no longer needs friends? Friends who can protect him and fight for him? If Sir Robert no longer needs strong men to watch his back, then truly, things have changed around here in my absence!'

'The world has changed in your absence, Hereward,' said Siward seriously, shaking his head to clear it of drink. 'The Count of Flanders has friends; powerful friends who keep him close. Friends he does not wish to offend and so he does what they tell him to.'

'You mean the Normans?' asked Martin.

Hereward's jaw dropped open when Siward answered.

'Of course the fucking Normans! Open your eyes. William is Duke in Normandy and King in England. His barons take the land; his bishops take the churches. Flanders is his ally because it cannot afford to be his enemy. William's army is like nothing seen in the world since the legions of Rome conquered all before them.'

Hereward snorted in derision, spraying his compatriots with wine and spittle.

'Do not underestimate the Normans when they fight, Hereward,' Siward said angrily, levelling a finger at his kinsman. 'They are well-equipped, disciplined and absolutely ruthless. When they have the scent of an enemy they simply do not stop until that enemy is destroyed. And they never – never – forget.'

Hereward brandished an empty mug, signalling to the serving boys in the shadows of the kitchen to bring more wine, then he slapped Martin on

129

the back with such force that Lightfoot's face pitched forward and smacked into the table.

'By all the Saints,' shouted Hereward, 'nay, by the sacred relics of Saint Oswald himself, is it possible that I am drinking with cowards who are willing to drop their eyes and tug their hair whenever one of those arrogant Norman bastards rides by and farts in their general direction?'

'Are you calling me a coward?' said Rufus as he tried to raise himself unsteadily from the table, only to sink down again on to the bench he was seated on.

'If I was, you would challenge me, old friend. I would expect no less of you, in fact, I would insist on it. That is what an Englishman would do, but a Norman would hide behind the stone walls of a castle until his army came to him and only when he was sure he outnumbered you, would he fight.'

'Perhaps,' said Siward gravely, 'that is why they win.'

'They do not always win!' Martin objected.

'There are few left alive who can remember their defeats. Have they not killed the King of England and taken his country?'

'They will not hold it,' growled Hereward. 'There are not enough Normans in the world to subdue all the English.'

'Oh, Hereward, open your eyes! William offers his nobles and his allies estates and riches which are far greater than the ones they already own in Normandy or Brittany or even Flanders. He is not short of men willing to claim such prizes. The Normans are moving into England just as your

130

ancestors and mine – men like your grandfather Toki and his father – came to settle in longships from the north. William's barons are taking the villains and serfs from their old lands and placing them on their new estates. They are there and they will stay there; it must be God's will that this is the fate of England.'

'But it is not mine!' shouted Hereward staggering to his feet and stumbling into the hanging carcase of a sheep. Steadying himself with one arm around the animal's haunches, he stretched out the other and extended a finger towards Martin Lightfoot, who was hunched over the table, sleeping deeply and snoring loudly. 'Nor is it his! My oldest friend, Martin the Light-footed, is as brave as a lion and as loyal as a dog. He has stood with me against these Norman thieves without fear. The Count will give us arms and men and money and we will return to England to claim what is rightfully mine. You and your cousin are welcome to join us unless you prefer kitchen work here in Flanders.'

Siward shook his head and looked to his cousin for support but found none as Rufus too had slumped forward on to the table.

'I doubt the Count will help you, Hereward. Have you not heard what we have been telling you? The nobles of Flanders and Brittany are allies of King William. They supply men, horses, ships, arms and grain to the army that has occupied England. In return, William grants them titles and estates. Do you not think that Count Robert has his eye on some rich corner of England he can call his own?'

Hereward gave Siward a look which few men had seen and survived unhurt.

'I will front Count Robert right now. He will see justice done for a man who has served him hard and true!' he shouted, slumping against the hanging carcase.

'It is night, Hereward, and the road to St Bertin is dark, let us go in the morning.'

'I will take a torch,' Hereward slurred, having difficulty speaking as well as remaining upright. 'I will be perfectly safe.'

'You may be,' said Siward reasonably, 'but will the good citizens of St Omer asleep in their beds be safe?'

Siward had known Hereward long enough to know that his fascination with fire increased with the amount of drink he had taken.

'Wait until morning and we'll go up to the abbey together. You pay your respects to Sir Robert and see Turfrida.'

Hereward stared blankly at him and slowly began to slide down the body of the hanging sheep as his knees buckled.

'Turfrida is staying at the abbey too,' said Siward.

For answer he received only a long stare, as if the candles in Hereward's eyes were dying out.

'Your wife, Turfrida,' Siward tried but Hereward had hit the kitchen floor.

Siward stood up and peered over the table at his inert companion, quickly deciding that the best policy was to let this particular sleeping dog lie.

It took the cousins Siward and Rufus the first three hours after dawn to prepare Hereward for an audience with the Count of Flanders. They were little helped by Martin Lightfoot who remained curled in a kitchen corner bemoaning the impurities of Flanders ale and the poor quality of German wine, though no such thought had occurred to him the night before.

Hereward did not complain at his treatment for it was as if he had been robbed of the power of speech. In silence, he allowed Siward to lead him to a horse trough in the kitchen yard and be sluiced with water until most of the sheep's blood had been rinsed from his beard and hair. Then, fittingly, it was with a pair of shearing clippers that Rufus trimmed the worst matted material from Hereward's beard. He wisely made no attempt to trim the long blond hair of which the young warrior was inordinately proud, but he did use a fine bone comb smeared with beeswax to bring it to order.

They found him a red wool shirt and smooth leather trousers with red leather gaiters and a short fleece cloak held at the throat by a large bronze pin shaped like a boar, one of Siward's most treasured possessions.

When Hereward called for his only remaining possession, his sword, to be polished and its edges sharpened, he was told that Sir Robert no longer received armed men into his hall unless they were captains of his guard, a rank which none of the four Englishmen now held.

Remembering the words of Siward the White, Hereward said: 'Perhaps the world has changed,

133

and not for the better,' and leaving Martin asleep, he set off with the two cousins to walk to the Abbey of St Bertin, where they were kept waiting until almost noon before Sir Robert, flanked by armed guards in full chain mail, summoned them to his presence.

The Count remained seated behind a refectory table upon which a procession of monks and clerks presented documents for his perusal or his seal, documents which he preferred to read rather than look his old friend in the eye.

'So, the famous English outlaw comes to Flanders to hide does he?' Sir Robert announced suddenly.

This was far from the welcome Hereward had expected and from any other man, such a welcome would have been answered with a blow, but Hereward was careful not to assault a lord of noble birth in front of so many witnesses.

'I hide from no man, my Lord. I come seeking only to serve Flanders as I once did willingly, bravely and without thought of profit for myself.'

'No one would ever question your bravery, Hereward, and it is beyond dispute that you served Flanders well as a master-at-arms. I should know this, for have I not myself fought at your side?'

'Then you cannot deny me, my Lord,' said Hereward with a smile.

'Deny you what, my old comrade?'

'Make me a knight of Flanders. Let me lead your army so that I may serve you and restore my fortunes.'

'But I thought that, dear Hereward, was the

very reason why you left the service of Flanders, to claim your fortune in England.'

'I returned to England to claim my birthright only to find it stolen by a Norman,' growled Hereward in a tone which made Count Robert, his guards and the monkish clerks stop whatever they were doing and look at him in earnest.

'Not stolen,' said the Count carefully, 'but appropriated as the spoils of a just war in pursuit of Duke William's rightful claim to the kingship of England.'

'A claim still disputed by many in England,' said Hereward severely, failing to notice the two monks at the end of the refectory table who were scribbling down his every word.

'Though not by you, my old friend, for were you not in the service of my father when he was Count of Flanders at the very time that Duke William's navy was sailing him to English shores and his battle with Harold Godwinson?'

'I held no allegiance to Harold the West Saxon.'

'Then you must recognize William as your rightful king, for surely you would not seek service again with Flanders, who are known to be an ally of Normandy, if you did not.'

'Do not confuse me with talk of kings, my Lord. I am a simple man who gives his loyalty to men who are loyal to him. I have no dealings with kings, I am a sworn man of Peterborough Abbey and have been since I was old enough to carry a sword.'

'And how has the abbot there repaid this loyalty of which you are so proud? Has he not outlawed you? Yet again?'

Hereward's jaw dropped and his face began to flush bright red.

'Do not think that Flanders is a small country far away from affairs in England, Hereward,' continued the Count. 'We have heard of your assault on Ogier the Breton, a true friend of King William and, therefore, of Flanders.'

'He had stolen Bourne Manor, which was mine by right!' stormed Hereward.

'Not, it seems, by the law of the Church, nor the law of the new king and you should not have pursued your claim by striking down and crippling a confidant of that king.'

'But those estates have been claimed by my family for three generations!' wailed Hereward in a voice which reminded the clerics of a frightened child.

'Claimed, but not granted, Hereward, never granted. Not under English law, let alone Norman.'

'The Count of Flanders knows much,' snarled Hereward.

'He knows that tales told by a fond grandfather around a winter hearth are just that – tales for children. When those children become men, they must accept the world for what it really is; a world of laws and property rights, and lords and kings whose will must be obeyed. Manors and estates are not granted lightly on the bedtime stories of an old Viking.'

'Be careful, my Lord, when you scorn my family.'

At this, several of the monks drew breath sharply.

'I give no insult, Hereward, but for the love of God, think before you speak and give insult to others who are beyond your station. I meant no slight on your family, for is not Abbot Brand both your uncle and the man who outlawed you?'

'He did so on the command of a Norman!'

'A Norman knight who has every right to command! We know of Sir Frederick of Oosterlese, we have greeted him many times here in Flanders. Indeed he was an advocate of this very Abbey of St Bertin. Oh, yes, Hereward, I say he "was" for Sir Frederick is no longer among the living. But perhaps you knew that already?'

Hereward remained silent, forbidding his temper and his tongue to betray him for once as twenty or more pairs of eyes bored into him. He remained silent and proud, his jaw jutting out but remaining firmly closed.

'What I suspect you do not know is that Sir Frederick's property has passed to his brother-in-law, Sir William de Warenne, a most noble Norman whom King William favours with the title of Earl of Surrey, wherever that happens to be.'

'Him I know well,' snarled Hereward.

'Then you know that he is not a man to offend,' said the Count quickly, as if preventing Hereward from saying something which might condemn him. 'And as he has inherited Sir Frederick's advocacy of this abbey, he is a man I cannot afford to offend either. Let me speak plain, Hereward, if Sir William had issued a warrant naming you as the murderer of Sir Frederick, then I would have had you put in chains and sent into Normandy to await his convenience. I would have no choice; but there is no warrant to date.'

'Perhaps Sir William is too busy taxing the new estates he has inherited.'

'Careful, Hereward,' warned the Count. 'Had it not crossed your foolish mind how I know so much of events in England? Do you not realize – and you a supposed sworn man of Peterborough – that the religious houses of St Bertin and Peterborough and Ely are closer linked than ever since William became king? He has encouraged it, and now it seems that news passes between them faster than heralds and messengers can safely ride. What happens in England is quickly known in Normandy and Flanders, but similarly, what happens in Flanders is reported in England. Your presence here is not a secret, Hereward.'

'I hide from no man,' Hereward said quietly so that the scribes had to strain their ears to catch his words. 'Though perhaps I should begin to hide from the monks who spy for Sir William.'

'Do not make an enemy of Sir William de Warenne, Hereward,' said the Count in the same whisper.

'It is too late for that,' said Hereward.

[iv]

It is not known, except by God, whether Hereward truly appreciated that his arrival in St Omer, his visit to the abbey at St Bertin and his interview with Count Robert had all been noted, recorded and reported by the holy brothers there. And that those reports would be circulated

138

between the monastic houses wherever Norman rule held sway, with a speed Hereward could not imagine.

Whilst it may have been that Hereward's movements from the moment he landed in St Omer were known within a week in Peterborough and Ely, it must always be remembered that news and rumour travel in all directions. Bad tidings often travel faster than good; all news requires is an open ear.

It came as no surprise to anyone, save her husband, that the Lady Turfrida was as well-informed, if not better, of events in England as was the Count of Flanders. Some said that because of her large entourage of monks, nuns and servants (as befitted her rank) coupled with her spider's webs of connections through her family business as merchants and traders, she was in fact better informed than the gracious Matilda, wife to the Duke of Normandy and King of England, herself.

Turfrida was a woman of no little education who could read and write as well as any monkish scribe or copyist and converse in Latin better than most bishops. She was a wealthy woman in the Old English way as she held property in her name and not merely land and rents, but also ships and warehouses. Perhaps only one or two of the most trusted sub-priors at St Bertin knew exactly how much gold and silver coin Turfrida had deposited there and as to deposits in other abbeys in Christian countries, only Turfrida herself knew.

Rumour of her wealth was widespread and this brought her the adoration of the monks of St

Bertin and the respect of Count Robert. It was even whispered that her lands in Flanders and Normandy were lightly taxed by command of Duke William in lieu of leased ships which supplied his armies in England.

Certainly, in Flanders Count Robert treated Turfrida as an equal and even entrusted her with keys to his houses in St Omer as well as to the Abbey of St Bertin. These she wore openly from an iron girdle-hanger tied around her waist with a silk belt, normally a badge of honour for the Lady of the Manor. Whether Count Robert's wife (for he was indeed married with fine daughters) regarded this as a slight upon her own position is not recorded, but then the Countess was from a strict Norman family and knew her place.

Yet not only clerics and nobles respected Turfrida; she was known and liked, if not loved, among the lower ranks as a woman of true Christian charity and as a herbalist and witch whose skill with herbs, plants, potions, balms and charms matched that of any court or monastery physician.

Those of an unkind disposition, and there are many, would describe Turfrida as a plain woman, tall and with a flat face with eyes, some would say, too far apart. Even her admirers and those who sought favour would hesitate before describing her as a notable beauty, but it was the sly whisperer who maintained that a woman of such an age could only control a full-blooded man such as Hereward by wealth or witchcraft.

No monk or priest can ever know what really transpires in the bed chamber of a man and wife, but whereas those of lowly birth may be observed

140

by their immediate family and, in winter, their livestock, those of noble station are watched by an army of maids, serving girls and scullery urchins who have no ties of kinship and wagging tongues in their mouths.

And so it was that word of Hereward's reunion with the wife he had not seen for over a year soon gained common currency in the alehouses, markets, wharves and docks of St Omer, though not before the news had run the length of the Abbey of St Bertin from scriptorium to brewhouse.

To no one's surprise (no one who knew him, that is), Hereward did not rush to the apartments of his pining wife immediately following his audience with Count Robert, though he left the abbey grounds at some speed. Hereward, Siward the White and Siward the Red, known now as Rufus, departed St Bertin as if the hounds of hell had been unleashed upon their trail.

At the western gate of the abbey they found two horses lightly tethered in the orchard there and though there were a dozen or more monks working in the nearby vegetable patch, the three bold Englishmen untied the animals and mounted them.

One brave monk shouted out that the horses were the property of the Count, to which Hereward replied: 'And I am the Count's man until someone pulls my arse from this saddle and tells me different!'

With Hereward and Siward riding one and Rufus the other, the horses set off at a gallop causing great damage to that season's choicest crop of

141

leeks. It is a story still told in the kitchens and scullery of St Bertin and sometimes embellished with the fact that the horses belonged to members of the Count's guard, one of whom was the unfortunate Folcard who had already lost one horse to Hereward and seemed to be making a habit of it. Whether this is true is not known.

What is firmly attested is that the riders paused only to collect Hereward's sword and Martin Lightfoot before descending upon the riverside taverns of St Omer with the force, but not the stealth, of an invading army. To their credit, they handed their borrowed horses to a passing carter and his son, ordering them to see the beasts safely to Count Robert's household where they would be rewarded by Folcard, the Master at Arms. They did this partly in jest at young Folcard's expense but also because they were now well aware that the Count could not, or would not, protect them from the hanging offence of horse thievery.

Pooling what little money the two Siwards held (for Hereward and Martin had not a nipped halfpenny between them), the four young Englishmen proceeded to do what young Englishmen abroad in a foreign land do all too often when they feel their pride or their person has been affronted. They began to try and drink the taverns of the town dry.

By noon on the second day, they had exhausted what little credit they had managed to obtain (mostly by threat and harassment) in two alehouses and so moved into a tavern which specialized in the best quality ciders from Normandy. For an evening they entertained the tavern crowd with bawdy songs from their homeland. Perhaps mercifully, this unholy choir sang in Old English and Danish so that the true bawdiness of their songs was not fully appreciated by the majority of the locals, though enough sailors and rivermen (for St Omer was a busy little port) did understand enough for a brawl to break out during which several heads were cracked by Hereward's iron-bound scabbard.

Dawn on the third day found the four friends asleep on the muddy banks of the River Aa, a sight which provided much amusement for the passing boats setting out for the salt marshes near the coast. It was the jeers of the boatmen which woke Hereward though it would have taken the trumpets of heaven or the drums of hell to stir any of his companions. Hereward himself tried, dispensing kicks and oaths equally among the three sleepers, even dragging the unyielding Martin Lightfoot to the edge of the river and dunking his head there repeatedly.

Abandoning his attempts to raise his countrymen, Hereward staggered back to the tavern from which they had been expelled at some point during the night.

The witnesses who saw him said that he walked with a bowlegged and unsteady gait, as a man would who had just landed from a long sea voyage, or a rider who had just dismounted from a fat horse after a journey on a cold winter's night.

Finding the door of the tavern barred, Hereward is said to have repeatedly beaten on it with his fists shouting 'Drink! Drink! And some bread, too.' When this brought no response from inside the tavern, Hereward's voice boomed out the challenge that the tavern-keeper must provide victuals for he had surely poisoned his unsuspecting customers with sour cider.

When this charge (regarded as a serious one by the taverners of Flanders) also went unanswered, Hereward began to scour the backs of the houses of the town until he had found a goodly supply of faggots and logs and dry straw from the eaves of a low roof and these he piled at the door of the tavern.

Taking a trusted piece of flint from a fold in the belt of his trousers, and half drawing his sword, he knelt as if in prayer before the makings of his fire and attempted to put spark to straw. So engrossed was he in this action (and still so befuddled from the night before) that he did not hear the approach of the five men, all wearing helmets and mail and carrying long Norman shields, until they had formed a half circle around him.

'You must come with us,' said one of the soldiers, though Hereward appeared not to have heard and continued to strike sparks with his flint.

'Your presence is required up at the abbey,' the soldier tried again.

'Did the Count send you?' Hereward growled, still striking. 'Because the Count can go fuck himself! I'm not going anywhere until I've had a drink.'

At a signal from their leader, two of the soldiers rammed into Hereward's kneeling frame with all their weight behind their shields, whilst a third clubbed him senseless with the thickest log from his own fire pile.

The leader of the guards kicked Hereward in the face just to make sure he had no possible fight in him and then once more for his own amusement.

'You fucking English are all the same: long-haired, loudmouthed, bloody arrogant and you can't hold your drink. But you're going to get yours, my fine drunken sot with the long blond tresses; oh yes. It's not the Count you have to worry about. It's your wife who wants to see you.

[vi]

Turfrida kept Hereward in the rooms which had been set aside for her private use at the abbey for two weeks, during which time he was allowed no contact with any other man. Messages from the Count, carried by monks or heralds, were dealt with at the door. All Englishmen were officially proscribed from the abbey grounds.

Turfrida's maids fetched and carried food and wine heavily diluted with water and were frequently sent on specific errands to the abbey infirmary or gardens for herbs and balms, particularly potions of peony and Christmas Rose, and occasionally they were dispatched into the marshes outside St Omer to search for plants and roots unknown to the abbey's own herbalists.

After the first week the curious ears at every door and under every window reported that the sounds of purging and the expulsion of bodily waste had lessened to the point that they were barely audible. In the second week, the eavesdroppers discerned different sounds, similar yet different to those they had heard and growing louder, not quieter. The ladies and maids of the chamber, and several of the monks, recognized instantly the song of lust unbridled yet even the most worldly of them could not distinguish some of the sounds as to whether they were made by a man or a woman or even an animal.

And then the noises from Turfrida's apartments stopped, for man and wife began to walk about the abbey grounds hand-in-hand and though many would have liked to overhear their conversations, none were invited to attend them and woe betide anyone found following on behind too closely or lurking with an inquisitive ear.

'And so, my young outlaw,' said Turfrida when they were alone in the abbey vegetable garden, 'what does fate have in store for you?'

'Since when does a wife talk to her husband as if he were a boy to be chided as if for stealing apples?' asked Hereward with a twinkle in his eyes.

'When a wife knows she is ten years older than her husband and when that husband would steal the last apple in the world from the hand of a martyred saint if he thought he could make cider out of it.'

'It was always said that I was marrying a woman of fine wit,' said Hereward with some grace. 'But it was also said she would be no more than five years older than her husband. Said by the prior who married us, as I recall.'

'You must learn, dear husband, that priests can bend a truth almost as much as women if the cause is just.'

'That I have learned of late in England. About the duplicity of priests. The wiles of women I have long known.'

'Then you would be wise to stay clear of women, my dear husband, even if your fate has been entwined with priests and will continue so to be.'

'You have seen my future?' Hereward asked seriously.

Turfrida laughed.

'Oh, my beautiful, golden-haired lad! I have some skills in witchcraft when it comes to healing or, occasionally, cursing but I have never pretended to be a soothsayer or diviner of the stars. All I do is look at the world as it is and it is not too difficult to see how it will be in one year's time, or five or even fifty. It is no great skill and no magic is involved. You could see it yourself if you ever looked about you at the world instead of trying to fight it or drink it or steal it.'

'If the future is so easy to divine, my witch-wife, then tell me what it holds for us!'

The woman took the man's hands in hers and gazed down upon his face, for she was a good head taller than Hereward.

'Your future is what you will make it – with God's blessing, of course. So, my noble warrior knight, what will it be?'

'I will be just that – a warrior knight,' said Hereward joyously. 'For am I not that already?'

'You are certainly a warrior, my love, or at least a fighter and a scrapper, but you are no knight. You were declared outlaw under Saxon law and Norman law in England.'

147

'Then I will serve Flanders and earn my nobility from Count Robert.'

'That is unlikely, dearest husband, for have you not seen that Flanders now sits up and begs when Normandy calls its name? The Count will not even employ you because he dare not risk the displeasure of Sir William de Warenne.'

'Him again! That man dogs my feet as if I had walked through shit.'

'I think perhaps that sometimes when you see a pile of shit, my love, you jump in it with both feet. Can you not see that Count Robert cannot help you even if he wanted to?'

'Why should he not want to? I served him well enough. His enemies were my enemies.'

'But the Count's friends are not your friends, Hereward. You must look elsewhere for friends and allies.'

'Where? God's face, woman, did you not say yourself that I am damned in England and in Flanders? Where would you have me go to find friends? France? France is a country not fit for brigands. It is not even a proper country.'

'My poor husband; a brave warrior without a country to fight for,' Turfrida said as if to a child. 'Come, sit down here with me.'

'Do not mock me, wife,' growled Hereward.

'Sit, husband, sit. I do not mock you. I want to tell you where you can find a country.'

And so Hereward sat on the grass whilst his wife combed and plaited his hair and beard with a fine silver-handled bone comb and told him where his future lay.

'You must look to your old loyalties, Hereward,

if you are to make something of yourself,' she told him as she stroked his hair.

'Since I was a boy and able to carry a shield, I have been a sworn man of Peterborough Abbey, but I have no future there, for the abbey is now in thrall to their Norman overlords, withholding my estates from me and proclaiming me outlaw.'

'I know, my husband, I know,' soothed Turfrida.

Perhaps it was the sweetness of her voice which distracted Hereward or perhaps it was, as some say, the power witches are known to have when handling human hair. Whichever it was, Hereward never asked his wife how she did know all that she knew, for he had confessed nothing to her about his ill-fated visit to England.

'Your uncle, Abbot Brand, is in a very difficult position. He cannot help you,' she said quietly.

'He *will* not help me!' snapped Hereward. 'Just as Count Robert will not.'

'Neither the old abbeys of England nor a small country like Flanders can stand against the Normans, there is only one power which can.'

Turfrida's voice must have weaved a charm for her husband stared at her as if she spoke in a tongue he never encountered before and it was the wife who had to break the silence.

'Denmark, Hereward, Denmark. Does not King Svein of Denmark covet the throne of England?'

'He does?' asked Hereward and Turfrida sighed heavily.

'Yes, my love, he does. It is widely known that the one thing King William fears is a Danish war fleet which will inspire a rebellion by those Englishmen who still have the spirit to deny him his new kingdom.'

'There are many in the east of England who would support a Danish king,' said Hereward excitedly, 'they always have. Indeed, my grandfather always said he would trust a dead Dane over a live Saxon any time.'

'As I said, husband, you must look to your older loyalties.'

'But my oath was given first to Peterborough Abbey. Above all, I am sworn to protect the abbey; that has to be my governing oath.'

'Yet you cannot protect the abbey at Peterborough from the Normans, Hereward. Not alone. No single man can.'

'My uncle, Abbot Brand, has defied King William and will continue to do so!'

Turfrida stroked her husband's face and ran a finger over his lips, willing him to remain calm and then she whispered what she had to say into Hereward's ear, as a rider would clam a horse.

'Not for long, husband, not for long. I fear that Abbot Brand is dying. It is said he took a cold to the stomach in late winter and has been poorly treated by those of his own infirmary. He now has a wasting disease which is beyond even my skill to cure. He is not expected to see out the end of the year. The monks of Peterborough are already preparing his funeral Mass.'

'How do you know this to be true, wife? Is it witchcraft that allows you to see into the future?'

'No witchcraft does that, Hereward,' said Turfrida softly, grooming her husband's hair to calm him. 'I do not see the future, I am merely

150

told of the present by those who know.'

'But how?'

Hereward turned his head towards his wife and his eyes – those peculiar eyes which could strike fear into men – seemed only large and innocent, like those of a young deer or a surprised kitten, and looking into them only made Turfrida laugh and take her husband's face in both hands.

'Oh, Hereward, if only you could read and write! You would learn such things! The world is big and extends far beyond Peterborough Abbey and the manor of Bourne, if only you could *see* it.'

'Make me see, wife. Use your charms to make me see my future,' Hereward said gently, with rare affection.

'I have said I cannot make you see your future, Hereward, but I can help you see your opportunities, if you will let me.'

'As your husband and master,' Hereward said with a boyish grin, 'I grant you leave so to do.'

Turfrida returned his smile and said: 'Without argument or contradiction, my master?'

'That I cannot promise, for I am a true Englishman who always tries the goods before he buys them. Was that not true of our marriage?'

'It was, dear husband, and you should remember that purchase was for life.'

'Then tell me of this life you see before us, woman, and make it plain so that a simple hard man can understand these magical opportunities you foresee.'

'It may not be a life we will be able to share, that you must understand from the start, but I believe it is the course, the only course, for a

151

warrior such as yourself.'

Hereward bristled with pride at these words and his wife knelt before him, stroking his face, and told him of his destiny.

'It is almost three years since William landed in England and though his power grows every day, the land is not yet quiet. There have been risings in Wales and unrest is brewing all across the north. Raiders from Ireland have landed in Cornwall and from Scotland, the rebels have invaded almost as far as York.

'Yet none of these uprisings will dislodge William from England because they are disunited; they have no single leader strong enough to challenge the Norman's claim. Those who could best have faced him died at Hastings. The only claimant to the throne which William truly fears will come from Denmark, for King Svein has a large fleet and an army skilled in battle. There are also many in England, especially the east – the land of the East Angles of old – who once owed their allegiance to Danish kings rather than Saxon ones.'

'God's truth, my own grandfather, Toki of Lincoln, was just such a man!' exclaimed Hereward with glee.

'Yes he was,' said Turfrida, 'which is why I said you must look to your older loyalties.'

'Did you?'

Turfrida sighed patiently before continuing.

'William fears that eastern England would rise in support of a Danish invasion and so for three years he has given the eastern shires little cause to look to Denmark for their salvation.'

'Apart from him stealing the land of honest

men and making them outlaws!'

'Hush, my sweet boy,' whispered Turfrida, placing a hand across Hereward's mouth. 'You will have your revenge. Just listen, do not try to think too much. William is winning, but subduing England is costing him dear.

'True, he has taken much but he needs more and until now he has resisted plundering the rich abbeys and monasteries of the eastern shires. He will not resist much longer and he will make his move soon, for the treasures of Peterborough and Ely, as well as the smaller monasteries, will prove too tempting. When Abbot Brand leaves this earth, William will take control of Peterborough Abbey. He already has a successor to your uncle in mind, a monk called Turold, who is of the house of Fecamp in Normandy.'

'A Norman? A Norman abbot at Peterborough? The brothers there would never elect a Norman.'

'There will be no election, Hereward; this Turold, who already serves William at Malmesbury, will be appointed on the king's authority. It is said he is almost as good a soldier as William himself; more soldier than monk, and it is true that the monks of Fecamp have a reputation for strict discipline and a love of hardship. There are many in the English Church who will welcome hard men like Turold, for they see the Church as too soft and too concerned with the wealth of this world, but yet there are many churchmen who would hate to see the treasures of the abbeys being weighed by the gloved hands of Normans. They would rather see them given to King Svein in payment for a Danish army of liberation.'

153

'There were Danish ships off the Suffolk coast as we travelled here,' said Hereward. 'We had to shelter at Ipswich. I didn't like Ipswich; the ale there did not agree with me and we ate herring which was rank.'

Turfrida allowed her eyes to flick upwards to the heavens before she said: 'They were certainly scouts or spies for Svein Estridsson, surveying King William's defences.'

'That is what they were?'

'Yes, Hereward,' Turfrida said patiently. 'In Denmark, many ships are being built or repaired and Bishop Christian of Aarhus is filling a war chest to pay for a big campaign next spring. When the Danes come, they will make their landfall on the east coast of England and they will look to the Fenlands for support.'

'How do you know all this, wife? How can you know what is in the minds of men, of kings and bishops in foreign lands?' asked Hereward, genuinely perplexed.

'The world is large, Hereward, but it is made small by traders and monks. My family have always been traders and here, in St Bertin, I am surrounded by monks, monks who travel in many lands and who write reports and letters for their Orders and their bishops and their Lords. And all these well-travelled, wise and worldly monks, they talk and gossip like fishwives among themselves and they do not fear it when a harmless woman such as I happens to overhear their chattering.'

'And so these monks...' Hereward began, puzzled and confused. 'They chatter and gossip

154

about *me?'*

'No, my dear husband, but they say that when King Svein comes over the water from Denmark, he will look to the men of the east, of the Fenlands, to support him.'

'They will, they will. As God is in his heaven, they will.'

'They will if there is a man to lead them, my husband. A man who can fight and inspire others to fight alongside him; a man who knows the country and a man who knows the abbeys of Peterborough and Crowland and Ely and knows where and how they store their wealth. A man who will make sure that the riches of those abbeys does not fall to the Normans.'

Hereward grabbed his wife's two hands in his and his eyes lit up as if with fire.

'I can do that.'

And thus were the plans laid for the plundering of Peterborough Abbey which would become the signal for the revolt of the Fenlands, which in turn would give birth to the legend of Hereward.

Plans laid in a monastery garden in Flanders, by a wife.

[vi]

Using Turfrida's purse, Hereward and his companions, Lightfoot and the two Siwards, equipped themselves with clothes, armour, weapons and horses from the best they could find in all Flanders. They even had the opportunity to blood their arms (and find them totally satisfactory) when they accompanied a party of St Bertin monks to Cambrai to enforce the collection of certain rents and taxes owed to the abbey.

The four English warriors displayed themselves openly in Flanders in those winter months, but made sure that they did nothing to cause affront to Count Robert and his Norman allies or, for that matter, the good burghers and taverners of St Omer. Hereward kept his countrymen close and Turfrida kept Hereward even closer.

In the court of Count Robert it was said openly that the long-haired English hard man had finally remembered what wives were for and was determined to over-winter in the warmth of Turfrida's bed, only to emerge with the coming of spring. There were also many coarse and venal suggestions that Hereward, who shared all hardships with his kinsmen, also shared his wife's bed with them, but such talk was unfounded or at least unproved.

In the first week of December, Hereward and his three companions slipped out of St Omer and took passage on a ship bound for Ipswich which had been secretly commissioned by Turfrida. It was only when their absence at Mass on Christmas Day was noticed did Count Robert hear of their departure.

Turfrida, left alone, remained silent on her husband's business in England, except to God and the priest who confessed her.

Some said she was with child and that Hereward was only one of several possible fathers; but this was not true.

Many said that she never saw Hereward again.

156

Which is also false; though it is true she never saw him alive again.

[vii]

Hereward and his three men-at-arms had spent Turfrida's money wisely, sparing no expense on the hardiest of horses (chosen with a view to a winter sea-crossing to England) and the highest quality cloaks of Flemish weave. These items proved the most formidable weapons in their armoury for the winter was a severe one and many across the land of the East Engles as they were known in history, went hungry.

Having landed at Ipswich, where they drank the ale suspiciously and avoided the herring, Hereward's gang, called 'genge' in the slow speech of Suffolk, rode westward towards the Fens on frosty roads and over crisp hardened heathlands. They took shelter where they could and paid for it with Flemish coins. Coins of any description were welcome in England that year, though there was little food to buy. In the hamlet of Nedeham, an alewife called Evoy offered one of her daughters to Martin Lightfoot for half a silver shilling, though he is said to have thought the price too high. In Stowmarket, the church of St Peter and St Paul had nothing to offer for the riders, but allowed the horses to be stabled for a week.

Only in the Abbey of St Edmunds, where the monks prayed eight times a day, did not eat meat and were all expected to work with their hands, did men and beasts fill their stomachs.

157

It was there they asked their goodly hosts why they had seen little sign of Norman soldiers on their journey (for they had not encountered a single one on the road) and were told that King William's army was busily engaged laying waste the rebellious north, having successfully laid waste the rebellious west country and rebellious Wales on the way.

This was told to them by the Almoner of the abbey, who received a small purse of coins in return.

When Hereward asked whether King William feared a rebellion in the east of England, the Almoner answered: 'If he does not, then perhaps he should, for hungry men quickly lose their fear of the lash and the lance.'

Hereward, pondering on these wise words, then asked if there was any news of Abbot Brand, for in this company he had no concern over declaring himself to be a sworn man of the sister abbey of Peterborough.

Sad had been the news in the November gone, he was told, of the passing of the noble Brand, who had been laid to rest with all dignity by the brothers of Peterborough.

And when he heard this news Hereward, for the first time his kinsmen could recall, wailed and wept until the tears soaked his beard.

[viii]

At the inland port of Soeham, which is still called Soegham by some from the Norse word *soggi*

158

meaning drenched or soaked land, they were welcomed by the few monks who still kept a vigil over the ancient ruins of the once proud abbey which had been named for St Felix, known to history as the Apostle of the East Engles.

There Martin Lightfoot was delighted by a diet entirely of smoked eel, for the fishermen of Soeham net in excess of four thousand of the creatures. Now, Martin confirmed, they were truly in Fen country and their passage to Ely would be by boat from here onwards.

They found boats and fenmen willing to row them with surprising ease, for there were many willing to throw in their lot with four armed men who walked tall and carried arms and showed no fear of the Normans. What did it matter if they were outlaws? Did not outlaws eat when others starved?

And so the gang of four had grown to four-and-twenty when they landed on the Isle of Eels and when serfs out on the marshes trapping wildfowl saw them, they ran in terror to the Abbey of Ely itself to raise the alarm thinking they were an invading army.

But the gentle and good Abbot Thurstan had been expecting them.

Hereward's motley company was offered food and drink in the abbey refectory and for many it was a meal the like of which they had seen only in their dreams.

Not only was there ale, both fresh and strong vatted, and also mead, but wine also, for the soil of Ely Island was rich enough to grow vines. For meat, which those in holy orders only ate when illness demanded or feast days allowed, there was, in abundance, venison, mutton, hare and otter, as well as goose, duck and the delicacy that is the fig-bird, known locally as the chiffchaff. From the rich waters surrounding the Isle came the famous eel as well as wolf-fish, pike, roach and lamprey.

'There is a ballad,' Hereward said as he feasted, 'which goes "Merrily sing the monks of Ely". I think we should change that to "Richly do they eat, the monks of Ely".'

Abbot Thurston took no offence at this rudeness for all could see that he dined simply on bread and coddled eggs.

'This bounty, which the Lord has provided, is in your honour, Hereward. Our brothers prepared it but do not partake. In winter we eat only once a day at midday. Only my loyal sacrist here insists I eat with you out of good manners and the need to keep up my strength, for I am rich only in years and each winter seems harder than the last.'

Thurston and his trusted sacrist, whose duties ranged far beyond the usual safekeeping of the abbey's books and valuables that many said he deserved the title of prior as deputy to the abbot, were the only brothers of Ely to sit at table with their visitors. Other monks, with true Christian humility, willingly acted as serving boys and kitchen skivvies while others busied themselves spreading clean straw as bedding in the storehouses but not, on the sacrist's orders, in either the kitchen or the brewhouse.

'Let us hope it has been a hard winter for those

Norman bastards and pray that their summer will be even harder,' said Hereward loudly.

'Fine words to many ears in Ely and the Fenlands,' said the abbot, 'but words best spoken softly off the Isle.'

'I fear no Norman!' said Hereward fiercely, chewing venison with relish and acknowledging the murmurs of the men feasting around him. 'I will not bow to one and I have never run from one. I would have brought the head of one as a present for the abbey's crows had I met one on my journey, but they must have known I was coming for they were all in hiding!'

The company roared their approval at this, with much banging of ale-pots on the table.

'Your followers seem to share your spirit, young Hereward,' Thurstan observed.

'My followers? Only three are kinsmen and comrades in arms. For the rest, I do not know their names or their families or their rank and most of them I have only seen for the first time these past two days.'

'Yet still they follow you, as will all men of the Fenlands.'

'Aye, follow us as far as the next meal,' said Martin Lightfoot, seated to Hereward's right. 'These Fen rats will not fight unless their stomachs are full.'

'All men will fight to fill their stomachs,' said Thurstan, 'and the stomachs of their wives and children. More will come, if they are shown the way.'

'And the way lies towards Peterborough, does it not?' asked Hereward, as he had been told to ask

161

by his wife.

'That is where it will begin,' said Thurstan with a heavy heart. 'I can see no other way. I am a man of God, with charity for all and malice towards none, but our Holy Church here in England is under threat from the invader. King William will strip our great religious houses of their treasure, their learning and their lands in order to pay off the barons and knights who keep him on his throne.

'Now that Abbot Brand has gone to God, there is no one to protect Peterborough and the King has already appointed his henchman Turold as abbot. It is rumoured that Turold will march on Peterborough within the month with an escort of a hundred and sixty knights. He will come not as a brother in Christ, but as a conquering hero.'

'Will the brothers of Peterborough stand and fight?'

'No, they will not resist,' said Thurstan, shaking his head.

'Then we must hurry,' said Hereward, smiling. 'This Norman abbot has a hundred and sixty knights, but I have three hard men of English stock to watch my back. That should be enough!'

And seated on Thurstan's left, the trusted sacrist, wrapped in a thick wool cloak, who had sat throughout the feast without eating or speaking, finally allowed himself to smile also.

[ix]

Though men will swear that it was a Danish horde

which sacked and ravished Peterborough Abbey that year, it was an act committed by Hereward and little more than two score men of the Fens. Men such as the fishermen Enchel and Ulfkell, the fowler Eadric and the villeins Winter and Liveret, whose true calling was as poachers. These were no soldiers, and they had few weapons between them, but they were all skilled boatmen who knew the rivers and weirs and floods of the Fens as well as they knew the folds and wrinkles of their wives' backsides, although some said afterwards that they were required to use less stealth in approaching Peterborough.

Hereward's motley company landed at the eastern hythe of the town at dawn, before the morning sun had chased away the river mist. They were challenged by two armed watchmen in the service of the Sheriff of Cambridge, who had been charged with guarding a consignment of hides taken as taxes.

Hereward himself felled one of them with his sword still in its heavy scabbard, and Siward the White slit the throat of the other, which was said to be the first man he had killed in England.

As the morning mist still swirled about them, Hereward and his men presented themselves at the Bolitho Gate of the abbey and demanded entrance.

From an upper storey window, a monk of tender years demanded to know what business armed men had in that holy place at that hour.

Hereward replied in the manner in which he had been taught by Abbot Thurstan before his force had rowed out from Ely.

163

'I come on business which is between me and your abbot. Tell him that Hereward, who is now a sworn man of King Svein Estridsson of Denmark, demands to see him.'

'Abbot Turold is not here,' said the young monk, 'but he approaches as we speak, accompanied by three hundred noble knights.'

'You show spirit, brother monk, for one so young and at such an early hour, but my spies tell me that your new Abbot Turold has but one hundred and sixty Norman lackeys with him and that they are all quartered to the west of Stamford. They will not be here this day.'

Now Hereward could not have known if this was true (though in fact, it was). He was merely repeating what he had been taught to say by Thurstan and his sacrist in such an eventuality.

'Open the gate, young brother monk, and if you have no abbot, then fetch me your prior,' Hereward demanded.

'Prior Athelwold is tending to one of our brethren who is sick and cannot be brought,' protested the monk.

'Then open the gate, my friend,' said Hereward, charming the monk above him with a smile, 'and let me go to him. I know the way to the infirmary and my business will be concluded the quicker.'

'I cannot do that, my Lord Hereward.'

The monk's words hit Hereward like a blow.

'You *know* me, monk?'

'I know you to be Hereward of Bourne and that you have been twice-outlawed and expelled from this abbey, for I am Godric, the youngest brother of the most pious Abbot Brand, and the last son born to Toki of Lincoln.'

'God's face!' exclaimed Hereward, 'That makes us kin!'

'I believe it makes me your uncle,' replied the monk.

Hereward turned to Martin Lightfoot who was, as always, watching his back.

'Is this not a sign, old friend? A sign that we were right to come home?'

'I would feel more welcome if your uncle there would unlock the gate for us,' replied Martin.

'I cannot let you in,' shouted down Godric. 'For I fear your purpose is unlawful and will defile the sanctity of this abbey which protects us from thieves.'

'I am no common thief!' yelled Hereward. 'I was a defender unto death of the sanctity of this house until I was deprived of my birthright and spurned. I return now only to protect the treasures of the abbey, to prevent them being stolen by the Normans who have stolen our country!'

At these noble words, the men of the Fens ranked with Hereward cheered in agreement, which surprised but pleased their leader. Only Martin Lightfoot whispered caution into his leader's ear.

'Fine words, Hereward, but that fucking gate is staying shut.'

'We shall see about that,' said Hereward.

Then he pointed to the mud huts of the peasants and serfs which were built leaning against the abbey walls, as was allowed in those days.

'Tell the men to torch those houses,' he commanded, then softly, he said to Martin: 'You remember those priests we burned in Scaldermariland for the Count of Flanders?'

'I remember how they screamed,' said Martin in agreement.

'Priests don't like fire,' said Hereward. 'And neither do monks.'

[xi]

The huts and hovels outside the Bolitho Gate burned well and smoke engulfed the town. Fearing for the very fabric of their house, for most of the abbey buildings were of wood in those days, the monks opened the gate to allow Hereward's plunderers unopposed access.

Some would later say how the Fen pirates had stormed the walls, killing and maiming the un-armed monks who tried to protect the abbey's treasure, causing much damage to a house of God. But most of these stories come from the testimony twice or thrice repeated, of the one brother of Peterborough who remained in the abbey to wel-come Abbot Turold and his one hundred and sixty Norman knights, who arrived the following day, having hastened from Stamford when they heard reports of smoke rising above Peterborough.

This solitary monk, who was called Leofwine the Tall, remained behind in the infirmary be-cause of a broken leg and had been tenderly nursed by Prior Athelwold himself. It was he who had to answer to the furious Turold for the fact that the abbey was empty of all its considerable deposits of jewels, gold and silver, as well as gold and silver church plate, many valuable books, property deeds and the wills of noble landowners and some of the finest wines in the abbey cellar. Strangely, the pharmacist's store within the infirmary appeared to have been left untouched although on closer inventory it was discovered that the abbey's entire stock of Christmas Rose root and peony had vanished. Shockingly, even the reliquary containing the bones of the arm of the blessed St Oswald had been plundered and ferried away eastwards over the flooded fens.

'What army of pirates could carry such treasure away so swiftly?' the new abbot, who was not known for either patience or delicacy, demanded of the bed-ridden monk.

'A mighty horde of Danish Vikings, my Lord Abbot,' Leofwine informed him, 'guided and aided by an army of rebellious Englishmen, who took our brave prior and all the brothers hostage.'

'King William will hear of this outrage,' swore Turold, 'and his wrath will be swift and terrible.'

Thus was born the story of the sack of Peterborough Abbey and the plundering of all its riches, though there was no Danish horde present, merely Hereward and his Fenmen in their shallow-draft boats. Apart from some burned hovels, little destruction was brought down on Peterborough and the abbey itself, though the poorer for the loss of many of its rich hangings, was in good enough condition for Abbot Turold to celebrate a Mass on the day of his arrival.

He did so with enthusiasm, calling for a blessing from God and the head of Hereward in almost the same breath.

Leofwine the Tall, of whom nothing more is heard, thought it wisest not to tell his new Norman master that the brothers of Peterborough, led by young Godric, had actually opened the gates to Hereward under cover of a screen of smoke from the fires he had started, and, furthermore, had helped load the abbey's treasures on to Hereward's fleet. Even Prior Athelwold himself thought it best to accompany the relic of St Oswald as it was spirited away. So much of what is said and written of the plundering of Peterborough is therefore not the truth of what actually transpired.

Abbot Turold's prophesy, however, that King William's wrath would be terrible; that alone was true enough.

Thirteen

Giraldus

Brother Thomas gives me too much – and too little!

There is too much here that cannot be disputed and too little to use in what I must write, for much of this is not suitable for a respectable, nay, honourable, family history.

Should I go to my patron (my client?) Baldwin Le Wac and tell him that if he wants Hereward as an ancestor, then he must have the Hereward who is an outlaw, a suspected murderer, a drunkard, a thief, a rebel and a plunderer of church property?

Such are the twisted values of the young nobility today, that my patron may well agree to this, for sometimes I believe we are living in a world where to say 'bad' means 'good'. The sainted martyrs up in heaven must surely weep at such a state of affairs.

But I have no illusions that my thoughts are centred on Baldwin's dubious family tree, for I am now far more interested in the writings of Brother Thomas. As God is my witness, I have not read anything like this before. He writes as if he were there when the events he described happened, but how could that be?

Only God can know truly what a wife says to a husband when they are alone and certainly only God and the wife will know if what she says is true, for usually the husband does not. Yet there are many things Thomas writes of which are palpably true and can be proved by reference to other books and chronicles of the time.

He mentions that when returning to Flanders, Hereward meets (and assaults) the young captain Folcard, suggesting that as a man-at-arms, Folcard had not found the right calling. Surely this must be the same Folcard who, after serving the Count of Flanders as an officer, relinquished his right to bear arms and became a brother of St Bertin. In latter years the monk Folcard had something of a reputation as an historian and philosopher, writing many books, some of which still exist today in cheap copies. Some scholars rate his talents moderately, though I myself was never comfortable with his longwinded style and bad Latin grammar.

The young monk Godric, claimed by Thomas to have actively helped the plunderers, is certainly known in the records of the English Church, going on to make his name as a brother in Ely and then in later life returning to Peterborough where he was elected abbot in the year of our Lord 1096. I was unaware, until this manuscript of Thomas, that Godric was the youngest brother of the noble Brand, though that may well explain his throwing in his lot with Hereward.

Most interesting of all in this account is the lack of Danes, for they play a major part in Hereward's story, as they had in the story of the east of England throughout history.

Thomas notes that Hereward and his companions stayed at Soegham before arriving in Ely, in the ruins of the Abbey of St Felix. Was this not the famous abbey destroyed by Danish raiders some two hundred years before Hereward's visit? (In 870 AD)

And it is now well-known, though it may not have been to Brother Thomas in his lifetime, that the Count of Flanders did indeed marry off one of his daughters to Cnut, son of King Svein of Denmark, and when Cnut succeeded his father to the Danish throne, Denmark and Flanders entered into alliance to invade England through its eastern shires, naturally, in the year 1085. But King William, for king he still was, got wind of the plan and by a combination of threat and generous bribery defeated the invasion before it even sailed and it is acknowledged that from that year, the power of Denmark and Flanders began to wane.

There is no doubt that King Svein and a Danish army had helped rebellious Northumbrians march against William at York, but that rebellion had been crushed and the whole of the north of England laid waste by Norman knights to such an extent that it took a generation or more for the land to recover enough to feed its much reduced population. Some would argue that the north of England never did recover and remains a desolation even unto these times.

William was said to have chased off the Danes himself, at least as far as the Humber river, a safe harbour long-used by raiding Norsemen. Did they sail from there down to the Fenlands when they heard of Hereward's attack on Peterborough, which would have been an attack in King William's unprotected rear?

Perhaps Brother Thomas will tell me.

It was said in the stories of the time and sung in the ballads of the taverns, that Hereward (with or without a Danish horde to assist him) was merely taking charge of the treasure to protect it from the Normans. What happened was to be proof positive that the treasure of Peterborough, including the relic of St Oswald, was protected by God, not by Hereward.

Fourteen

Thomas

Hereward the Firestarter

[i]

As Hereward's victorious raiding party returned to Ely across the Fens, they attracted more followers and their squadron of shallow-draught river boats became a small fleet.

At Chatteris, several of the monks of the abbey founded there by Countess Aelfwein a hundred years before, offered to join the company on seeing the monks of Peterborough rowing alongside the rough men of the Fens. It is certain some did, though Hereward lost interest in them when they admitted that Chatteris had not treasures to match those of Peterborough.

On the wooded island that rose from the flooded lands which was known as Were-my-hill-long Wood, though many called it Langwood Fen, the pirates (for so they called themselves) camped for two nights whilst Hereward and his lieutenants oversaw the better distribution of their loot into the sturdiest craft in their fleet.

Much of this work was done at night and in secret by Hereward, Martin Lightfoot and the two Siwards, much to the consternation of Prior

172

Athelwold and Brother Godric. Their fears were laid to rest when Hereward entrusted the security of Peterborough's icons and bejewelled altar pieces, as well as the abbey's books and scrolls and, of course, the relic of St Oswald, to Godric alone, granting him exclusive use of three boats to be crewed only by monks.

Into two small skiffs, certain valuables were packed and these boats were to be commanded by Hereward and Martin, their only crew being two Fenmen who went by the names of Winter and Liveret.

The rest of the company were formed under the command of Siward the White and Siward the Red, or Rufus, with the remaining treasure of Peterborough distributed between them as weight and bulk allowed, and Hereward gave the command – and none disputed his right to command – to sail and row for Ely the next morning, where they would be greeted as heroes.

But when the dawn came, two boats were found to have already sailed.

[ii]

What happened next is known only to God and his humble servant, Thomas of Ely, who writes this book, which none are likely to read.

Hereward and his servant Lightfoot made their way by river and through fen, not to Ely, but to the isle of Littleport to the north, to the very place where Martin Lightfoot had been born and where he and Hereward had sheltered

173

whilst outlawed and, some would say, where they had planned the (unproved) murder of Sir William de Warenne's brother-in-law Frederick in Norfolk.

Being an island like Ely, though smaller and even more remote, Littleport was a place hidden from prying eyes and deaf to enquiring lips, save for those born or inbred there. The one exception to this rule was the stilt-walker they called Hraga, the 'Heron', whose skill at crossing the flooded fens was valued higher than the fact he came from Norfolk.

Hereward and Martin would have sought out Hraga as soon as they reached Littleport, for he was known to them and trusted by them, and with his help they would have directed their boatmen, Winter and Liveret, to a secret place in order to bury or conceal that proportion of the Peterborough hoard they had appropriated for themselves.

They did this because it was the plan to which Hereward and Martin were working, a plan which was laid out for Hereward in a monastery garden in Flanders and which had then been repeated for Martin Lightfoot's ears to insure that Hereward remembered it. It was a plan which could be shared only between those with ties of kinship or loyalty.

Which is why when Hereward and Martin eventually returned to Ely, they returned alone, though none asked the whereabouts of Winter and Liveret for the inhabitants of the Isle of Ely had other visitors to occupy them.

The Danes had arrived.

Thwarted in his attempts to unseat William, who was now becoming known as 'the Conqueror', by aiding the rebellion in the north, King Svein Estridsson of Denmark had sailed his fleet into the large tidal bay which separates Norfolk from Lincolnshire (now known as The Wash.) and taken his smaller craft by way of the port of Lynn and the river Ouse at great speed to Ely.

King Svein was accompanied by his brother Bjorn, Bishop Christian of Aarhus, some twenty Danish monks and over three hundred warriors who had spent the season campaigning in northern England though had not a pennyweight of plunder between them to show for it.

They brought with them over three hundred empty bellies in need of filling immediately and demands for further supplies to be sent down river to the men and ships they had left on the coast. For this reason, their arrival on the Isle of Ely was greeted with much despair rather than the joy expected for a liberating army come to remove the repression of the Normans.

At that time the Island of Eels, though rich in game, fish and wildfowl, and fertile in the soil which stood above the water level, supported some eighty families and the monkish community. The previous winter had been harsh and much of the abbey's stores of food had been distributed off-island to the poor and needy thanks to the charity of Abbot Thurston. The arrival of three hundred hungry mouths, therefore, caused much consternation in the chapels and cloisters of Ely.

King Svein, his bodyguard, his bishops and his monks, occupied the largest house they could find and sent word to Ely Abbey, calling for an immediate council, but before that was convened, a private council took place between Abbot Thurston and his sacrist.

'So we have preserved the treasure of Peterborough from the clutches of one invader only to find another invader on our doorstep,' said Thurston gloomily, for he was by nature a gentle man and was much burdened by the thought of what lay ahead.

'The Danish king was not only expected,' the sacrist pointed out, 'he was invited.'

'I had not expected him so quickly, that is all.'

'His men are hungry and his ships empty of plunder. They attempted to re-supply their expedition by seizing food in the north. The Viking word for such a seizure is *herfang* I believe.'

'Stolen food is stolen food in any language, my brother, and the true community of this abbey will starve rather than partake of stolen food, under the rules of the blessed St Benedict himself.'

'Quite so, my Lord Abbot, though I fear that temptation will not be sent to test us, for the Danish *herfang* failed. King William's cavalry chased the raiders back to their ships before they could scourge the countryside and then he himself ordered crops and barns burned, destroying everything, almost as if he wished to scorch the very earth itself.'

'The Danes did not fight?'

'No, Abbot, they did not, but their king was not at that moment with them. He has only recently joined his army from Denmark, accompanied by our brother-in-Christ Bishop Christian. Now he is with them, the Danish army will have more backbone and here on Ely they feel they have a secure camp from which to operate, for not even the Conqueror will invade the Fens.'

'I pray you do not underestimate the Normans, my friend, for we have cast our lot in with outlaws and invaders and if William does come, he will not be merciful.'

'What we do, we do for the good of the church in England, Father Abbot. We cannot stand idly by and watch the Normans strip our country bare. The time is right, dear Abbot. William is stretched thin, his armies and his treasury exhausted. The men of the Fens will rise up with our Danish allies and Norman rule will crumble.'

Thurston nodded his head slowly, deep in thought.

'I only hope our allies agree with you. Come, give me your good hand and let us pray together before our council with King Svein. Is the treasure of Peterborough safe?'

'It is safely stored within the treasury, but the first Danish ships arrived before the cousins Siward and Rufus had completed unloading their boats, therefore King Svein will be well aware of what lies within our walls and we must rely on the sanctity of our abbey to protect it.'

'And on the influence of Bishop Christian,' said Thurston, 'for he is an honest and holy man.'

'And a Dane,' said the sacrist.

177

'Who are our allies, are they not? Perhaps we should pray for God's protection from our allies as well as our enemies.'

'And perhaps we should add a prayer for protection from our own men,' added the younger monk.

'Hereward?' asked the abbot, his brow furrowed. 'Where exactly *is* Hereward?'

'Hereward and Lightfoot took a proportion of the valuables from the Peterborough plunder and are busy hiding it in a secret place, which is almost certainly in Littleport, the birthplace of Martin Lightfoot.'

'You know our young hero well, my brother.'

'I have followed his career with interest,' conceded the sacrist.

'And do we know how large a portion of the Peterborough treasure our loyal outlaw has taken to his secret nest?'

'Only those deposits, though they are substantial, made by the Lady Turfrida's family before the Normans came, and also some jewels bequeathed to the abbey by the Lady Aedina of Bourne seven years ago.'

'His mother?'

'That is so. I remember that particular deposit well. Hereward claims it by right of inheritance and Turfrida's fortune by right of marriage under Norman law.'

'Hereward is not one to put such faith in Norman law,' Thurstan mused. 'Are you sure that he has only taken what he was supposed to take?'

'Brother Godric assures me so and Prior Athelwold sleeps with one eye open to make sure the abbey's relics and valuables do not go astray.'

'With the Danes here on the island, he will need to forgo sleep.'

'Which is why, dear Abbot, we must seek the protection of Bishop Christian.'

'Do not hurry an old man, brother, though you are quite correct. We must go and treat with our Danish guests, remembering that we lie to no man before God, but before Danes we do not necessarily have to tell the whole truth. Though it is a pity Hereward is not here yet. I am sure he would have impressed them. Whatever else you may say, he does leave a lasting impression on men who meet him.'

The sacrist agreed with that thought, but remained silent and Abbot Thurstan took silence to mean doubt.

'You are sure that Hereward will come, now he has his share of plunder?'

'Quite sure.'

'Why so?'

'Because we can give him something he values far higher than mere gold or silver, rubies or amber.'

'Of course,' said Thurstan. 'Earthly glory in freeing England of the Normans and heavenly gratitude for protecting the English Church.'

'I was thinking of the deeds to the manor of Bourne,' said the sacrist.

[iv]

To make the Danes as comfortable, and therefore

as quiet, as possible, Thurstan gave instructions for ale, bread and pickled fish to be provided without question or limit, for like all Norsemen the Danes were particularly fond of ale and pickled fish and recognized the need for bread to assist in the digestion of both.

The abbot, wisely, ordered all supplies of malted barley, wheat, oats and rye on the entire Isle to be brought into Ely where the abbey's brewhouse and bakery would be working all the hours of God's day and night. All the honey on the island was also collected, for it was well-known that the Danes set great store by English honey calling it probably the best honey in the world.

When Thurstan and his sacrist, accompanied by Prior Athelwold, Brother Godric and Siward and Rufus, who now styled themselves 'Captains of Ely', reported for the arranged council with the Danes, they were thanked for the hospitality by Bishop Christian, a true man of the Church who spent many hours in prayer seeking forgiveness for the actions of his flock.

Svein Estridsson, King of Denmark, was, however, not a man to waste time on diplomatic niceties and with his fierce-looking bodyguard of mailed and helmeted axe-men, his *huscarls* as they were known, at his side, he saw no reason to be tactful.

'I have seen many here on this Island of Eels as it is called, who can claim kinship with me and my people,' he announced from his table, 'for was it not their Danish ancestors who settled in this place in days gone by, bringing with them the word of Christ?'

180

Every English head in the hall which heard that also remembered that the Danes had brought fire and sword in abundance before they had turned from raiding to farming, though none voiced the thought. Similarly, Abbot Thurston and the monks present decided as one that this was not an appropriate time to debate theology and the coming of Christianity to England.

'And I see men, or I am told I see men, who would not suffer to live under Norman rule. It is those men I have come to help, but only if those men can show that they can help themselves, unlike their countrymen in the north, who flee at the first clip-clop of a Norman horse.'

Thurstan knew it was time for him to speak, knowing that some would call his words treason, but his heart was heavy because he knew his words would lead to death and destruction and he was in truth the most gentle and unwarlike of churchmen.

'The men of the Fenlands will fight alongside their Danish cousins,' declared the abbot, 'for their land, for their homes, for their freedom and for their Church.'

'Then tell us, where is the army of these Fenmen camped? I have seen no stockade, no watchtowers, no ditches or even gates which could protect this place.'

And the brother of King Svein, the warrior Bjorn, seated on his left, added: 'Nor have I seen a single blacksmith working a lit forge to make weapons.'

'The Fenman's weapons are his heart and the island on which he lives, for the paths across the

181

Fens are few and hold many dangers and much fear for the Normans, who prefer to build castles of stone and then hide in them.'

'Brave words, Abbot, but it is strong arms and sharp blades which win battles,' replied the Dane.

'You will not find the men of Ely lacking when it comes to throwing off an oppressor,' said Thurstan's sacrist, speaking for the first time.

'I may find them lacking, Monk, if I can find them at all. If they can conceal themselves from me, then the Normans will never find them! I have tried to recall the songs and sagas which concern the brave deeds in battle of the men of the Fens, but I can recall not a single one. Please, good monks of Ely, refresh an old man's memory. Or perhaps your noble general would like to step forward and sing of your battle honours? Is he here? You do have a general to command you, don't you? Or do you leave the fighting to your monks?'

This speech drew much mirth and grunts of approval from the ranks of King Svein's *huscarls,* who had all been blooded in battle if not against the Normans, then in the wars fought by Denmark against Norway and Wendland (An area on the Baltic coast roughly where modern day Germany borders Poland.)

From the assembled Englishmen, it was Siward the White (who could easily have been mistaken for one of the King's bodyguard) who stepped forward.

'I am Siward, a Captain of Ely,' he announced bravely, 'and have sworn allegiance to that noble knight Hereward, who is our general; the general we will follow into battle.'

Abbot Thurstan turned to his sacrist and raised his eyebrows in a quizzical fashion, but whether this was to question whether Hereward was a 'knight' or indeed a 'general' of Ely, or even 'noble', remained unsaid.

'And where did this great general of yours learn his trade, if I might be so bold as to ask?'

If anything, it was Siward who was the bolder, but Danes, and Vikings in general, will listen to any man who is willing to speak to them as equals before they kill him.

'My Lord Hereward was master-at-arms to the Count of Flanders and trained armies both for him and his son Robert, who is now Count. He fought for Flanders in campaigns against the Duke of Guines, besieged cities and invaded the Frisian lands by land and sea. He defeated the giant German warrior Hoibrict in single combat and took the German's wife-to-be for his own. In England, he found his family estates sequestered by the Norman invaders, but he refuses to bow to their will and vows to reclaim them. No Norman knight will meet him in combat, though he has challenged many. They have declared him outlaw and sought to deny him food and shelter, but everywhere he goes in the east of England he is saluted and called a champion of the oppressed.'

'Surely there will be sagas written about this hero,' said Svein with humour, 'though your English poets are known for their slowness and long-windedness. I confess I have not heard of this Hereward. Is he afraid of nothing?'

'Hereward knows not the meaning of fear,' answered Siward. 'He does not hide from his enemies, but rides towards them, seeking them out. And havoc and destruction follow in his wake.'

'As God is my witness,' said Abbot Thurstan, 'I can attest to the truth of that.'

'Then where is this warrior chief? Will he not drink with fellow hard men who have crossed the cold seas to lock shields with him against a common enemy?'

'I know nothing would give him greater pleasure,' declared the sacrist before Siward could answer the Dane. 'Hereward is in the outlying villages of the Fens, recruiting more men to the banners of England and Denmark. Your most welcome arrival was earlier than expected. I am sure he is hurrying here as we speak.'

'And who might you be, brother monk, to speak at this council?' growled King Svein, a man happier conversing with warriors than with priests.

Yet there was one priest to whom he always deferred and that was Bishop Christian, seated on his right, a man who, although a Dane, was also a member of the great brotherhood of the Church.

'The Sacrist of Ely is well-known to us,' soothed the Bishop. 'He is known in many countries for his logic and the clarity of expression of his letters and despatches.'

'A left-handed scribbler?' muttered the King's brother Bjorn. 'That is something I have not seen before.'

But Bjorn's accent was so guttural and slowed by ale that few heard him clearly and even less understood his words.

184

'My sacrist speaks for me and for Ely,' said Thurstan, 'and in his role as curator of the earthly valuables of this abbey, meagre though they are, he now also has charge of the treasures of Peterborough Abbey which are much more extensive.'

'A prize of legend even in Denmark,' agreed Bishop Christian, addressing the King. 'It is said that Peterborough is the second-richest abbey in England, and its treasures include the relic of blessed St Oswald, a rubbing of which upon infected skin can cure – in the truly penitent – all common diseases and some not yet known to the Church.'

'And these treasures are now here, on this Isle of Ely?' King Svein asked for he could scarcely believe his luck.

'Indeed they are,' said Thurstan. 'They were harvested from under the very nose of the new Norman abbot, a warrior monk named Turold, and his army of Norman cavalry and spirited across the Fens to Ely by brave Hereward and his band of loyal Englishmen.'

King Svein raised his ale cup in salute to this speech and then asked: 'All of it?' at which Thurston looked puzzled.

'Was *all* the plunder of Peterborough brought here?' Svein insisted.

'I see my Lord Svein is worried about the holy relic of St Oswald,' the sacrist intervened (for it was every monk's duty to protect their abbot from having to tell a lie). 'Let him rest assured that the arm of the blessed Saint is among the treasure, along with the entire contents of the

185

abbey's inventory of holy property. Athelwold, the noble Prior of Peterborough, has even travelled here with the treasure and is willing to see it granted to the protection of Bishop Christian from this day forth.'

All in the Danish company shouted their approval at this and there was much stamping of feet and slamming of shields, such was their delight at the acquisition of such plunder without the need to fight and shed blood.

Alone in that hall, only Bjorn, the King's brother, did not join in the laughter and celebration; whispering, but not softly enough, in Svein's ear: 'I doubt this Prior Athelwold had much say in the matter, and I do not trust the crippled monk who speaks so smoothly. If this Peterborough treasure is so great, William and the Normans will not let it go without a fight.'

King Svein put down his ale cup (which was immediately refilled by one of the serving monks) and gently stroked the scars on Bjorn's face.

'You worry too much, little brother, but not without cause.' Rising from his seat, King Svein turned again to the abbot and his retinue. 'Do the men of Ely know the disposition of the enemy we share? For surely King William will come seeking the great treasure of Peterborough if he thinks he has a claim to it.'

'William thinks he has a claim to everything in England,' said Thurstan sourly. 'The Normans will come.'

'And in what strength?'

'We cannot know for sure,' answered the sacrist, 'but Abbot Turold, to whom William gave

Peterborough Abbey, was himself accompanied by one hundred and sixty mounted knights. I understand that those troops have been placed at the disposal of Baron Ivo Taillebois, or Ivo the Woodcutter as we would say, who is the Sheriff of Lincoln and one of William's most respected military commanders.'

'You understand a lot, Brother Monk,' said the Danish Lord Bjorn with an ill-concealed sneer.

'The Church in England is like an ancient oak, its branches reach everywhere,' replied the sacrist with all humility.

'Then be careful this Norman woodcutter does not lop those branches for kindling,' snapped Bjorn, at which his brother Svein held up a hand to both calm and silence him.

'My brother is right to be cautious,' said the King. 'Too many Vikings and Saxons have already underestimated the Normans' skill in battle. Many longships have sailed from the north these past four years and many have returned empty. We need to know more before we challenge King William.'

'By accepting the treasure of Peterborough into your protection, you have already challenged him, my Lord,' said the sacrist, 'or that is how William will view it.'

Svein was taken aback by the boldness of this, for he was after all a king and kings are not familiar with plain speaking.

'You have a bold tongue in your head, monk,' said Svein.

'Pray that it stays there,' added Bjorn, but the sacrist was not afraid.

187

'Baron Ivo is already on the road, riding south for Cambridge Castle. There he will join forces with Sir William de Warennes, one of King William's most trusted knights and one who has no reason to love the east of England.'

'This knight Warennes, of him I have heard,' admitted Svein. 'Stories of his skill at arms match only the rumours of his wealth and both have reached us in Denmark. Why does he hate these eastern shires?'

'His brother-in-law was murdered here, my Lord,' said the sacrist. Many a Fenman winced at the memory of that crime. 'Though no murderer was ever brought to justice.'

'So this Warenne, he has declared a blood feud?' asked Svein, with some concern, for blood feuds were, from history, notoriously long and dangerous quests which could span many generations.

'The Normans do not have the same concept of blood feud as was once held in this country,' the sacrist tried to reassure him. 'They are a much more practical people in many ways and Sir William de Warennes cannot deny that he has inherited great wealth due to the death of his brother-in-law. But memory of that crime will still haunt him and he will show no mercy when he invades these lands.'

'But I thought the Isle of Ely has always defied invaders in the past, at least those who have come from the land. Have I been misinformed?'

'You have not, my Lord,' said Thurstan. 'No army has penetrated the Fens unless it has come as you yourself have, by river from the sea.'

'And I must say our passage was easy and

quick. What is to stop King William following in the wake of my ships and so trapping my army here, with their backs against these Fenland marshes and swamps? My longships are fast and ferocious in attack but they need open water, not flooded fields if they are to be used in a battle.'

'William's navy is sorely stretched supplying his armies in the west country and fending off raiders from Ireland,' said the sacrist.

'Is William not capable of finding more ships when he needs them? That is what we kings do,' answered Svein with some cunning.

'He has scoured the coasts of Normandy and Flanders for any vessel which can float, but no more are available to him.'

'God's teeth, but you are well-informed Brother Monk! Do you have spies everywhere? Can they tell me where King William sleeps this night?'

'It is thought the King is camped at Salisbury in the west. Any threat to Ely will come from Sir William de Warenne in Cambridge.'

'And what will Sir William have for breakfast before he marches out to attack us? Can you tell me that, Monk?'

This jest, if it were a jest, raised a thunder of laughter from Svein's bodyguard but the sacrist did not drop his gaze from the Danish king as he knew that to the Danes, a whipped dog deserves only further whippings.

'That I cannot tell you, my Lord, but without doubt it will be food stolen from an English table.'

At this, it was the turn of the men of Ely to cheer their approval.

The *huscarl* Bjorn, who was becoming impatient

189

with all this talk, slammed his pot on the table for silence before he spoke.

'Whether this Norman has a full belly or not is of little matter. If he comes to fight, he will find a fight waiting for him. There is no question of that, only the question of *where* will he come?'

Abbot Thurstan stepped forward to supply the answer.

'On the southern tip of the Isle at the village of Aldreth, there is a causeway which stretches almost two miles across the old west river and Ouse Fen. It is the easiest and most obvious approach from Cambridge and the route taken by all travellers who do not know the secret ways across the Fens.'

'So there are secret ways?' pressed Bjorn.

'As long as there have been Fens, the Fenmen have found ways to cross them with speed and in stealth, but these pathways are travelled by lone fishermen or wildfowlers with their dogs and flat-bottomed boats which they push with poles rather than row with oars. They are not paths so much as places where the water is the depth of no more than a hand-span, yet a few inches to either side and the brown waters can swallow a horse and rider leaving no trace.'

'And these paths are unknown to the Normans?' asked King Svein.

'They are known only to those born and bred on the Isle and we have no traitors on Ely, for all true men here are blessed and protected by the shrine of the blessed St Ethelreda.'

Svein looked to his Bishop of Aarhus for guidance.

'St Ethelreda, who was also known as Audrey, was a most virginal woman, one of the founders of the Abbey at Ely. If the men here are sworn to her blessed memory, then they are to be trusted.'

Svein seemed pleased with this reassurance.

'So if an attack comes, it will come across this causeway from Cambridge? I have heard of this place Cambridge. It is said there is nothing worth stealing there.'

'It is a town of little consequence in the affairs of the world,' agreed Thurstan.

'And this causeway, where does it run?'

'From a small village on the isle called Aldreth, some five miles from here across what we call Grunty Fen.'

'And what defences does this causeway at Aldreth boast?'

But the King of Denmark did not receive a satisfactory answer, for at exactly that moment a voice boomed out from the back of the hall.

'Defences? Why do we need defences when we intend to attack?'

'Hereward...' whispered the sacrist as if to himself.

'Step forward, bold fellow,' shouted Bjorn, 'and make yourself known to Svein Estridsson, King of the Danes.'

Hereward did indeed step boldly forward, with Martin Lightfoot one pace behind his right shoulder, his sword in its wooden scabbard resting on his left shoulder.

He nodded and smiled a silent greeting to his comrades Siward and Rufus, and made a slightly more courteous bow as he faced Abbot Thurstan.

191

Then he turned on his heel to face the pride of Denmark aligned at the feasting table.

'I am Hereward,' he said loudly, 'once a liege man of Peterborough now a sworn man of Ely. Have I missed anything?'

[v]

Even as Hereward was meeting with his Danish allies – an alliance quickly sealed in a drinking bout which went on throughout the night, endearing Hereward to the *huscarls* if not the abbey's brewers and maltsters – another council of war was taking place in Cambridge Castle, a little over twenty miles to the south.

This was a more sober affair and whilst a secret council between two of the most senior Norman nobles in the land was not recorded word-by-word, many things were written down by scribes as orders or requisitions, or even letters reporting matters to the king. And much of substance was overheard. The Normans had yet to remember that English walls had ears.

Baron Ivo Taillebois was, even by Norman standards, a blunt man who liked to say that he spoke his mind plainly, taking things as he found them. Which is to say that he spoke loudly without fear of contradiction and never felt it necessary to listen to an answer.

'God save me from fucking priests who think they have been robbed of a rich living! If that bugger Turold doesn't stop whining and start cracking some heads, I'll slit his throat myself

192

just to shut him up.'

Sir William de Warenne eyed Baron Ivo with amusement. He had always thought of Ivo as a bear of a man, with no more culture than the roughest of the soldiery he commanded, which was perhaps why King William trusted him so much.

'You must try to forgive Turold, my dear Ivo. There he was, promised the title of Abbot of the second-richest monastery in the country after years of loyal service to the King. He is even given an honour guard of knights with which to impress the locals, but he arrives at his sinecure to find the abbey in flames and its wealth stolen from under his nose by outlaws and rebels and he has to conduct a Mass in an empty church. Surely, that is enough to make a bishop weep?'

'Abbot Turold should look to his own before he asks me to send my men into the forests and swamps looking for outlaws. They might as well be chasing wild geese.'

'What can you possibly mean by that, Ivo?'

'I stopped at Peterborough on my way down from Lincoln. The abbey there was not in flames, it was hardly singed. The fires had been started in some peasant hovels against the walls, but they were no great loss. What was interesting was that the gates had not been broken, they had been *opened*. That was a robbery which was conducted from the inside.'

'Are you accusing the good brothers of Peterborough of conspiring with outlaws and rebels, Ivo? That is outrageous.'

'It is the bloody truth! All the monks have dis-

193

appeared along with the treasure, even their prior! We should outlaw the lot of them and hunt them down as common thieves.'

'Well, we shall certainly hunt them down, but I do not think they are common thieves. The King suspects this robbery is to pay for an uprising in the eastern shires.'

'Come, come, Sir William. You know as well as I do that the King sees rebellion behind every tree and under every rock, not just in England but in Normandy also.'

'In most cases, he has just cause to do so,' said Sir William dryly, 'and it is not for us to question the King's judgement.'

'I question no one, least of all King William. I value my neck too much for that. And there is wisdom in treating this outrage as open rebellion, as we can order our men to grant no quarter and have them lay about with fire and desolation as we did in the north. Peasants with empty bellies do not enjoy having to shelter and feed rogue outlaws and robbers. We'll have them soon enough.'

'Are you sure they went into the Fen country?'

'Where else could they go? They came by boat, they left by boat. They would have scuttled back across those marshes like eels. That's where they will be hiding, on that damned Isle of Eels. For too long that place has been a hiding hole for outlaws and disobedient priests.'

'The Abbot of Ely is the man Thurstan, is he not?' asked Sir William, though he knew the answer to his own question.

'He is, and the old fool is known to favour all things English above anything Norman – and he does not keep his views to himself,' Baron Ivo said with venom. 'If Ely had been half as rich as Peterborough, the King would have had Turold installed there a year ago. It was to be the next on the list. The King has been too generous towards the abbeys of the east; that was his first mistake – generosity.'

'I think you will find that King William has had a change of heart now that the abbeys are harbouring rebels. You are sure it was Hereward at Peterborough?'

'The whores and drunkards of the town fairly boast that it was. We did not have to apply the usual pressure to find out who did this robbery in broad daylight, they seemed quite proud that it was one of their own. Hereward was named by many, as was a man called Lightfoot who seemed to be his servant.'

'His servant; and perhaps more,' said Sir William softly.

'You know these outlaws, Sir William?'

'Hereward and I have crossed paths in Flanders and in London. I think he may also have crossed the path of my brother-in-law in Norfolk the year before last.'

'Sir Frederick? The most noble knight so cruelly murdered whilst out hunting? By all the Saints, it is no wonder you have a personal interest in this rogue.'

'It is nothing personal, Ivo, it is strictly good business.'

'Business? What do you mean?'

'Think, my dear Baron, think. If you are a shepherd and you find a mad dog in among your flock, you kill the beast as quickly as you can, do you not? Otherwise you will have less sheep to shear next season. That is only good sense.'

'This Hereward is known to you by sight?' Baron Taillebois asked and when Sir William nodded in acknowledgement, he said: 'Then you will be able to describe him?'

'He is short and stocky, as the English would say, but strong. He has golden blond hair and he wears it long in the Danish fashion; so long that in Flanders some called him beautiful as a girl. He also has the strangest eyes. One is blue and the other is brown, which is a sure sign of madness in both man and beast.'

Baron Ivo tugged at his beard and allowed himself a smile.

'So this Hereward is truly a mad dog. Even in the stinking swamps of the Fenland, a man like that should not be hard to find.'

'Not hard at all,' said Sir William, 'for he will come and find you.'

[vi]

June gave way to July and the weather was warm and fine and the days long and all the men and monks on Ely worked every hour there was light, trawling the fens with nets and emptying the fish pools created by the weirs built across the many rivers and streams which flowed there. Likewise, they trapped every wild fowl that came within reach either on land or water, harvested every grain and vegetable whether truly ripe or not and stripped every hedgerow of berries certainly not ripe.

Such action was necessary, for as the news of Hereward's raid on Peterborough spread, men of the Fenlands did indeed flock to Ely to follow his banner and took comfort from the sight of what seemed to them (for they did not travel much) a mighty Danish army led by a Danish king, encamped on the Isle.

All these mouths had to be fed, including the sizeable number of warriors King Svein had left as a rearguard with his long-ships anchored near Lynne. As a consequence, no matter how much food was garnered into Ely, it appeared as if the same amount was needed to be ferried down the River Ouse to resupply the Danish fleet.

'These fucking Danes do nothing but sit on their arses and eat!' complained Hereward to his companions.

'It is what Danes do,' said Martin Lightfoot, 'and they do it very well.'

'I thought these boys were supposed to be hard men,' complained Rufus, who was always more ready for action than his cousin, 'but they don't seem interested in taking on the Normans at all.'

'Why should they be?' asked Siward. 'They have full bellies, their ships are in a safe harbour and more treasure than they could hope to gain in a year of raiding has been handed to them as a gift, by us – who did all the work.'

'The treasure of Peterborough has been given over to the protection of Bishop Christian,' Martin answered him. 'That way, if William the Norman Bastard wants it, he will have to take on the King

197

of Denmark and then we will have a war which will free England from the invader.'

'Does he need it that badly, though?' argued Siward.

'It does not matter whether he needs it or not,' said Martin, who had thought long and hard about the matter. 'He has proclaimed himself King of England and he cannot allow the treasures of the English Church to be stolen from under his long Norman nose by a gang of common outlaws like us.'

Hereward slapped the scabbard of his firesteel sword with the palm of his hand.

'By God, if a Norman tongue had said that, I would have cut it out!' he shouted.

Even Lightfoot, who thought he knew all his master's moods, was taken aback by this outburst.

'Said what, Hereward?'

'That we are *common* outlaws! We are *noble* outlaws! We do not steal anything that is not ours by right and we do not steal food from the tables of starving Englishmen. What right have they to liken us to common thieves they would rather see hanged than meet in a fair fight? Why don't they come out of their castles and fight?'

'Perhaps,' said Rufus, 'they are waiting for an invitation to a battle from the King of Denmark.'

'Then they will be waiting until their beards grow to their knees, for King Svein's army has been here over a month and seems reluctant to move further than the abbey's kitchens,' said Siward. 'It would need a Norman spear point up their fundaments to get them moving.'

Hereward slapped his scabbard again with both

hands, as if he were beating a drum, and his face split with a huge smile.

'Then let us go and find some Norman spear points!'

That night Hereward, his three trusted companions and some fifty chosen men of the Fens left Ely for the south of the Isle and the causeway at Aldreth which led into Cambridgeshire.

They marched quietly and did not light any torches until they were clear of the Danish camp and even then, only when they were among the tall, lush reeds on the secret pathways through the watery landscape. It was said that even on the very edge of Grunty Fen itself – a marsh land bigger than many a lake in the middle of the Isle of Ely – none of Hereward's men got wet feet that night thanks to the knowledge of the Fenmen who guided their steps, and they were seen by no living thing except perhaps the fox or the owl.

In Ely, only the sacrist of the abbey was aware of their departure, for Martin Lightfoot had disturbed him at evening prayers and begged for a blessing on their adventure and also a supply of the root of the Christmas Rose from the infirmary.

[vii]

It being summer and the water levels low, the causeway at Aldreth stood proud of the brown waters of Ouse Fen and the old west river, stretching two miles from north to south until it merged with the firmer ground rising to the

199

north-west of Cambridge. This was a land so flat that even the smallest rise in the ground was regarded as valuable as a mountain-top when it came to spotting the approach of an enemy.

Hereward was well aware of such strategies, for much of what he knew of warfare he had learned in the service of the Count of Flanders in the lowlands and flooded coastal islands of Frisia, Walchern and Scaldermur; lands which were similar in many respects to the Fens. And the men of the Fens, though they themselves were not trained soldiers, knew that anyone crossing the causeway could be seen coming from a great distance from the southern aspect.

It was therefore to the astonishment of his own men, as well as Norman eyes to the south (and there were many), when Hereward, Lightfoot, Siward and Rufus, their sheathed swords and axes carried across their shoulders as animals wear a yoke, marched four abreast across the exposed causeway in broad daylight.

The men who had followed Hereward from Ely he commanded to stay on the Isle, and in the main they were happy to do so and took great heart from seeing their leaders march proudly and openly towards the territory of the enemy.

They were even more heartened to see their brave vanguard halt their march when over half-way across and sit down on the sunken logs and reed bundles of the causeway and proceed to build and light a fire over which to roast a duck they had trapped that very morning.

Perhaps it was the impudence of men openly displaying arms advancing towards them, or (as many would say later) the smell of roasting duck which drew the Norman patrol from the southern bank.

Eighteen Norman troopers rode out carefully across the dry causeway that day, although some tales would later say eighty. The four Englishmen appeared not to notice them, though their progress was slow and careful, until they were close enough to hear the Norman ponies shying and squeaking at the smell which assailed their nostrils.

The Norman cavalrymen were confused, not realizing that their horses had scented not the roasting duck, but the poisonous fumes of vapour which a stagnant marsh gives off in summer, and in the spot where the Englishmen had camped, the fumes were strong indeed, and in that they had chosen well.

No record was ever kept of what was said by the two parties that day on the causeway, but it is almost certain that Hereward made the first insult. Certainly, many Fenmen, from the safety of the Isle, saw him stand and advance towards the mounted captain of the Norman patrol, and many would say that it was God who unsheathed Hereward's sword (for no mere mortal could have acted so fast) and a few would live to tell their grandchildren that they were there the day that one blow from Hereward's flashing blade severed the front leg of a Norman pony, pitching it and its rider to the earth, where both were rapidly dispatched.

Some of those Fenmen would also swear that that was the moment when the two warrior cousins, Siward and Rufus, cried out aloud, 'So it begins!' as they launched themselves into the attack.

The causeway, being narrow, was easily defended by three such reckless warriors, but they were not foolish enough to rely simply on their skill with broadsword and axe, for even in a confined space, a mounted knight in armour has many advantages.

And so after inflicting death on four Normans and severe wounds on several more, Hereward, Siward and Rufus conducted their retreat across the causeway as they had planned, for whilst the fighting was at its height, Martin Lightfoot had been busy spreading the Englishmen's camp fire across the breadth of the causeway, where the flames quickly took hold in the dry reeds and rushes and were fanned by the marsh vapours trapped therein.

With bloodied blades, the English heroes leapt through the wall of flame which rapidly rose to above the height of a man and ran towards their Fenmen comrades who cheered them loudly across the causeway as the Norman patrol turned back in disarray. As they got closer to the Isle of Ely, the Fenmen urging them home could see that though their beards and hair were singed and still smouldering, all four were laughing as they ran and several of the witnesses swore that Hereward shouted 'By God I feel alive again!' to the heavens.

Such as it can be recorded, that battle of the causeway was to be but the opening move in the siege of the Isle of Ely, which some chroniclers have said lasted seven years. But they are mistaken in that and must have been thinking of Troy.

The one thing which is recorded is the dispatch sent to Sir William de Warenne from Baron Ivo Taillebois, who observed the battle of the causeway from a wooded rise on the Cambridge bank.

Having seen his cavalry patrol attacked and routed, then thwarted by fire, Baron Ivo sent these simple words back to Cambridge Castle: 'We are going to need a bigger army.'

Just as Baron Taillebois sent a rider south to Cambridge, so did Hereward send a runner north to Ely; naturally choosing Martin Lightfoot, who had earned his very name by being a fleet-footed messenger in his youth.

The message carried by the Norman rider brought an instant response from Sir William de Warenne, who, acting with supreme authority (in the absence of King William), assembled a squadron of cavalry and a troop of mounted crossbow men and set out immediately at their head for the Aldreth causeway.

In Ely, a crowd had gathered near the abbey gates to greet Lightfoot, for they were aware that something had taken place to the south as the column of smoke from the fired causeway was clearly visible across the flat Fens.

Before Abbot Thurstan and his sacrist and Bishop Christian of Aarhus, Martin told his story; a story of a valiant defence of the Aldreth causeway against impossible odds and how Hereward routed the mass ranks of Norman cavalry with fire and sword. But if he had been expecting a

Roman triumph or a hero's garland, he would be disappointed.

Thurstan showed concern only for the souls of those killed, even though they were all Norman, and gave instructions for prayers to be said that evening. Bishop Christian questioned Martin closely as to the number and rank of the Norman forces which were claimed to have 'invaded' the Isle and said sourly that thanks must certainly be offered to God for his intervention in aiding Hereward and only three companions to defeat such a host of enemies. But it was the attitude of the Sacrist of Ely which seemed to puzzle poor Martin the most, for the dry, soft spoken monk, who kept his arms folded within the deep sleeves of his thick robes despite the heat of summer, was only interested in the damage the fire had done to the causeway.

'The fire there will burn all night,' said Martin proudly, 'as marsh fires often do, and no Norman will be able to cross the gap over to the Isle.'

'Nor we escape from it,' said the sacrist to himself.

And so it was a much chastened Martin Lightfoot who returned to Aldreth that night with pack horses and a hay cart carrying food, picks, shovels, mattocks and a supply of pitch torches. He was accompanied by fifty or more men of the Fens, who had been told to bring their hunting bows and as many arrows as they could carry. All this was as Hereward had commanded, but he had also made one other request which was not fulfilled; for the Danish army of King Svein did not march to assist him in the defence of the causeway.

Had he heard Martin Lightfoot's boast that no Norman would cross the causeway on to the Isle, Sir William de Warenne would have agreed with him once he had seen it for himself.

But neither Ivo nor De Warenne were men easily daunted.

Firstly, Sir William demanded a report on the casualties suffered by Ivo's men, as every good commander should. He was told that four troopers had been sent to God and a further five had been maimed or crippled, along with three horses killed. Baron Ivo explained that the blood on the front of his tunic was not his own but that of a horse he had been forced to spike between the eyes after its tendons had been severed by an English axe.

Next, Sir William dispatched riders to Huntingdon, Nottingham and even Warwick, demanding reinforcements and sent scouts all along the south bank of the river to commandeer not only supplies of food, but also any flat-bottomed boat capable of holding two men, their weapons and armour.

Then he set one troop to work as woodcutters, chopping down every tree or sapling thicker than a man's arm they could find. It was Sir William's plan to repair the fire damage to the causeway and to put his cavalry on to the Isle as quickly as possible, but in this he was to be thwarted.

Whilst smoke still rose from the burning reeds

and marsh grass which grew on the causeway and shielded them from the Isle, Sir William's men carried a great quantity of logs out on to the causeway to the breach and began to lay them over the burned areas. But if the Normans could hide behind a curtain of smoke, that same curtain could also protect Hereward, who advanced from the Ely shore with a handful of men each with a wet cloth wrapped about their face which protected their throats from the foul smoke and gave them a fearsome appearance when they burst upon the Normans.

But Sir William's men, though taken by surprise, were not unprepared for such an attack. As the English, disguised in masks and hoods, burst among them, blades flashing, the Norman troops, acting as loggers, did not give fight, but dropped their axes and turned to flee.

Some were hacked down before they could follow the plan to flee and some were caught because Hereward and his gang were fleeter of foot, spurred on by bloodlust. And then, sensing another victory, the defenders of Ely raised a cheer and removed their masks the better to jeer at the backs of the fleeing Normans, though the Normans did not flee very far. Some fifty or sixty paces down the causeway, from out of the tall bulrushes which grew where the causeway edged the water, there arose twenty of Sir William's best crossbowmen who had spent the day silently hidden in the reeds.

Among the Fenland rebels, only Hereward and Rufus, who was at his side that day, had ever seen a crossbow used in anger against men and when five of their number were hit in the first volley, the heart and fight went out of them. Leaving three dead lying among the smouldering reeds and abandoned logs, Hereward and Rufus each dragged a wounded man over the breach and back through the smoke towards the Isle.

Even with a man hefted across his shoulder (the man struggling silently and in vain to pull a bolt from his throat) Hereward warned his men to stay to the sides of the causeway, for he knew that a second volley from the Norman crossbows would come through the smoke screen behind them, along the line of the causeway. It was, he reasoned later, exactly what he would have done and so it proved and three more of his men fell thus to bolts fired blindly but cunningly by unseen enemies.

And so the two opposing forces probed and jousted for control of the causeway. Neither wished to destroy it; for Sir William it was the most direct route for getting cavalry on to the Isle, for Hereward it was the route by which his Danish allies would cross when they chose to give battle – if they ever did.

In the bloodiest encounter, Baron Ivo himself led a charge of knights along the causeway. It was a foolhardy attack but after a week among the sour vapours and blood-sucking insects of the marshy Fens, his patience was sorely tried, and in truth, the attack almost succeeded.

Sharp Norman eyes from the Cambridge bank had seen that each morning, just as dawn was breaking, many of Hereward's men would make their way into the Fen or along the river bank, to see to the traps and snares they had laid the night before, for these, it must be remembered, were born Fenmen first and soldiers only second.

With Hereward's garrison so depleted, Baron Ivo advanced his men in a column four-abreast, for the causeway was not wide enough for more, and only slowing in their charge for their horse to pick their way across that part of the causeway which one side had burned and the other attempted to shore up with cut branches and logs. Careful though they were there, two of the horses on the right flank, along with their riders, stumbled and fell from the causeway and into the Great Ouse Fen, which was still covered by a layer of morning mist. The frightened horses threw their riders and Baron Ivo's knights, heavily encumbered with sword, spear, shield, helmet and chain mail, simply disappeared and were left to drown in the brackish water. (Though it is said that these horses of these knights survived long enough to be pulled on to the banks of the Isle and be taken to Ely where they were eaten by Danes.)

Once they had crossed the breach, the Norman cavalry had the advantage, for there seemed none left on the Ely side of the causeway to oppose them and the charge gathered speed, the horses in the van being pressed by those behind who had no room for movement to either side.

When the leading horsemen, Baron Ivo among them, were within sight of the Ely end of the causeway and well within bowshot (though not a single arrow had been loosed at them), the tall reeds parted and out on to the causeway was pushed a hay-cart the width of the causeway save for only room for one man to pass on foot, and as high as a cottage, loaded as it was with hay, dry rushes and marsh grass and squares of dried peat, which the men of the Fens use as fuel in the winter.

Tied to each corner of the cart was a blazing pitch torch and more torches were thrown on to its load as Hereward and his kinsman pushed the cart from behind towards the advancing cavalry.

As the cart, now full alight and a terrifying orange ball of flame in the early morning light, progressed with steadfast purpose towards them, so the horsemen attempted to slow their mounts, knowing full well there was not room enough to turn them. Had the Norman cavalry been less experienced – for these were all battle-hardened men and horses – then panic and even greater slaughter would have resulted. As it was, they managed to halt their charge and at the command of Baron Ivo, turn their shying mounts away from the moving wall of flame which blocked their progress, and retreat back along the causeway, pursued by the trundling ball of flame and smoke.

A handful of the bravest of Ivo's knights, though none could be counted as cowards, disputed his order to retreat, feeling ashamed to flee before what they suspected, rightly, to be a much inferior force.

Ignoring the Baron's shouted orders, five of these knights dismounted, slapped their horses away and formed a line across the causeway with swords drawn and shields held over their hearts, shouting a challenge for the Englishmen to step from behind their fire-cart and meet them in hand-to-hand combat.

But no enemy stepped from behind the cart, as it was pushed harder into their line and to avoid the flames they had to jump clear, abandoning their weapons in fear of falling into the water. Only then did a soot-smeared and begrimed Hereward, his face black and his eyes glowing like coals, show himself, along with those other devils Siward and Rufus, and the three of them did hack each Norman knight to pieces, one by one, piece by piece.

Thus did three Englishmen rout a column of Norman cavalry on the causeway at Aldreth and for the first, though not the last, time was Hereward named as a Firestarter by his enemies.

[ix]

Unlike Baron Taillebois, Sir William de Warenne was to prove a much more patient commander. Having requisitioned a dozen or more flat-bottomed boats from the honest fishermen and wild-fowlers of Cambridgeshire, Sir William placed two cross-bowmen in each and told them to pole or 'punt' (for the water was in many places too shallow and tangled with marsh grasses to use oars) both upstream and down the old Ouse river, leaving no tributary or inlet which led into the Isle unexplored. To the west, upstream, these patrols would reach the edges of Chatteris Fen though without encountering any human form, for this was the least populated side of the Isle of Eels. To the east, down the Ouse river, their orders were to proceed as far as Theoford (today known as Little

Thetford), which means Little Ford, a mile or more from Ely itself, though no further, for the object of these patrols was spy out the watery land and to take prisoners, not deliver hostages to the enemy.

One patrol was successful in this, returning to Sir William's camp having captured an old lamprey-fisherman by the name of Alnod, a small, hunched man with skin like tanned leather. This Alnod, who had been born on the Isle of Eels and whose soul was in the care of the church of St Ethelreda, had no particular reason to love his Norman overlords, especially when Sir William's expert torturers, who had accompanied him since his arrival from Normandy (for it is always better to have men you can trust in such occupations), began to apply hot irons to the soles of his feet.

At first, Alnod protested that he was a humble fisherman who knew nothing of the rebels of Ely or their disposition and strength, though he thanked his captors when they allowed him to remove his one good pair of waterproof boots before the questioning began in earnest. Feet can heal, but good boots are a luxury for poor men. And as the irons scored his feet and the stink of burning meat reached his nose, he remembered that though he did not love the Normans, he had equally no reason to love the Danes who had eaten his entire stock of smoked fish and eels which meant that his family would go hungry that winter.

Thus did Sir William, careful not to betray his surprise, learn of the Danish army at Ely, and over supper he shared the news with Baron Ivo,

211

choosing his moment badly, for the baron almost choked on the rabbit (stewed whole with rosemary) he was biting into at the time.

'Fucking Danes!' he roared, still crunching flesh and bone, 'Why don't they give us a decent fight or just piss off back where they came from?'

'You were never suited to the role of ambassador, were you, old friend?' said Sir William. 'But you pose a good question. Why have the Danes come to Ely and not thrown in their lot with Hereward's rebels?'

'Perhaps they do not like the idea of fighting alongside outlaw scum and I cannot blame them for that. But why do you talk of ambassadors?'

'My dear Baron, if the Danish King is here on Ely, then we must treat with him.'

'What makes you think he is?'

'We know he sailed from Denmark–'

'We do?'

'Yes, we do, along with Bishop Christian of Aarhus, to rally his fleet after King William drove them from the Humber. But what would bring Svein Estridsson and Bishop Christian across the sea from Denmark? Not a charitable concern for the tired and hungry men of their army, surely?'

'The treasure of Peterborough!' exclaimed Baron Ivo.

'Exactly. The Danes failed to win anything assisting the rebels in the north and so now they come to help rebels in the east and Peterborough pays for their hire.'

'They have done little to earn their blood money so far.'

'Indeed they have not and we, my dear Baron,

212

must ensure that that state of affairs continues,' said Sir William, waving away a serving boy and helping himself from a flagon of finest German wine.

'I'm not frightened of a few Danish pirates,' said Baron Ivo, sucking rabbit juice loudly from his fingers. 'The days of the raiders in longships are over; they just don't know it yet.'

'Wise words, Ivo, but our forces here are not strong enough to take on a Danish army and this cursed Island of Eels is not the place to use your cavalry to best effect, as we have already discovered.'

'We should send word to the King for more men and siege engines so we can keep them contained and grind them down.'

'A decent enough plan, but I was thinking that instead of keeping them on the Isle, we should encourage them to escape.'

Taillebois was so astonished by this, he paused in his eating of a cold rib of beef.

'Let them escape, to spread their rebellion to the rest of the country like some sort of plague?'

'God's faith, no! We encourage the Danish army to leave, then we will see how bravely our English rebels fight when they stand alone.'

'And how, pray, do we do that?'

'We simply suggest it to them, my dear Ivo. That is why we need an ambassador.'

[x]

Having organized the defenders of the causeway

in throwing up a series of defensive earthworks made from blocks of cut peat (which when dry would have the advantage of forming fire-traps), Hereward left Siward in charge at Aldreth and accompanied by Martin Lightfoot, he hastened to Ely Abbey to plead his case for attack rather than defence.

If the two warriors, riding captured Norman ponies and wearing shirts of chain mail from which the blood had been carefully washed, had expected to be greeted as heroes, then they were sorely disappointed. Yeomen, serfs, women and monks working in the fields and among the reeds did not raise their eyes as they rode by, even though Hereward was keen to shout to them the news that no Norman had crossed over to the Isle and lived.

As they rode through the Danish encampment to reach the abbey, they did receive a greeting of sorts, but the calls from the Danish warriors sitting in the sunshine, sewing their clothing or honing their weapons, were more jeers than cheers. Martin Lightfoot was glad that his master's ear for an insult was not as keen as his, as he felt sure Hereward's temper was strained so that a single word might have him set about his allies as enthusiastically as he did his enemies.

At the abbey itself, Hereward demanded to see Thurstan immediately and was shown by a surly monk to the Chapel of St Ethelreda where the abbot was at private prayer with Bishop Christian. Not even Hereward would disturb an abbot and a bishop at their devotions, or at least not when the abbot was a true Englishman and the bishop had an army camped within earshot. And so he and Lightfoot made themselves comfortable on a pile of reeds cut and dried for the annual re-thatching of the chapel's roof and demanded, none too courteously, that they be brought fresh ale and bread.

'There is neither to be had in Ely this day,' snarled the surly monk. 'Your friends the Danes have supped their fill and then sent everything the brewers and bakers could provide down the river to the sea, where the rest of their army sits in its long-ships contemplating their own arseholes!'

'Harsh words, brother monk,' said Hereward with a smile, which many men more worldly than that aged monk had mistaken as sincere before now. 'Has no one thought to send for ale from the villages on the Isle? Do not places like Witchford and Theoford have brewhouses too?'

'Aye, but for them that live there. Abbot Thurstan will allow no monk to partake of stolen food or ale; that is his rule and strict in the observance is he.'

'Dear God, would you have us drink stagnant water from a sewer ditch like the dogs do? Is this the thanks a fighting man gets for defending God's holy places?'

'If God had called on you to fight for Ely then he would have blessed us with a bigger barley harvest and a larger brewhouse!'

Even as he said these words, the monk knew that he had angered Hereward beyond control and yet was still unable to raise his hands fast enough to deflect the first blow to the head from the heavy scabbard.

By the time a voice shouted 'Desist!' the monk

215

was bruised, battered and almost senseless, cowering under the chapel's overhanging thatched eaves.

His saviour was Thurstan himself, who had appeared at the door of the chapel with Bishop Christian of Aarhus at his side and his sacrist, as was the custom, standing just behind his right shoulder. They had been brought from their prayers by the sound of the old monk's head bouncing off the wooden walls.

'What is the meaning of this assault, Hereward?' demanded Thurstan.

Hereward looked down at the cowering monk and then at the fistful of the monk's habit he held, as if seeing it, and unfortunate brother, for the first time.

'He... I... We only called for ale...'

Thurstan stretched out an arm and placed it over Hereward's shoulder.

'Come, walk with me, my son, down to the hythe. There is much to discuss.'

As the abbot led the warrior away, Bishop Christian followed a discreet distance behind whilst the sacrist signalled with a jerk of his head that he wished to speak with Martin Lightfoot and hissed in his ear: 'Has he been taking the Christmas Rose root?'

'All of it,' whispered back Lightfoot. 'We need more supplies.'

The sacrist looked at him in wonder and then the two of them took the path to the hythe.

The wharves and landings at Ely had been planted into the mud of the river bank so that the men of the Isle could land and trade their daily catches of eels, lampreys, pike and wolf-fish for which they were famous. But a local fisherman in his shallow punt would have been hard pressed to find anywhere to dock on that warm day in late July, for the hythe was crowded with the transports of King Svein's Danish army, tied up and packed so closely together that it was impossible to see the river running under their keels. These were not, of course, the ships of the Danish fleet, which were anchored some twenty-five miles away on the coast at Lynne, but much smaller keels, mostly appropriated from the fishermen of Norfolk and more suited to the inland waterways than the ocean-going Danish longship.

Hereward looked at the array of small craft all tied to each other, stretching across the river almost to the marshes which surrounded the smaller isle and village of Stuntney across the Ouse.

'God's face!' cursed Hereward, 'a man could walk from Ely to Stuntney across this bridge of boats.'

'You see our problem, my son,' said Thurston, his arm still around the young warrior.

'I see a problem sure enough. You have all these boats lying idle here, when my Fenmen at Aldreth could have the use of them to harry and disrupt our Norman foes, who gather strength on the Cambridge side every day.'

The abbot shook his head slowly and took a firmer grip on Hereward's shoulder.

'No, my son, you miss my meaning. This chaos of empty boats here is but a sign of a larger disease. No traders can reach us from the coast because they fear our Danish allies. Even if they could, where would they unload or take on cargo? No traders come along the old west river, for that passes near Aldreth and the causeway and nothing comes downriver from Cambridge, for the Normans make sure of that.'

'Then give me some of these boats and fighting men to paddle them and I will take the war to the Normans and spread such havoc that they will wish they had stayed in Normandy!' cried Hereward.

'Brave and noble words, my young warrior, but can you not see that the Isle of Ely is starving itself to death? We cannot sustain this unnatural situation.'

At this, Hereward broke free of Abbot Thurstan's embrace and reached for his sword, though he did not draw it. Martin Lightfoot plunged forward to place himself between the warrior and the monk, calling out 'My Lords, be calm, calm.'

'If this is an unnatural situation,' snarled Hereward, 'then it is not of my making. I was charged with leading the men of the Fens, to have them follow me to Peterborough to save the treasure of the abbey there from falling into the hands of the Normans. This I did without loss or harm to a single man or monk. And when it drew the Normans' vengeance, as we knew it would, who is it that has defended this Isle and this abbey? My Fenmen, without any help from your slack-arsed Danish flock, my Lord Bishop.'

'Hereward! You must not speak to Bishop Christian like that!' Thurstan chastised him.

'I will do more than speak, my Abbot, I will come here at night and set fire to this beautiful bridge of ships! Perhaps that might stir the stumps of our Danish allies and kindle some of the fighting spirit my grandfather sang of.'

'You must understand, my son,' said Bishop Christian, determined to show no fear of Hereward, 'that King Svein came to this land expecting a popular uprising against William the Bastard and recognition that the claims of Denmark to the throne of England are more legitimate than those of Normandy.'

'And have we not recognized Svein Estridsson by entrusting him with the treasure of Peterborough and have we not denied the Normans the causeway at Aldreth for a month now with our own blood?'

The sacrist noted the staring visage which Hereward presented and moved close to Bishop Christian's side, for he knew the young Englishman far better than the Danish bishop did.

'You have, Hereward, you and your men of the Fens,' soothed Thurstan, 'no one can deny that. God has seen how you have fought to protect his English Church, but King Svein expected to see all of England rise up and cast out our oppressors. That has not happened, Hereward. England is not in flames.'

'It soon could be!' said Hereward with a grin. 'Let me take these Danish hard men off the Isle so we can carry the fight to the so-called knights of Normandy. Give me those boats and some Fenmen to guide them and we can attack Cambridge by river whilst fat Baron Ivo Taillebois and his cavalry sit watching the causeway at Aldreth.'

'What are you saying, my son? Do you think we

219

can lay siege to Cambridge Castle *and* defend Ely?'

'Why not? They would not expect it.'

Bishop Christian held up his right hand as if in blessing.

'My brothers, we are dreaming. Svein will not approve of a plan which involves besieging a stone castle. The Danish army has no siege engines and it is a style of warfare which does not suit them.'

'Then bring up your reserves, the men who guard your longships on the coast.'

'King Svein and Prince Bjorn will not agree to leaving the fleet undefended. If King William's navy catches them against the coast they could be scattered or sunk.'

'And then the Danes would have no means of escape,' said Martin Lightfoot to the irritation of all but Hereward.

'King Svein does not look to flee,' said the Bishop sternly, 'neither does he wish to sacrifice his army defending another man's country to little purpose or profit. Remember, Hereward, you have been fighting for a month, most of Svein's army spent last year aiding the rebels in the north, rebels whose spirits failed at their first sight of King William. Many of the men have not seen their wives and homes for two years. They will not settle for another winter here.'

'Then make them fight!' cried Hereward. 'Get their blood up! I will lead them if their own captains will not.'

'Careful, my son,' murmured the abbot as he saw Bishop Christian's face darken.

'Careful, my Lord Bishop,' murmured the

sacrist just as quietly.

'The King of Denmark will fight when he de-cides he will fight and his men will follow him, no other. As a bishop I must do as God commands. As a man, you, Hereward, must do as kings command. Both of us must obey without question. It is the way of things. Now go and find what food and drink you can, and take some rest, for you look weary.'

And with that, Bishop Christian turned his back and walked away, which was truly the action of one who firmly believed in the protection of God, for Hereward in that moment did not look tired. His eyes flashed and his chest heaved. On his forearms and shoulder, his veins throbbed where the blood boiled and his mouth opened and closed but, and perhaps this was God's mercy, no sound came from his lips.

[xi]

Later, as Thurstan made his way to evening prayers in the abbey, he enquired of his sacrist the whereabouts of Hereward and his groom, Light-foot.

'They have gone to Littleport,' replied the sacrist.

'You saw them yourself?'

'One of the fishwives working down on the hythe repairing nets was told to observe them. It is thought they have gone there to collect more men and supplies.'

'And perhaps to check on anything they might

have buried there?'

'I would be surprised if they did not.'

'The men who went there with them, after Peterborough, two Fenmen called Winter and...'

'Liveret,' completed the sacrist. 'They were eel-fishers, known to us.'

'What happened to them? They never returned to Ely.'

'Only God can know their fate now, my Lord, but I dispensed alms to the widows and families yesterday.'

Thurstan bowed his head and said a silent prayer before continuing.

'Do you think Hereward will come back?'

'Where else can he go?' the sacrist replied. 'Beyond the Isle of Eels he is an outlaw and by now the barons will have put a price on his head. In any case, there is a fight to be fought here and Hereward runs towards a fight, not away.'

'Do you think he will hold to his threat to burn the Danes' boats?'

'Fire is proving to be his favourite weapon and who but God knows what is in Hereward's mind?'

'Perhaps we should warn Prince Bjorn...' The abbot stopped in hesitation.

'I have already advised him to treble the guard on the river tonight,' said the sacrist with a sigh.

But the Danish boats and the hythes and wharves of Ely were not troubled that night. Hereward and Lightfoot had indeed gone to Martin's birthplace of Littleport which, in summer and with the level of the River Ouse low, could be approached on foot from Ely with little difficulty, providing a man knew the paths through the marshes. Only in winter and when the spring tides flooded the Fens, was Littleport truly an island like the Isle of Eels.

How long they stayed there is not known for sure, though it is said they found a supply of ale and wine enough to last a week. This was not unusual for a proportion of the goods traded into and out of Ely had for generations found their way into hidey-holes in Littleport. They did recruit men from the village to join their fight, along with stilt-walkers from Burnt Fen and Middle Fen who followed the instructions of Hraga the Heron, the Norfolk incomer who had made the Fens his home.

With Hraga acting as a sure-footed guide, Hereward took some forty men on to the Isle and by night they marched to Aldreth, across the secret paths of Grunty Fen to the west of Ely, well out of sight of any curious Danish eyes, for he had no wish to reveal the cargo his men carried.

On his arrival at Aldreth Hereward was, for once, greeted as a hero for the defenders of the causeway were honestly pleased to mark his return. Some had perhaps heard that he and Light-foot were to visit Littleport and maybe doubted that he would return at all. But they took courage and fresh heart from seeing him again and, being Fenmen, as soon as they saw the cargo he had brought, their spirits soared even higher.

For what Hereward's troop had carried from Littleport in tied bundles, were pairs of Fenland stilts fashioned from ash wood, each taller than one man sat on the shoulders of another. When strapped to the legs of a man used to balancing

223

on them, they made him almost thrice the height of a grown man and, if practised in the art it was said that a stilt-walker could outpace a trotting pony over even ground. It was where the ground was uneven, though, that the stilt-walker came into his own, for the marshes, reed-beds, ditches and dykes of the Fens were no obstacle to a man on stilts though often a death-trap for a man on a horse. At the height of summer, with their levels low and their flow gentle, not even the rivers of the Fenlands daunted such as Hraga the Heron, who could stride across a river where man with weapons and armour would have to seek out a ford or a ferry.

Of the defenders of Aldreth only Siward and Rufus, who were not Fenmen by birth, questioned Hereward as to why he had brought them a supply of long spears without iron points, at which Hereward had laughed loudly.

'These are not spears, but they are weapons. They will allow us to walk into the Norman camp and steal as many spears as we can carry.'

'Walk? Just walk across that causeway into the Norman camp?' asked Rufus, disbelieving his own ears.

'Not across the causeway,' said Hereward, the sparkle back in his eyes. 'We will walk on water! Though some of us may need to do some training first!'

And so it was that for a week, Hereward, Lightfoot and Hraga would lead thirty selected Fenmen into the marsh so that they were out of sight of Norman eyes on the Cambridge side of the causeway, and they would, with some cursing, much laughter and the occasional broken bone, perfect the art of walking whilst ten feet off the ground. To many of them, it came naturally for if they had not stilt-walked before, they had seen their fathers do so, and most were good enough to balance and use the short Fenland hunting-bow with considerable accuracy over short distances.

In many aspects of the science of stilt-walking, Hereward deferred to Martin Lightfoot, who was far more adept than he, although all deferred to Hraga the Heron and it was easy to see how he had come by his name, for not only could he move effortlessly over the marshes, but then he could stand as if hovering in the air over his prey before striking down with spear or arrow.

During this period of training, the Normans suspected nothing and each day would continue their probing attacks against the rebels. These they did by skirmishers of crossbowmen, who would remain out of throwing range of the defenders and unleash bolts at the every head foolish enough to rise up above the peat earthworks Hereward had ordered built. Alternatively, small boats with two or three crossbowmen would approach alongside the causeway, taking advantage of the tall reeds until they were level with the defenders and then they would fire their weapons, catching several Fenmen by surprise initially. But Fenmen are born hunters and will often spend days in the reeds and bull-rushes waiting for the slightest sound or movement to betray the presence of a wild pig or a young deer. Siward placed his best hunters on the flanks of the causeway, themselves hidden in the reeds, and when a stalk twitched or a ripple of water spread without cause or a bird took sudden flight, then the attackers would find themselves attacked, with arrows or spears or by a sudden rush of Fenmen through the shallower waters. Many a Norman boat was overturned and many a Norman soldier, unsure of where to place his feet on such treacherous ground, was sent to God with a blow from a sharpened hoe or had their throat slit with a shearing knife or their head held under the brown water until they choked and drowned. In these encounters, both sides took casualties. Neither took prisoners.

Yet since Ivo Taillebois' ill-fated cavalry charge, the Normans had seemed content to harry the defenders, to keep them contained and to deprive them of a full night's rest, rather than try and draw them out and into battle. Siward and Rufus put this down to cowardice on the part of the Norman knights not wishing to stand toe-to-toe with honest Englishmen who had right, and God, on their side.

In front of his men – for he was a good captain of men at arms – Hereward could not but agree with this claim, but in his heart he knew that when Normans had met Englishmen in open battle, the result had always favoured the invader. Here in the Fens, Hereward had found the only ground on which a smaller force of men on foot had the advantage over a larger, better equipped, better disciplined, more battle-hardened Norman army. For had he not seen almost exactly the same conditions when fighting in Friesia for the Count of Flanders?

When his own men, brave, trained and well-armed though they were, had been unable to crush the elusive water rats of Scaldermariland and Walchern in a flooded landscape almost a copy of the Fens (though without the religious houses and deep devotion to God).

Furthermore, Hereward was a good enough general to know that his Norman opponents grew stronger every day whereas his army was limited to the Fenmen he had led from Ely to Aldreth and the support of the men of Littleport he had recruited. In total, though, this was an army of not much more than 120 souls, stout in heart and all sworn defenders of the holy shrine of Ely, but poorly armed and all with wives and children on the Isle expecting to be provided with food for the winter.

And when he thought of three hundred Danish warriors sitting at their ease in Ely, eating and drinking – especially the drinking – from the larders and storehouses of the Isle, he knew he must bring the Danes into the fight, and soon. To do that, he must first enrage the Normans.

He was confident he could do that.

[xii]

The Norman camp on the Cambridge side of the Aldreth causeway had been fixed due south of Aldreth on firm ground which rose to a slight hill and the village of Cottenham, where the church there was used by Baron Ivo's knights for their prayers and the blessing of their weapons.

At the time of Hereward's attack, Baron Ivo's

knights numbered one hundred, though the numbers in the camp were swelled by hostlers, fathers, blacksmiths, cooks and bakers and even a dozen or more loose women from Cambridge who had followed the camp, as women from Cambridge were prone to do.

On the night in question, Baron Taillebois and Sir William de Warenne were both in Cambridge Castle, receiving messengers not only from King William, who was in Salisbury overseeing the torture and execution of rebels from the west country, but also from the estate managers in Norfolk overseeing the lands which had belonged to Sir William's murdered brother-in-law.

It was perhaps because their two commanders were elsewhere that the camp was lax in its defences that night, but then the Normans thought they had little to fear. The causeway from Aldreth was well-defended, but what other approach was there to watch? Between their camp and the rebels on Ely was a mile of marshy fenland as well as the River Ouse and so far there had been no sign that the rebels had the will or ability to launch an attack by boat, or any attack at all beyond the causeway itself.

Siward and Rufus were left in charge of the English end of the causeway and ordered to show torches to occupy the attention of Norman lookouts, to which they did not object for they had showed no aptitude at all for stilt-walking. And the diversion worked well enough, for the raiding party crossed the Ouse Fen and the river itself no more than a quarter of a mile downstream.

Once on dry land Hereward and some thirty of

his comrades dismounted from their high and unnatural legs, hiding their stilts in a small copse of trees all except for three pairs which the men carried up the rising ground as they followed the scent of wood smoke and roasting duck fat which wafted on the night air from the Norman camp.

Hereward had planned his attack not to secure any lasting military advantage or territory, but to spread the maximum fear and confusion he could and as part of this strategy he had insisted on all the warriors of the raiding party coating their faces in a mixture of peat and ash until their black faces gleamed like devils in the firelight. None wore armour or carried a shield, but each had a longsword strapped to their backs and a short bow and quiver of twenty arrows hanging from their necks. Three of the best hunters carried only fire arrows made from wool clippings, sawdust and beeswax. All, being Fenmen, carried a short blade normally used for cutting reeds or gutting fish, but equally useful for a Norman throat.

Being careful to approach downwind (for whilst the smell of an honest Englishman may go un-noticed by a Norman knight, the same could not be said of his horse), Hereward's forces eased their way through the grass and scrub towards the tents and fires of the enemy until they were within bow shot and the accents of Normandy and Brittany could be clearly heard, if not understood.

Many a commander would have ordered a sur-prise attack with a volley of arrows out of the dark, but for Hereward that was not enough. Disregard-ing all thoughts of personal safety and well-being, Hereward, Lightfoot and Hraga the Heron strapped on their stilts, tying them to their legs with leather thongs, and had their comrades haul them upright. Slowly, and with great concentration for their hands were occupied notching arrows to their bows, these three giants advanced slowly towards the camp where the unsuspecting Normans slept or sat around their fires playing dice or knelt at prayer.

Indeed it was Hraga the Heron, being a good Christian man of Norfolk, who had mooted that it did not seem just to attack an unsuspecting enemy whilst they were at their devotions, to which Hereward had answered that they were merely men seeking God and he was there to hasten their passage to Him.

Several of those surprised Norman knights must have felt that Satan and his dark angels themselves had come to claim them, for the three stilt-walkers were among them, close enough to kill, before any alarm was raised. In fact the tale was told that Hereward was able to kick over the stew pot hanging from the dog irons over one fire with his right stilt before the Normans sitting cross-legged on the ground realized his presence. When they looked up expecting to see a man, they saw a giant with a black face and flashing eyes, roaring with laughter and they were in awe to the extent that Hereward was able to put an arrow through the throat of one of them and into the shoulder and thigh of two others before they managed to start screaming.

The commotion was the signal for Hereward's raiders to launch their fire arrows towards the Norman tents but avoiding their horses, picketed near a copse of young trees. The tents, many with sleeping soldiers still in them, caught fire quickly, lighting the whole camp area so that Normans running in panic became easy targets for the other bowmen.

And through all this fire and death strode three dark giant figures, dispensing a fair proportion of death themselves and instilling so much terror that not one of the three stilt-walkers was challenged, even though a single blow could have toppled them and left them at the mercy of their enemies.

Such was the confusion among the Normans that their shouts and screams could be heard across the moonlit fens by the small garrison holding the Aldreth causeway who were soon able to see flames licking the sky above the main camp; but either out of duty or because they were afraid, they stayed at their posts as ordered.

When their arrows were all fired, the English stilt-men strode out of the ruined camp and into the trees where they cut themselves free of the unnatural legs and felt firm ground under their feet. Drawing his firesteel blade from the scabbard on his back, Hereward gathered his men together and led them at the run back across the camp site they had just devastated.

Any wounded Norman soldiers who had not taken to the dark trees (for few would have been frightened enough to risk escape across the treacherous fens even in daylight) were set upon and killed with blade or club. Some took heart from the fact that they could see they were fighting men and not giant demons, and struck back,

231

inflicting wounds on several of the English before they fell.

Whilst Lightfoot attended to a terrified string of Norman horses still tethered at the edge of the smouldering camp, Hereward began to collect up discarded weapons and armour and Hraga did what he could for their own wounded. Those who could ride (for not all Fenmen were familiar with horses) dressed themselves in the mail coats and helmets of the dead Normans, and Hereward blessed the night which meant his more timid followers could not see the blood and brain matter in some of the helms he placed on their heads. Those with no experience of horseflesh, unless cooked, and the wounded were tied in pairs to the most docile animals and given long Norman shields for protection.

Thus did Hereward's make-shift cavalry make its first and only charge down the slope to the Aldreth causeway, hoping to take the Norman guards there by surprise.

The subterfuge lasted only as long as Hereward's temper. As he led his horsemen in ragged formation on to the causeway, Normans began to emerge from their earthworks and bivouacs, bringing torches so they could identify the night riders.

A tall, clean-shaven sergeant holding a torch aloft had the misfortune to step in front of Hereward's horse and demand, in a thick Breton accent, what had caused the commotion at the Cottenham camp, thinking that he was talking to a brother-in-arms. (For Hereward, with his long hair tucked inside an iron helmet and holding the

232

edge of a long shield up to his face, would have been unrecognizable even to those who knew him well.)

Hereward thought about the question as the sergeant waved the torch near his face and then, after he had considered it long enough, he answered: 'Why, I did, of course!'

And in one swift movement Hereward reached behind his helmet to the handle of his sword and drawing it, slashed downwards, severing the sergeant's arm, at the shoulder and he watched the separated arm still holding a burning torch in a gloved hand fall to the causeway and ignite a patch of dry reeds before, with a whoop of joy, he spurred his horse towards Aldreth.

The Normans were taken by surprise at first but were quick to recover their courage, for these were men of Baron Taillebois picked for their proven bravery and they took pride in their chosen profession. They threw torches at the rebel riders and the crossbows began to sing, taking a heavy toll on the poorer riders and wounded at the rear.

Of the thirty Fenmen who had stilt-walked off the Isle of Eels that night with Hereward, fourteen rode back across the causeway with him to be cheered home by Siward and Rufus and the other defenders behind their peat barricades. Two men, and the horse they were riding, had been seen to plunge off the causeway and into the marshy water, never to surface. A further one died of his wounds and one more was crippled for what remained of his life on this Earth, when his stolen Norman pony tripped on a root and stumbled, flinging him through the air where a broken back awaited his landing.

The rest had either fallen or been taken by the Normans at the south end of the causeway who were anxious to revenge their sergeant who had bled to death during the night.

As the rising sun dispersed the early morning mist across that mysterious landscape, the jubilant defenders of Ely ceased in their singing of hymns of victory one by one, as they saw the Normans building a bonfire on the causeway out of the stilts they had abandoned the very night before.

When the pyre, taller than a man on horseback, was well ablaze, the Fenmen saw the bodies of their comrades being flung on to it by the Normans.

From the screams they heard on the Isle it was clear that some of those being pushed into the flames had been taken alive. At that distance, however, not even the sharpest-eyed Fen-man could see if the prisoners had lost their hands or feet before they burned, for such was the traditional legal punishment for treason.

[xiii]

'The King says that if this rebellious scum want a war, then we must oblige them,' Sir William informed Baron Ivo. 'He is sending warships around the Norfolk coast to worry the Danish fleet and he's sending you more troops and his best engineers and artillerymen. He has ordered a full siege of the Isle of Ely. Nothing is to get in;

no one is to get out. No monk or priest is to be harmed, but otherwise he wants no prisoners. There is only one exception to this general order: King Svein and his army are to depart unchallenged first.'

'And just how the fair fuck do we arrange that?'

'Why, my dear Ivo, we simply ask them to leave. We make them an offer they simply cannot allow themselves to refuse.'

'We do, do we? Just like that?'

'Yes, Baron, just like that. I will need the services of one of your best knights for a delicate and dangerous mission.'

'There's always Sir Deda. He's a bit slow but brave enough and he's one of my wife's cousins. How dangerous is this mission?'

'If he falls foul of Hereward and his gang, it could be deadly.'

'Sir Deda's your man,' said Baron Ivo. 'He wouldn't be missed that much.'

[xiv]

Although he had his hair cropped in the military style and he bore his arms and armour with all the dignity of a veteran of many campaigns, young Sir Deda had something of an unworldly pallor to his skin and whenever he moved his hands, which were rarely un-gloved, it was with delicate affectation. He looked like a man more comfortable playing the harp or singing in a choir of monks, than on the battlefield or training ground.

Many said he was better suited to the life of a

235

monk rather than that of a soldier and that he had only offered to serve William of Normandy in the hope of finding a wife in England and despite more than three years of searching he had yet to find an English widow to suit his purpose. (Saxon women he found too dark and maids of Danish stock not delicate enough for his taste.) Certainly, he travelled well in the company of monks and even knew the song *Dulce cantaverunt monachi in Ely, dum Canatus rex navigaret prope ibi*, and could even sing it in the Old English, *Merie sungen de muneches binnen Ely da Cnut ching reu der by* (Sweetly sang the monks of Ely when (the boat of) King Canute rowed near.) in which it was supposed to have been written by King Cnut himself, though few scholars really believe this as kings are rarely musical.

No one doubted Sir Deda's skill in several languages, nor his dedication to following the orders of Baron Taillebois, for he had a healthy respect for the Baron's temper, but few would have made him their first choice for a most secret and highly important mission into the heart of enemy territory. And to go unarmed, save for his personal eating dagger, and without a bodyguard was thought foolhardy by many, or the sign of a man who had the utmost faith in his God.

Wearing a long brown cloak with the hood covering his head, despite the warm summer, Sir Deda was indistinguishable from the four monks who sat at the oars of the small boat launched on the River Cam a half mile upstream from the confluence with the Ouse to the south of Theoford on the Isle of Ely itself.

Up until that afternoon in late August, Sir William de Warenne had resisted the temptation to send any force other than a scouting patrol to attack the rebellious Isle at Theoford. To a military eye, Theoford presented easily the most vulnerable spot to any hostile attack, for although there was no causeway as there was at Aldreth, the river here was narrow and low, it being summer, and was overlooked by higher ground on the small Isle of Stuntney, which only truly became an island during the winter flooding of the Fens.

As a consequence, the defences at Theoford comprised little more than some young boys who acted as runners and three old women of Ely who spent the days weaving baskets from bulrushes whilst keeping one eye on the river.

Since the arrival of the Danes, whose camp lay between Theoford and Ely, there had been little traffic on the rivers which skirted the Isle, which was hardly surprising for a traveller on these roads of the wetlands might fall prey to piratical Danes, rebellious Englishmen or vengeful Normans. Therefore the sight of a small boat containing five monkish figures coming from the south caused some excitement among the women, who set a pair of boys running on the riverside paths through the tall reeds (which kept them invisible to both the river and the Danish camp) to Ely Abbey. There they were told to seek out Abbot Thurstan or one of the brotherhood and give them the news that more good and holy men would be landing at Ely before Vespers.

Thus it was that when the rowing boat docked at the hythe of Ely amidst all the craft already tied there, its passengers were met by a welcoming party of Abbot Thurstan, his sacrist and a dozen monks of the abbey bearing wooden platters of bread and bowls of curds and freshly boiled green beans.

'From wherever you come, brothers, you are welcome here in Ely,' announced Thurstan as the visitors stepped on to the wooden planking of the hythe and this was the signal for the monks bearing platters to begin a chant to the glory of God for watching over the travellers.

The chant, though harmonious enough, was quickly cut short by the first monk who stepped ashore, flung back his cowl and held up his right arm to command silence.

'These men who rowed me here may well be your brothers in holy orders, but I am not,' the visitor said haughtily. 'I am Sir Deda, sworn man of Baron Ivo Taillebois and a knight in the service of William, King of England and Duke of Normandy. I come here unarmed and in a spirit of truce.'

The sacrist bowed towards the Norman knight and indicated the abbot with his left hand.

'This is Thurstan, the father of our abbey and our guide and leader in all matters of...'

Once more Sir Deda flung up his arm for silence.

'My business here is not with Ely Abbey or its rebellious followers. I carry words from one king to another, so take me to King Svein of Denmark with all speed, for he will not thank you if I am delayed. If God smiles on my errand, I may well join you in the abbey for prayers at Compline, for

238

I have heard that monks of Ely sing sweetly.'

[xiv]

It was Godric, youngest brother of the late Abbot Brand of Peterborough and uncle to Hereward, who took the news from Ely to the defenders of Aldreth, guided by the daughter of a reed-cutter across the swamps of Grunty Fen.

In his later years, when he was much wiser and so highly thought of that his fellow monks at Peterborough were to elect him abbot there, Godric was to share his memories of those times. He would say that he had never felt such fear as he did when he had to leave Ely under cover of darkness without alerting the Danish army to his departure, until that is, he had to cross Grunty Fen with no torch and only a young girl, who might have been a mute for all she spoke, to guide his feet. But even then, the terrors of the night and the swamp, with its bubbling, stinking mud holes and its unseen animals rustling and splashing within the reeds, were nought as compared to the fear instilled in him by the eyes of Hereward as he told his story as dawn broke over the Aldreth camp.

'The Norman emissary arrived three days ago, having been rowed down the river by brothers from the Priory near Cambridge,' Godric began his tale. 'He called himself Sir Deda and held himself in a courtly manor, proudly declaring his liege lords to be Baron Ivo Taillebois and King William, though he had been sent to Ely by Sir

William de Warenne, whom he described as the Norman king's champion and captain of his armies in the east of England.'

'I don't suppose that arrogant bastard De Warenne wants to surrender to us, does he?'

Hereward's remarks drew much laughter from his grizzled men, although his own face remained serious as if he had not meant it as a jest. So Godric replied seriously.

'My Lord Hereward, this Sir Deda brought a message from King William himself and for the ears of King Svein of Denmark alone, although Bishop Christian insisted that he and Abbot Thurstan and his sacrist be included in the negotiations, to which Svein agreed as he holds Bishop Christian in high regard.'

'When do we get to hear what they heard?' snapped Martin Lightfoot.

'They say that women talk too much,' observed Siward the White, 'but surely monks have longer tongues.'

'Which sometimes have to be removed,' growled Hereward menacingly.

Godric was almost certain that Hereward would not harm a blood relative. After all, that was why he was here, was it not? But being almost certain is not the same as having complete faith and so he hurried on with his tale.

'King William wished the King of Denmark to know that the ships of the Danish fleet have been discovered at anchor near the town of Lynne on the coast, and that William's own fleet of warships is being assembled at Ipswich. They will be ready to sail within a week.'

'Excellent news!' shouted Hereward, slapping the scabbard of his sword with the flat of his hand. 'Now the Danes will have to fight.'

It was Martin, the only one who could always speak plain to Hereward without fear, who held up a hand in caution.

'What if the Danish fleet breaks out and scatters?'

'They will not scatter without their king,' said Hereward confidently.

'No, my Lord Hereward, they will not,' said Godric and every Englishman's gaze turned on him in such a way that the spittle dried in the young monk's mouth.

'Speak on, Holy Brother,' said Lightfoot. 'We may not like the message but we do not kill the messenger.'

Which, if Martin had remembered certain campaigns with Hereward in Flanders, was not actually true.

'The Danish fleet will not leave English waters without their king, for their king will be sailing with them. Sir Deda brought with him an offer of free and unchallenged passage to the coast for Svein and all his army now on the Isle of Ely on condition that they leave within a week.'

'Hah!' spat Hereward. 'And they expect a Danish warrior like Svein to turn tail and run, do they?'

'The Danish king has already agreed to the proposal,' said Godric softly.

'What in the kingdom of God could make him agree to that?'

'The treasure of Peterborough,' Lightfoot answered quietly.

'It is true. King William will forgo all legal claims to the plunder of Peterborough Abbey so long as the holy relic of St Oswald's arm is given into the care of a trustworthy holy man.'

'Let me guess,' said Hereward angrily, 'he found just such a holy man in the fat form of Bishop Christian, a loyal lapdog who will do as he is told.'

'Bishop Christian has sworn to safeguard the treasure, to be sure, but it is Prior Athelwold of Peterborough himself who has taken charge of the holy relic. He and all the brothers of Peterborough who came to Ely with you, my Lord Hereward, are to accompany all the wonders of Peterborough to pray for their protection on the voyage to Denmark.'

'So the pirate king of Denmark steals not only the treasure of Peterborough but also the monks of Peterborough!' laughed Hereward.

'It is a sound ploy,' said Siward, 'for William will not attack the Danish ships if they carry holy men of the English Church.'

'Why wouldn't he?' asked Hereward aloud, as though such a concept was foreign to him.

'William of Normandy may steal from the church and his brother Bishop Odo may wish to shape it in the image of the strict houses of Fecamp and Normandy, but he does not make war on the English Church,' said Godric with conviction. 'He is a king, but even kings answer to God in the end.'

'If they do not answer to Hereward first!'

Hereward's hand grabbed the handle of his sword, but Lightfoot placed his own hand over his master's and spoke soothingly as he would to a horse he did not know but was intent on stealing.

'King Svein the Danish pirate does not have *all* the treasure of Peterborough,' said Martin close enough for only Hereward to hear, 'and the Isle of Eels now has three hundred less lazy mouths to feed.'

Hereward's face transformed.

'God's face, my old friend, you're right! Why should we feed an army that does not fight? It is the men of the Fens who have held off every Norman attack so far; it is the men of the Fens who have unseated Norman knights, scattered their camp and stolen their horses. Let the Danes go and the Normans come, for we know how to make them welcome!'

The defenders of Aldreth who were there to hear this speech, hungry and stinking though they were, all cheered as if a great victory had been announced.

'And when do the Danes scuttle away?' Hereward asked Godric.

'They began to load their rowing boats yesterday,' answered the young monk.

'Then I must go to Ely and bid them farewell!' said Hereward loudly, a broad grin across his face, although the faces of his men were full of consternation at this plan.

'Is that wise, Hereward?' asked Lightfoot, for only he dare whilst Hereward still held a sword.

'Surely it is only courteous to say goodbye to our Danish cousins?'

'Be careful, my captain,' warned Siward. 'If

William has put a price on your head, our noble allies might try and claim it.'

Hereward continued to smile at his men and especially his young uncle.

'They have to catch me first, my friend. You, Brother Godric, take off your clothes.'

[xv]

Beyond Ely and beyond Littleport, the River Ouse (now combined with the Cam, which some call the Grant or Granta) broadens out to form the Wellstream, as it was called in the Fens, and then the Ouse Magna or Great Ouse which meets the sea at Lynne.

In the winter months when the Fen waters are at their highest and the rivers run their fastest, it was a common sight to see twenty or more boats at any one time working the Wellstream, with wool and barley being shipped downstream to the port of Lynne passing cargoes of salt and herring heading upstream for Ely.

But on that first day of September when the Danish army of King Svein left Ely, all the traffic on the river floated only one way and so low was the water that anyone observing the scene might have mistaken the slow-moving flotilla for a single, heavily laden raft. Many of the small craft were indeed roped together as one would lash logs into a raft, those containing the treasure of Peterborough being situated in the middle of the flotilla – for there were many creeks and tributaries which wandered off the Wellstream before

244

it met the sea – on boats commanded by trusted *huscarls* of the King.

Svein Estridsson and his brother Bjorn were among the last to disembark from the hythe at Ely, but only after a Mass celebrated jointly by Bishop Christian and Abbot Thurstan. The monks of Ely provided a choir but were said not to sing sweetly that day, for it was a day of sad farewells to Prior Athelwold and their brothers from Peterborough who were departing with the Danes. They took with them prayers aplenty from their Ely brethren, for all knew they were embarking on a perilous journey, but were given great heart when the arm of St Oswald was shown to them. Surely such a holy relic would hold a watch over them whatever was to come. Of this, none doubted.

As Bishop Christian made his final blessing over Thurstan and the monks of Ely, the abbot begged him to persuade King Svein to leave the small boats the Danes were using at Lynne, for many of them had been stolen by the Danes from the lawful fishermen of that town and as a result they had suffered a summer of hardship, being thus deprived of a means of feeding their families.

Bishop Christian, impressed and somewhat humbled by the charitable concerns of Thurstan for others, made King Svein swear to do so on the spot, to which he agreed with kingly grace for once re-united with his longships, he would have no need of such small inland craft.

When it was time for Svein and his brother and their bodyguards to board their boats, the Danish king took Abbot Thurstan to one side in farewell.

'The people of Ely do not show themselves, Abbot,' said Svein. 'Is that because they are sad to see us go, or happy?'

'They are simple people, my Lord, and they are afraid,' replied Thurstan. 'Afraid they have defied a Norman king who will now come to extract vengeance.'

'You worry unduly, good Abbot,' Svein counselled. 'What has happened here on the Isle of Eels is but a pinprick to William they call the Conqueror. The men of the Fens lead no great rebellion against the Normans, perhaps no one in England ever will. Your grand scheme to save the English Church failed because you left it too late to throw off the Norman yoke. Perhaps it is also too late to expect to see a Danish king on an English throne ever again. My bringing my army here this summer was in vain.'

'But not without profit.'

The voice was not that of Abbot Thurstan.

'Your sacrist is known for his sharp mind,' observed King Svein, 'but seeking fame for a prying nose and sharp tongue is a dangerous business.'

'Forgive my brother in Christ,' pleaded Thurstan. 'He fears what will become of us.'

'I should think nothing will become of you,' said the Dane, 'though among the noble men of my country, that is a curse and not a blessing. With my army gone from these lands, William has no opponent worthy enough to give him battle. He may fine the abbey and he may well grant much of your land to one of his pet Barons,

246

but he will not make war on monks. He needs men who can read and write; men who know the law and can administer it even if it is now Norman law, not Danish or Saxon. He has a country to run and he is a very practical king.'

'But what of the Fenmen who have defied his soldiers these past months?' cried Thurstan.

The King of the Danes shrugged his shoulders.

'He may be tempted to deal with them as he did the rebels in the north, laying waste the very land so that neither man nor beast could live off it again for a generation. There again, the land here is richer and more fertile, a worthy prize for a Norman lord, so perhaps William will merely treat the rebels as outlaws, hanging the ones he finds and declaring the rest *silvaticus* and banishing them to the forests. Should he wish to make an example of the men of Ely, then he will charge them with treason and the punishment will be that they live, but they lose either a foot or a hand.'

And Svein turned to the Sacrist of Ely and said: 'But I thought you, of all men, would have known that.'

[xvi]

As the last Danish boat creaked away from the hythe and began to float slowly (for all the boats were heavily laden) into the Wellstream, Abbot Thurstan assembled his choir of monks around him for a final prayer for the safety of their departing brothers

247

Deep in contemplation, the innocent and un-worldly Thurstan failed to notice that his congregation comprised thirteen robed and hooded monks rather than the twelve that had been present earlier. But this did not escape the sharp-eyed sacrist.

'My Lord Abbot, we have a stranger in our midst,' he said with a catch in his voice which betrayed his nervousness.

'No stranger,' shouted Hereward throwing back his disguise, 'but a sworn defender of Ely and from the looks of things, the only one you have left!'

Thurstan dismissed the choir, ordering the monks to return to their duties in the fields and gardens, and then he asked Hereward and the sacrist to accompany him into the abbey court-yard.

'Walk with me, my son, and let me show you why we have no need of defenders for Ely any more,' said the abbot, speaking no more, as he saw it, than the truth.

'Look about you, Hereward, and see that our dairy has no cows, our granaries are empty of grain and the fires in our brewhouse and bakery lie cold. Our brethren survive on oat porridge and the few vegetables not yet ripe enough for the Danes to steal. They even stripped the hedgerows of blackberries before they left. If they are lucky, the people of this Isle will have some smoked eel hidden in places where the Danes have not searched, for their crops this season have been eaten or stolen, their animals slaughtered and the game and fowl they would normally hunt have been scared away. Every scrap of iron has been taken from our smithies, along with most of our seasoned timber and pitch. A year's supply of firewood has gone on their campfires and there has been virtually no trade along the rivers since Easter. Winter is coming to Ely, Hereward, and it will be a hard and hungry one for all who live here.'

'It seems as if the King of Denmark has been an expensive guest,' said Hereward. 'Perhaps it was a mistake to invite him here.'

Hereward spoke in a tone which made the sacrist slow his walk and fall back a pace, but Thurstan, who rarely recognized the worst in men, continued his confession.

'You may be right, my son, though only God will judge us in the end. We did what we thought we must for the protection of the English Church here in the eastern shires, but what we did was too little and too late. If it is God's will that the Church in England succumbs to Norman influence, then we must beg His forgiveness for questioning His divine plan and I must do penance for my vanity and presumption.'

'And what penance do the rest of us do to William the Norman, Abbot? Or do we just pray to him in the hope that he will forgive us our sins? There is many a Norman knight floating face down in the reeds at Aldreth who will claim that we certainly sinned against them!'

'Do not blaspheme, Hereward. There has been no widespread rebellion against William. His throne is not threatened and with the leaving of the Danes there is no foreign army now on

249

English soil. Peace and prosperity is what William desires. He has no need to take vengeance on this abbey.'

Hereward turned on his heel so that his face was but an inch from that of the abbot's and the sacrist, standing back, saw Thurstan's hand scrabble for the wooden crucifix hanging around his neck as though the good priest had suddenly found himself in an evil place.

'William will not make war on monks for he needs those who can read and write. Is that not what King Svein told you?'

Thurstan recoiled his head in surprise but Hereward pressed even closer.

'Do not look so shocked, dear Abbot, I over-heard everything and I saw everything. It was quite comfortable in the thatch of that barn on the hythe and since dawn I have watched the brothers of Ely help load Danish boats not only with the treasure of Peterborough but with food taken from the families of men who guard the causeway at Aldreth.

'And why do these holy men do this? Because they know William does not make war on monks. But the Normans will come and they will have their vengeance; for it is what hard men of arms do. It is what I would do, and the people who will suffer are the lowly men of the Fens who have stood shoulder-to-shoulder with me at Aldreth while the Danes have sat here sunning them-selves eating their harvest and stealing their stores. What should I tell them, Holy Father?'

'Tell them to throw their weapons into the Fens and to return to their nets and their fields. If the

Normans come, we must throw ourselves on their mercy just as we seek the mercy of God each day,' answered Thurstan.

'And how will your flock tend their nets if the Normans have cut off their hands, or plough their fields if they have no feet to walk on? You would have them grovel in front of the Normans and beg for punishment? I have seen how Normans treat a whipped dog; they whip it some more so that it stays whipped!'

'My brave, hot-headed boy,' Thurstan began, reaching out to place a hand on Hereward's head, but Hereward jumped back a pace as if the abbot's touch would sting him. 'What else can we do? Without the army of King Svein we cannot hope to defeat the Normans in battle. Our cause is lost. Perhaps it was doomed from the start. It is over, Hereward.'

'No!' cried Hereward defiantly. 'I have been outlawed twice. It will not happen a third time! I will not allow those Norman pigs to walk on to the Isle of Ely unopposed.'

'But we cannot defeat them,' said the sacrist who had not dared to speak until now. 'We have no army to match theirs and Ely is close to starving.'

'We have an army of Fenmen who have held off the best of Baron Taillebois' men for two months and if they are hungry, so much the better, for hungry men fight harder, especially when they fight for their homes.

'With winter coming, the waters in the rivers and Fens will rise and the Isle of Ely will have defences as good as any Norman castle. We do not have to beat the Normans in battle; we merely have to shed enough of their blood to make them change their mind about coming here. It is not over, my dear Abbot, it has only just begun!'

[xii]

As was customary in all Benedictine houses, the monks ate their last meal of the day before darkness fell.

And it was thus, over a bowl of mashed turnip boiled with oregano in the gloom of the abbey refectory, that Abbot Thurstan allowed himself to show his despair in front of all the brothers of Ely.

'Why couldn't he take what he has hidden away on Littleport and just go?'

'What he has secreted from the plunder of Peterborough belonged either to his wife or his mother. There is only one thing which Hereward truly believes is *his* in his own right as a man,' said the sacrist, lowering his voice in the hope that Thurstan would follow his example, 'and that is the manor and estates of Bourne in Lincolnshire.'

'Are these estates large and rich? Do they come with a hundred tenants prosperous enough to pay their rents on time or perhaps a thousand sheep waiting to be fleeced?'

'No, they are not. It is a small estate with one house of any quality and far from significant among all the holdings of Peterborough Abbey.'

'But it is important to Hereward?'

'As important as life itself, for he believes it to be

his birthright, promised him by his grandfather, Toki of Lincoln, although Toki's claims were never proven by a church court in his lifetime. Legally, the ownership of the estate is still in dispute, though with a Norman abbot in charge of Peterborough, any claim not by a Norman is unlikely to be heard.'

'So why does Hereward persist? How does he think he can ever take the lordship of Bourne from his sworn enemies?'

'By making it worth their while to let him have it,' the sacrist said quietly. 'He has learned a valuable lesson today.'

'Explain yourself my faithful *consiliator*,' said Thurstan, using the Latin word for 'counsellor' though in Italian it is said to imply something more sinister.

'Hereward has seen King Svein and his army depart these lands safely with plunder he did not have to fight for; and he leaves with the blessing of King William. This shows him that William is willing to pay off a troublesome enemy rather than go to the expense of battle. Hereward hopes to make himself so troublesome to the Normans that William will pay him off because it will be cheaper than waging a war against him. He has picked a good place to do so, for here in the Fens a small force of a few men who know the back waters and secret paths through the marshes, can evade and harass an army many times their size. Hereward will fight until King William pays his price and his price will be the manor of Bourne.'

Thurstan looked at his sacrist in bemused wonderment.

'I thought you said you could control Hereward!' he hissed and the monks stared for they had never heard such venom from the sweet abbot before.

'I said his wife thought she could control him,' replied the sacrist. 'But she is a witch.'

'She would have to be,' said Thurstan, all hope gone from his voice.

Fifteen

Giraldus

Well, this is more like it. Here is history I can work with. At last I have a noble purpose for Baldwin le Wac's notorious ancestor if such he be (which I doubt), for now Hereward stands alone against terrible odds, to fight for what he considers his birthright: the very manor of Bourne today owned by my patron Baldwin.

Now I am far happier in my appointed task. Whilst it is never easy to extol the virtues of a known outlaw, drunkard and plunderer, these are the bricks I have and from them I must build my house of truth, or at least convincing history. Like a spider, I must spin a truth from the most heroic parts of Brother Thomas's story of Hereward and ignore the more unsavoury parts, of which there are many.

I will not dwell on the fact that Hereward and his ever-present shadow Martin Lightfoot could almost certainly be murderers, not only of Sir William de Warenne's brother-in-law Sir Frederick, but also of the two Fenmen, Winter and Liveret, who are not heard of again once they had served their purpose on the Isle of Littleport. Their only crime was to have witnessed the hiding of certain of the treasures of Peterborough which Hereward called his own and then, like the funeral servants of a Pharaoh in ancient Egypt, they were killed to protect a secret they had never wanted to have.

The Norman invader Sir Frederick may well have made other enemies who might have murdered him, though no other suspect has ever been named, and certainly Hereward felt insulted and aggrieved. Such a killing could be dressed in many ways – as an old-fashioned Saxon blood feud or as a hot-tempered exchange of insults which led to violence, or even as an honourable challenge to personal combat (though that seems unlikely). Yet there is no way the slitting of the throats of two loyal followers can be justified in this world, though it will be judged in the next.

True, I am able to use Brother Thomas's account to justify the skill of Hereward as a brave warrior and a leader of men. His defence of the causeway at Aldreth shows military skill and stratagems of the highest order, for it must be remembered that Hereward's army was small and made up of fishermen and farmers who knew nothing of war, whereas both Baron Taillebois and Sir William de Warenne, whose descendents still take the title Earl of Surrey, were tried and tested generals with well-armed and well-trained soldiers at their command. Both were to be counted among King William's most loyal military advisers as well as fearless knights in their own right. This will please my patron, though I still have no idea how to claim a family link with Hereward.

The story of Hereward's attack on the Norman camp at Cottenham is little known elsewhere, although many a tale and song tells of Hereward's skill as a stilt-walker. But Thomas's description of this skirmish is not, as far as I can find, copied in any other chronicles of the time.

The one place I did expect to find it was in the chronicles of the abbey at Crowland, which has already been mentioned in the story of Hereward, although such is the bad luck which has surrounded that abbey, it is a wonder that even its name survives.

In the days of which Thomas writes, Crowland was known as a monastery famed for its learning and a nunnery respected for its sanctity and charity. It was, however, a poor abbey, certainly in comparison to the houses of Peterborough and Ely. The monks there, unable to rely on rents or tithes or generous patron, took matters into their own hands and began to profit from the only wealth they had: their knowledge, which they began to share with anyone who could pay. Famously, the monks rented a barn at Cottenham near Cambridge and began to give a series of lectures on language, logic, theology, philosophy, mathematics and astronomy, to which men of substance would send their sons from many miles distance. So popular were these Cottenham lectures by the educated Crowland monks that many of those who attended sought lodgings in the town of Cambridge and there was talk of moving the monks' lectures from Cottenham to there. But then good sense prevailed and it was quickly realized that such a sordid backwater as Cambridge, with its filthy alehouses and even filthier whores, would never be a suitable place for the pursuit of education.

And so the monks continued their lectures at Cottenham and made such profits from their teaching that the Abbey of Crowland began to grow in size and grandeur. But perhaps they strived too much and were guilty of the sin of pride or perhaps God did not favour their attempts to educate those who did not couple their learning with devotion to the spiritual life, for every expansion of Crowland Abbey was met with catastrophe. Shoddy buildings collapsed and fire destroyed the abbey's library more than once. Under Abbot Joffrid of Orleans (a Norman placement, naturally) every attempt to build at Crowland seemed to be cursed and in the Year of Our Lord 1109 there was even an earthquake sent to rattle the very foundations of the abbey.

So perhaps it is not a surprise that any rolls or chronicles of Crowland which may have mentioned Hereward (and been consulted by Brother Thomas), no longer survive. In the absence of such sources, I must use my God-given skill as a historian and create a logical sequence of events from memory and imagination – as historians have done throughout history.

One thing is well known and that is the fate of the treasure of Peterborough, for it is a true story of the church and proof, if ever proof were needed, of the miracles that can be brought about when a holy relic of a blessed Saint is involved.

King William was true to his word for once, as King Svein and his army were allowed to leave Ely unhindered and make their way down the Great Ouse to the sea at Lynne where their longships and the rest of their army waited. The treasure of Peterborough – along with Prior Athelwold and the monks of Peterborough – were transferred to the ocean-going longships in which King Svein, his brother Bjorn and Bishop Christian were to travel and then, true to his word also, Svein returned all the small river craft and fen boats to the local fishermen in accordance with Abbot Thurstan's plea.

Watched by Norman warships from William's navy which had sailed around the coast from Ipswich, the Danish fleet set sail for their homeland and many thought that England had seen the last of the holy relic of St Oswald's arm. But where William had been content to allow the Danes this victory without cost, God had not.

On the first day of the voyage and only just out of sight of the English coast, a storm of unusual severity sprang up to the amazement of all and without warning. Storms are not unknown in September, but many whose livelihood depends on the weather were astonished at the ferocity of this storm. All along the eastern coast of England, fishermen and fishwives had reported signs of a storm coming – birds flying low and seaweed clocks drying out unnaturally quickly – but when they had sought guidance from their parish priests, they had been told firmly that this was idle talk and that no severe tempest was expected at this time of year.

But tempest there came and the Danish fleet was scattered by the storm, with over a third of King Svein's longships being sent to the bottom of the sea or smashed high up on to the desolate sandy shores of Lincolnshire. Some were even said to have been blown as far away as Ireland; some, humiliatingly, made landfall on the coast of Norway rather than Denmark. Yet every ship which contained a piece of the Peterborough treasure or a monk of Peterborough, retained its position in the fleet and remained afloat thanks to the constant prayers of the brave Prior Athelwold in the teeth of the storm.

Much impressed with the obvious power of the arm of St Oswald and the devotion of the Prior and monks of Peterborough, Bishop Christian swore before God that if King Svein and the treasure reached Denmark intact, it would be a sign that the treasure should remain as one horde rather than melted down or dispersed as was customary.

Not being a natural sailor, King Svein agreed to this oath and when the tempest had passed gave thanks to God, for every ship which carried a monk or part of the Peterborough treasure arrived safely in Denmark. Despite the temptations of so much gold and silver, the vow was carried out and on the instructions of Bishop Christian, a church was built at Aarhus exclusively for the shelter of the treasure and Prior Athelwold and his brothers.

There it remained, watched over by the monks

of Peterborough and the holy relic of St Oswald's arm for several years – some say three, some say more – until, miracle of miracles, King Svein ordered his ships to return the treasure and its guardians to England.

Not a monk had been harmed, not a coin or jewel stolen, not a crucifix or a cup damaged, or so the story went, although Athelwold and his monks swore never to set sail on an ocean again. This story became a lesson and was widely preached throughout England, proving the mercy of God and the strength of prayer, although not within the precincts of Peterborough.

Now ensconced as the abbot there, the Norman Turold was not trusted by Athelwold and his English monks who took the treasure to Ramsey Abbey, some ten miles away across the Fens. There it stayed for many years despite demands for its return by Abbot Turold and many a tortuous debate within the ecclesiastical courts.

Where the treasure is today is probably known only to a handful of sacrists in the abbeys of eastern England whose role it is to record the valuables of every religious house.

And one sacrist in particular, that of Ely, is playing a large part in the story of Hereward. If half of what Thomas has written is true, then this sacrist showed all the cunning of a lawyer.

Whoever this servant of Christ was, he was much trusted by the pious Thurstan; perhaps too much. According to Brother Thomas's book, the sacrist was also recognized by Bishop Christian who claims he was known in many countries. If this sacrist was a noted traveller, then he never wrote about his voyages, or if he did, no copies exist for I consulted every written book whilst writing my own histories of Ireland and Wales. But it is possible that the sacrist had some skill in writing, for does not Bjorn, the Danish king's brother, dismiss him as a 'left-handed scribbler'? There again, Prince Bjorn disparages him as 'a crippled monk' but then one should not put much faith in the judgement of Danish princes when it comes to matters of poetry and learning. King Svein himself is recorded as being very rude about old English poets, though the sagas of Denmark and Norway are equally as boring and usually twice as long. Thankfully, many of the Norse sagas which told tales of a time of pagan gods and unnatural practices, have been destroyed by conscientious bishops of our holy church.

I will write to the present Abbot of Ely to ask if there is any record of the sacrist who served Thurstan in the time of Hereward. I have already written to enquire as to the provenance of this book of Brother Thomas's but have not yet received a reply.

It seems that an old man, shivering here in his cell in Lincoln, is of no consequence to the younger monks of this order, whatever his achievements in the past. But I have said for many years now that the order can no longer attract the right calibre of novices any more.

Sixteen

Thomas

Hereward the Water-Walker

[i]

When no fewer than three messengers from the Norfolk coast had reported to Sir William de Warenne that the Danish fleet had indeed left the shores of England, then did the battle for the Isle of Ely begin in earnest.

The Normans, and Baron Ivo in particular, were confident that without the support of Svein's Danish army, Hereward and his gang of outlaws (for now they were so called by the Normans) would quickly lose their stomach for a fight.

What they had not counted on was that the English defenders of Ely had taken heart from the way they had denied the Normans the causeway at Aldreth with no help from the Danes, and the fact that they saw Hereward as their true leader. Many would say that those Fenland fighters were indeed more frightened of Hereward than of King William and there would be much truth in that.

Baron Ivo also took no account of the experience of Hereward (and his captains, Siward and Rufus and even Martin Lightfoot) among the armies of the Count of Flanders and assumed, falsely, that his troops faced an unruly peasant mob with no appreciation of military stratagems which could be easily crushed into submission.

But Hereward was no fool when it came to matters of warfare. He knew that with the Danes gone from the Isle, the Normans would launch an all-out attack in greater numbers than had been seen before and even though he had no knowledge of the reinforcements being sent by King William, Hereward realized he was already outnumbered by at least three-to-one.

His advantage was the Isle of Ely itself. Hereward's men knew its secret pathways and where patches of innocent flag-irises concealed mud pits and sinking sands which could suck in and swallow a horse and its rider. The Fenmen also knew where areas of still, dark water and rotting vegetation gave off noxious fumes which could be ignited, raising spectres of yellow flame as if from the fires of hell itself. Furthermore, they had seen the effect on Norman cavalry horses of burning deposits of peat in the marshes, for once alight, the peat burned for days and appeared to the terrified horse to be burning *under* the surface water. In truth, such a sight had the same effect on many a Norman trooper who had never been asked to march or ride or fight in such a land.

Hereward was also an experienced enough general to know that when a small army has to defend a large area – in this case an island seven miles long and four miles wide – it must either spread itself thinly or concentrate its strength and be prepared to move quickly to meet the threat of the enemy. And here the landscape again favoured

263

the defenders for the rivers and fens which surrounded the Isle were an army in themselves. For the attackers, who wished to employ their strongest weapon, their cavalry, the soundest footing, if not the safest, remained the causeway at Aldreth. In truth there were few alternative approaches to the Isle without a fleet of boats to carry both men and horses. Only at Theoford was the river narrow enough and shallow enough (in summer) for riders to cross; but fording a river is not a natural thing for armoured horses carrying knights and especially not under fire from bowmen hidden in the reeds on the far bank.

So Baron Ivo, falsely confident, put his faith in the largest attack on the causeway yet in the hope of catching the defenders down-hearted and also, it must be said, in the hope of crushing the rebellious Fenmen before King William had to be asked for more troops or, even worse, decide to take command of the battle personally.

Ignoring the counsel of Sir William de Warenne, who urged caution, Baron Ivo mustered his army at Cottenham and joined his knights in a four hour fast and prayer vigil before a dawn attack on the causeway.

The Baron's plan involved no fewer than two hundred horsemen supported by a hundred foot-soldiers and fifty crossbowmen and was, in all simplicity, a single, fast strike across the causeway to storm the peat earthworks thrown up by the defenders.

But Hereward and his captains were ready.

Whilst the Danes were being bribed by the envoy of Sir Deda, there had been few serious attacks on the causeway and Siward had used the hiatus to good effect. During daylight they had reinforced their earthworks at Aldreth and by night the defenders had crept far out on to the causeway itself and with bill, hook and scythe had created pits which they filled with dry reeds and peat. Into these pits was poured sparing quantities of precious whale oil which Hereward had brought from Ely, having been left behind by Bishop Christian's monks who preferred to carry the treasures of Peterborough in their boats rather than oil for lamps which they would not use while at sea.

Their preparations made, Hereward assembled his entire force of little more than a hundred men and boys of the Fens at Aldreth. Had the Normans but known it, the rest of the Isle of Ely at that time was completely undefended and Ely itself inhabited purely by monks and women, neither of which would fight.

Hereward took great care in the placement of the men he had, for he was aware that in arms, armour and discipline, they were no match for Baron Ivo's troops. Once again he put Siward the White in charge of the earthworks they had thrown up at the end of the causeway with the bulk of the men who were armed with captured Norman weapons and had undergone a rudimentary training, although no amount of training would persuade the Fenmen to use Norman crossbows which they regarded as heavy and cumbersome and some even thought of them as instruments of the Devil.

Hereward then chose two parties of younger

men and boys who had some skill with a hunting bow and who could swim, one party under his command, one under the captaincy of Rufus, to lie in wait in the reeds, waist-deep in the water at either side of the causeway where they would be almost within arm's length, but out of the sight, of riders on the path itself.

To make sure that the Normans kept their eyes on the Aldreth end of the causeway rather than have them wander to the reed beds on either side, Hereward instructed Martin and Hraga the Heron to construct a fresh pair of stilts as long as a man could use and keep his balance. It was the Norfolk man, Hraga, though not a warrior by nature, who rose to the challenge and fashioned a pair of stilts some twenty feet long. Thus when mounted on them, he would be a man more than four times taller than a mortal man and twice the height of the proudest knight on horseback.

As the most experienced stilt-man, Hraga insisted it should be he who strapped on these extended wooden limbs but even with his years of striding across fen and dyke, his movements were limited and he had to be hauled upright by means of a rope pulled by Martin Lightfoot. Yet with the aid of a third long willow sapling as a staff he found he could maintain his balance and gave the impression of a three-legged giant conjured by the wildest nightmare.

It was then that Brother Godric, who had chosen to remain with the men at Aldreth, showed his worth; not as a warrior (for the rules of his order forbad that) but as an apothecary. Sensing what Hereward had in mind, Godric disclosed that in his monk's satchel he carried various medicaments including crushed madder root. The madder, a plant much grown in Norfolk, was known to the Fenmen as a cure for the dropsy, though as many would testify, it was more famous for turning the patient's piss red and much valued as a dye for cloth. By grinding the madder root and boiling it in his own piss, then mixing with wet clay, Godric was able to produce a paint which he applied to Hraga's face and arms and which, when dried, gave him a terrible appearance as if he had bathed in the blood of men.

So fearful a sight was Hraga that Hereward made sure that all his men had seen him before he mounted his stilts and had further seen him receive a holy blessing from Brother Godric, to reassure them that Hraga fought on their side and was not a demon summoned from hell by their enemies. Although all at Aldreth hoped and prayed that he would appear as a demon to their attackers.

They heard their attackers long before they saw them, for even through the thick morning mist, the jangle of metal and the coughing of horses drifted over from the hill at Cottenham as the Norman cavalry approached the causeway with sure foot and steady purpose.

The Normans, however, waited until the mist cleared and the September sun reflected off the watery earth before they began to ride, three-abreast, on to and across the causeway, the cavalry in the van and infantry bringing up the rear.

Baron Ivo, who prided himself on eyesight almost as keen as any of his hawks or falcons, was one of the first riders to see the giant apparition appear at the far distant end of the causeway, even though he was not at the head of the Norman column, but rather some way back, surrounded by his personal bodyguard of knights who owed him their loyalty. Yet he could see quickly the effect which the towering stick figure, who it seemed was holding a spear or club as tall as a tree, was having on his advance guard for the horses in front of him were slowing their pace and stumbling against each other.

'Keep going, keep going,' Baron Ivo was heard to command. 'God is with us. Get the horses across and we'll let the crossbows take down this shouting devil.'

For the giant defending the causeway was by now shouting insults and curses at them; and though few would have been able to understand the thick speech of Norfolk, the intent was very clear. The advancing riders could also see that the giant's face and arms and chest were bright red and even the most hardened of Ivo's hard men thought this truly the mark of a devil.

'It is a man, only a man walking on sticks!' yelled Ivo, spurring his horse. 'Get close and bring him down, bring him down!'

With his archers bringing up the rear, the baron knew that his best course was to get his horsemen across the narrow causeway as quickly as possible before panic gripped man and beast. And therein lay his undoing for the narrow causeway became even narrower at the Aldreth end thanks to Siward's earthworks of peat blocks, and Hraga the red demon seemingly floating above them screaming and waving a long spear held the Normans' gaze skywards as their horses gathered speed.

Such was the spectacle of Hraga's dancing, screaming and cursing, that Ivo and his bodyguard were at first unaware that the leading horses in the column had stumbled and fallen into one of the pits the defenders had dug and lined with dry fuel.

Then a second rank of horses, unable to stop themselves, had fallen on top of them, crushing the bones of animals and riders. Following riders instinctively pulled their reins to avoid going where the ground seemed to have given way in front of them, only to find their horse pushed from behind and several veered off to the sides of the causeway and into the water.

By this time, arrows were beginning to sing into the melee from the earthworks, where Siward's bowmen were concealed and despite the screams of wounded horses, the curses of Hraga, looming over the slaughter, could still be heard.

Yet Ivo Taillebois was no coward and he realized that if his men were to acquit themselves honourably, he would have to set them a good example. Dismounting, he urged his bodyguard to do the same and ordered the horses to the rear and called for the crossbowmen to be brought up. He armed himself with a long shield and a short iron mace and bellowing, 'Make room! Make room' he pushed and levered his way through the crush of his own cavalry in order to fight on foot.

'Come on, you lazy bastards!' he yelled to his companions.

At least a dozen of his bodyguard copied his actions, risking the arrows of the Fenmen and the frenzied kicking of their own cavalry horses; and now on foot, to them the giant red demon on stilts looked even taller. But they took heart from the way Baron Ivo strode purposefully over the first pit, stepping on the head of one of his men trapped by a broken-boned horse to do so, and then when Ivo casually swatted away an English arrow with his mace. (A feat of extraordinary fortune which he was never to claim, whilst sober, that he could repeat.)

'Show yourselves, you water rats!' shouted Ivo and his knights took up his battle cry as they walked towards the Aldreth earthworks, their shields held high in front of them, each one pricked by ten or more arrows.

The defenders did indeed show themselves, but not where Baron Ivo expected them to, for his challenge was answered from behind and the flanks. Rising up from the waters and reeds at each side of the causeway came the men led by Hereward and Rufus, who had until now remained silent and invisible. They were lightly armed, mostly with knives and bill-hooks but also tinder-boxes and flints and they attacked from below, once they had gained the causeway, stooping low between the legs of the Norman horses so that few of the riders even saw them.

In this crouching mode of attack, following Hereward's example, the Fenmen cut the girths of Norman saddles and slashed at the hocks of Norman horses. They even, as Hereward had taught them, slid a hand like a lover up under the mail coat of a rider to stick a knife into the thigh of an unsuspecting rider if a decent slash at his hamstrings had not presented itself. And then the Fenmen did what they had come to do and they struck tinder and torched the traps of straw and peat and oil they had laid.

To the Normans it seemed as if the very roof of hell had fallen in and they were falling in after it. Horses bolted, threw their riders and charged for the Cottenham shore, sending in the process many other horses and riders into the water. As fire took hold across the breadth of the causeway, Hereward sought out Rufus in the smoke and blood and confusion and gave the order to swim for the Aldreth shore.

Baron Ivo, on foot, saw his army disappear behind a curtain of fire and smoke and ordered his knights to retreat back across the now burning pits wherein his advance guard lay, many still alive if trapped and praying to the Saints for mercy.

By the end of that day, fifty-seven Norman knights were wounded, dead or unaccounted for (as bodies which enter the waters of the Fens rarely emerge again) and a similar number of horses were lost or lamed.

The defenders of the Isle of Ely suffered only one casualty. In his joy at their victory, Hraga the Heron fell from his unnaturally long stilts and broke his neck.

Such are the fortunes of war.

[iii]

'I told you we needed a bigger fucking army!'
'Keep calm, my dear Baron, you will soon have

271

all the troops you could possibly want,' said Sir William de Warenne soothingly, 'but I think what you now need is a bigger causeway.'

The two Norman commanders sat astride their horses on a small hill between the causeway and the camp at Cottenham. From there they could have seen the entire length of the causeway to Aldreth, were it not for the pall of smoke which rose high into the afternoon sky some two-thirds of the way along its length. The sight which did meet their eyes was one of a line of straggling troops with smoke-blackened faces, many leading limping horses, or horses slung with the dead and wounded, towards Cottenham, whilst on the causeway itself skirmishers of crossbowmen edged near to the fire pits where their comrades and their horses still burned, and fired bolts blindly towards the enemy. This strategy did score a surprising number of hits on the unsuspecting Fenmen who had yet to learn the benefits to the common soldier of staying behind well-constructed earthworks.

The fires which Hereward's men had started were to burn for almost a week, but even on that first afternoon after the battle with Ivo's cavalry, it was clear that the causeway had been dangerously weakened as spars and bundles of logs broke loose and floated slowly down the River Ouse.

'Those holes in the causeway,' said Sir William, pointing with his riding whip, 'will need packing or bridging before we can risk putting a horse on them.'

'A company of the King's siege engineers could do it, but they would be under fire from those earthworks. If these rebels had any sense, they could make it very hot work for them,' replied the Baron, sniffing the air which carried the scent of burning horseflesh up from the Fen.

'Oh, I think those rebels have sense and courage,' said Sir William calmly, 'but what they lack is numbers. The King's engineers and wood-cutters will be here in two days, but we will not use them all on the causeway. Take your crossbowmen and a troop of infantry and strip Cottenham and Cambridge of every door, hatch and shutter. Have the men turn them into shields and tell them to strengthen their own shields, then show them how to march in close formation in the Roman fashion, holding their shields in front and above their heads. They are to form a shield for the engineers as they repair the causeway.'

'How long will it take working like that?' asked Ivo. 'I thought the idea was to finish this lot off before the King decided to come here in person.'

'That is my hope, Ivo, and do not worry about how long the work takes. That does not matter, for we are not going to attack across the causeway again.'

'Then just how the fuck do we get to Ely?'

Sir William allowed himself a smile.

'Whilst your men are distracting the rebels here, I will take my men and most of the engineers down the river to a place called Theoford, which is not only much nearer to Ely itself, but is where the river can be forded and with a pontoon bridge we can even get cavalry across.'

'You seem well-informed about the approaches to Ely, Sir William, for one who has never been

273

there,' said Ivo dryly.

'I have not, but others have, my dear Baron. The monks who rowed our cousin Deda on his mission to the Danish king were told to keep their eyes and ears open and report back to me. They say it would be possible to camp at a place called Stuntney and attack Theoford from there.'

'So now we have damned monks to do our fighting for us?'

'Monks do not fight for us, Ivo, they watch and they write and they talk and sometimes that can be worth a thousand seasoned warriors.'

'If you say so; I have as little to do with them as possible.'

'You should not dismiss them, old friend. Your eternal soul may yet need their help.'

'We have a family priest for all that sort of thing,' growled Ivo, 'I brought him over from Normandy specially. He does what he's told. Mind you, can't say I'm not grateful for the way the local monks are tending to the wounded.'

The baron nodded to Cottenham up the hill where wounded men and horses were limping and stumbling for whatever treatment they could find.

'They have their uses,' mused Sir William nudging his horse forward. 'Come, we should go and cheer our men.'

The two knights trotted their horses into the Cottenham camp, where both men and horses were being stripped of their chain mail so their wounds could be sutured or bound. Casks of ale had been brought on ox carts from Cambridge by the monks from the small priory there, along with herbs, balms and ointments, including supplies of bog-myrtle which was used not only for flavouring the ale (to be replaced in brewing, some 500 years later, by hops, imported from Flanders) but was also an effective means of keeping midges and flies away from open wounds.

The monks tending to and praying over the injured soldiery had lit several fires with charcoal in small iron braziers or stoves. In these they would heat up small irons with which to cauterize bleeding wounds where a knife had been stuck or an arrow removed. As a consequence, the camp would ring to the sudden screams of men and horses, although the men were granted the small mercy of biting down on a thick twig wrapped in muslin before the glowing iron was applied.

Sir William and Baron Ivo rode into the middle of the camp and halted. Sir William stood up in his stirrups and spoke clearly so all around could hear him.

'Soldiers of the King! You all know me and know that I am an honest knight and a faithful lord to those who are faithful to me. I tell you to take heart and not despair. God is with us and we will flush out this rebel scum soon enough. King William himself is on his way here, having crushed all rebellions in the north and west. Here he will put an end to the rebellious English once and for all. He brings fresh troops, more horses, siege engines and all manner of weapons of war. In Ely they are filled with curiosity and keep asking, "Why doesn't he come?" I tell them to be calm, be calm. He's coming! He's coming!'

Bruised and sore though they were, the soldiers

275

raised a cheer at this, which pleased Sir William.

Yet as they turned their horses towards Cambridge, Baron Ivo leaned towards Sir William and whispered so that none other could hear. 'Was it wise to tell them the King is coming? There were many monks there, and do not monks have ears and loose lips?'

'Oh, I do hope so,' answered Sir William softly.

[iii]

'We must always remember that God is with us,' said Abbot Thurstan.

'And so will be King William soon,' replied his sacrist with ill grace.

'King William does not make war on holy men and neither does Sir William de Warennes, who is a cultured man and known to be fearful for the state of his immortal soul.'

'Perhaps he has reason to be.'

'Let us not be uncharitable, my brother. We must pray for guidance for our abbey, our brothers in Christ and the flock of this Isle,' said Thurstan as he knelt before the shrine of St Etheldreda in the abbey church.

Abbot Thurstan, though, was a worldly enough priest to believe that the advice of men could sometimes smooth the path for the guidance of God.

'You are sure the King comes to Ely?' he whispered to his sacrist who knelt at his side.

The sacrist crossed himself as if to ward off the devil before replying.

'He is coming for he has said so himself. There is little to delay him in the west now, for he has crushed all others who stood against him and Ely will be the place he seals his victory of England. We thought we would be the first in a rising against the Normans; instead we are the last and we are alone.'

'Then our plan was doomed from the start, old friend. We are guilty of the sin of pride if we ever thought it would succeed.'

'Perhaps so, Father Abbot, but what we did, we did for the good of the Church in England.'

'We may have thought so, but we were blinded by our own vanity into thinking we could challenge a king. All we did was make him angry, and to continue to defy him will only increase his wrath. How long can the Isle be defended?'

'I am no soldier, Father Abbot, but I know that the families of the men who fight with Hereward are going hungry and winter is not yet upon us.'

'Will the men fight while their wives and children starve?'

'They will fight for Hereward, it seems; but then perhaps they do not know how the Normans punish rebels. There again, perhaps they do and that is why they fight.'

'These are good Christian men. We cannot let them suffer mutilation and death and see their families starve.'

'As always, dear Father, your charity sets an example to us all, but it is difficult to see how this business can end peaceably.'

'Have faith, my son, for God is with us.'

'But so is Hereward.'

277

The defenders of Aldreth had adopted a pronounced stoop when they walked, which came to be known as the 'Aldreth Crouch' as men became accustomed to presenting a low target for the Norman crossbowmen who would loose a bolt at any sign of movement around the English earthworks. For the wild-fowlers and poachers among them, this was almost a natural posture for they were used to spending many hours crouched in the reeds hunting their prey. But for the farmers and callow youths, who were more comfortable standing behind or pulling a plough, the defence of the causeway was a hazardous matter.

Neither fowler nor plough-boy could go about their natural business, which was, of course, to provide food for the table, as Hereward's ranks were stretched thin and whilst he was sure his men loved him, he knew that if they were allowed to visit their farms or their traps or nets to the north of the Isle, he might never see them again.

To keep his men busy during the day, Hereward had Siward and Rufus drill them in sword-play and the use of long spears against charging cavalry. When they were not training, they were put to making arrows or collecting Norman crossbow bolts from where they had landed or where they protruded from the peat earthworks (or sometimes English flesh), and removing the heavy iron tips so that they could be used in their own arrows or sent to the abbey blacksmith in Ely.

By night, Martin Lightfoot led small bands of those who had the skills of poaching down the edges of the ruined and still smouldering causeway. Half-crawling, half-swimming, these raiders would come so close to the Norman pickets that they could hear their whispers and prayers – for all soldiers whisper and pray in the dark – and slide like snakes on to the causeway until they reached the fire pits when men and horses had met their doom. In absolute silence, these raiders clambered over the dead and removed every weapon and piece of armour or mail they could without arousing the suspicion of the nearby Norman sentinels. Martin Lightfoot showed himself to be fearless on these raids, returning to Aldreth not with swords or axes but with large joints of horse meat which were gleefully roasted over the defenders' camp fires. He even boasted that when they had eaten all the dead horses, he would bring them a Norman knight's meaty thigh and perhaps one of the joints now roasting was man rather than beast, as in the darkness it was difficult to tell exactly what he was butchering. Although the Fenmen laughed at Lightfoot's joke, they took care to examine their meat that night, though such was their hunger, none refused their share save Brother Godric, for it was the custom of the Benedictines to eat only fruit and vegetables and when none were available, they would squash their appetites by chewing caraway seeds as the Roman legions of Julius Caesar had been said to do.

It was Hereward's plan to keep his small army together and to be prepared to move at an instant to any point on the Isle where danger threatened, for what he knew he must do was to deny the Normans a single foothold on the firm soil of Ely, where he knew his men would not stand in an open battle. If he could keep the Normans on the Cambridge bank of the Ouse and harry them from the reed beds and the marshes until the autumn rains and high tides which usually came in November flooded the Fens and thus strengthened the natural defences of the Isle of Eels, then, and only if he had cost them enough in men and supplies, might the Normans be willing to talk peace.

In this, Hereward was deluded on several counts.

Having little grasp of what was happening beyond the Fenlands, he did not know that after four years of Norman rule, their authority imposed with some thirty-six castles (there were over 100 by 1086.), England was tired of rebellion, hungry and, in some areas of the north, desolate.

King William had crushed all who had stood against him – envious earls in Northumbria, pretenders to the throne with Scottish support and Welsh rebels – and he had seen off Viking raiders from Dublin in the west and bought off the Danish invasion in the east. Now only Hereward and his outlaws defied the King and a king like William could not allow himself, after defeating far more distinguished foes, to be bested by a mercenary and outlaw with no title or land.

Though Hereward did not realize it, he was no longer an itch under the skin of the Normans. He had become an ugly and very visible boil in need of lancing.

Hereward had also no understanding of history, otherwise he would have remembered how William of Normandy had come to England in the first place and not have pinned so much hope on the rising rivers and flooded Fens of autumn.

[v]

In the last week of September, the defenders of Aldreth heard sounds and saw sights which were beyond anything they had experienced before.

King William's companies of engineers had arrived and Baron Taillebois had immediately assigned one third of their strength to the causeway. From dawn until dusk each day, the sound of wood being chopped and the creaking of cart wheels echoed over the flat Fen. Many among the defenders swore they could see the woods below Cottenham shrinking before their very eyes as Norman loggers felled trees with such speed it was as if the invisible hand of God was wielding a scythe to clear the land for the plough.

More carts than the Fenmen had ever seen on the Isle of Ely arrived at the southern tip of the causeway, along with more people than many had seen in one place in their short and sheltered lives. These were not soldiers, however, rather villeins and serfs pressed from the fields around Cambridge and among them, common thieves and convicted criminals from the town's numerous jails.

Under the lash of their Norman overseers, these poor wretches were made to carry the felled

281

timber along the causeway to where the engineers were hammering the thickest logs into the pilings of the causeway close to the breach where Siward's pits and Hereward's fire-starting had fatally weakened it. At first the Fenmen watching from behind their earthworks (for the Norman work continued in full view, albeit out of bow-shot) thought that all the activity was designed to repair the causeway sufficient to allow cavalry across. It soon became clear that whatever the Normans were constructing, they were building it several yards short of the gaping, fire-blackened holes in the causeway.

Hereward's tactics of fire-starting here played against him, for the flames which had destroyed the causeway had spread to the reed-beds at the edges and thus destroyed the small forest of rushes and water grasses in which birds nested, frogs and toads spawned. Those reeds, had they not been reduced to charred stubble, would have provided safe cover not only for the fish and fowl of the Fens but also hidden any spies sent out by the defenders.

As it was, Hereward and his captains were reduced to observing the industry of the enemy at a distance from slits they had gouged in the peat blocks of the earthworks at the north end of the causeway.

'Is it a bridge they're building?' Rufus asked his cousin.

'It would be kind of them to repair the causeway for Ely,' Siward replied, 'but I do not think that is their purpose even though they have brought enough slaves for the job. They have more mouths to feed among their serfs than we have fighting men.'

'Martin, you have the sharpest eyes,' Hereward instructed. 'Look to that third wagon and tell me what you see.'

'It's rope,' said Martin, squinting through the spy hole he had cut. 'Lots and lots of rope; thick rope in coils, enough to rig the sails of a ship.'

'They are building a ship instead of a bridge?' asked Rufus, though the other captains paid him little mind.

'We have seen this before,' said Hereward.

'We have?'

'Martin and I have, in Flanders, at the siege of Guines. Count Robert had a troop of Norman engineers serving him there.'

'That bunch of arrogant bastards?' snarled Lightfoot. 'They made it clear they didn't think we were good enough to be in their company and you never saw them when the fighting got face-to-face.'

'That was not their purpose,' snapped Hereward.

'Then what was their purpose, my Lord Hereward?'

Hereward turned to find Brother Godric at his shoulder although he had not heard him approach.

'Their purpose, my young uncle, was to build a *ballista* with which to bombard us.'

'Then we let them finish it and we charge out and burn it!' Rufus said laughing.

Hereward shook his head.

'No, for they will build a siege tower to protect it

283

and their damned crossbows will fire bolts down on any who approach.'

'Then we are doomed,' cried Godric.

'Nonsense!' laughed Hereward, slapping the young monk on the shoulders. 'Our hearts should be full at such news as this, for now we know King William is taking us seriously!'

[vi]

It was only fitting, therefore, that Hereward began to treat the Norman threat with seriousness.

Keeping his main force of armed men at Aldreth, though with orders to be prepared to move to anywhere on the Isle at his command, Hereward chose half a dozen young boys and girls to act as his runners. Martin Lightfoot, who had in his youth served Hereward's grandfather in this way, positioned the youths a mile apart on the edge of the Isle from Aldreth to Ely. Each was armed with a knife and flint and tinder, for if they were surprised they were expected to fight as best they could, or at least fire the reeds to signal their young comrades in this chain of spies. Martin also showed them how to construct a rudimentary shelter or 'hide' such as the fowlers and hunters would use to disguise them from their prey. In this exercise, he learned more than he taught, for the children of the Isle of Ely were natural born poachers and well versed in the skills of remaining unseen in the Fens.

These extra eyes in the reeds soon repaid Hereward generously for within two days his child spies had reported the arrival of a Norman force on the small isle of Stuntney across the river from Theoford and he and Lightfoot hastened to see for themselves, closely following in the steps of their young scout. By means of paths through the marsh which neither man had ever known were there, and by heeding the advice of their seven-year-old guide to avoid patches of the flag-iris plant (for these flowers often grow not on firm ground but on the surface of deep pools of standing water and have trapped many an unsuspecting walker), the two warriors concealed themselves on the river bank south of Theoford and observed their enemy.

They saw a familiar site.

'They are constructing another *ballista*,' murmured Lightfoot.

'And they are bringing up enough timber to build another watchtower to guard it,' agreed Hereward, then he added sourly: 'Thanks to the help of the peasants of Stuntney.'

As at the Aldreth causeway, the Normans had impressed man, woman and child into their building work, hauling logs, sawing timber, unloading carts and establishing kitchens for the growing camp. In all activities they were urged to greater efforts by the blessings of priests or the whips of the overseers.

'I do not think they work for the Normans willingly,' said Lightfoot, 'but out of fear. The same fear which will infect the village of Theoford if those bastards start to bombard them with stone and fire.'

Hereward pondered this before he replied:

285

'They will not find enough stone here in the Fens, it will be fire and the cottages of Theoford are wood and thatch. They will burn well. How many families live in the place?'

'Five, perhaps six. The men are with us at Aldreth, so only old women and children will remain there.'

'Send one of the runners back to fetch Godric. He is to gather the people of Theoford and take them into the abbey in Ely. They will be safe there. Then get some men with axes and find as much rope as you can. If the Normans can build, so can we.'

'Hereward, we do not have the skill to build a siege engine.'

'I do not intend to. Leave that game to the Normans. Let them pound away at an empty village or empty earthworks. I want our men here today, save for Siward and his best archers. Let them guard the causeway, while the rest of us build rafts.'

'Rafts?'

'Rafts; so that we may cross the river in force. While the Normans occupy themselves upstream at Aldreth and downstream at Stuntney, we will cross in middle-stream and set a fire in their rear that will surely toast their fat arses!'

[vii]

Brother Godric arrived at Ely Abbey around the hour known as *terce,* which is to say some two hours after dawn at that time of year, leading a straggling band of old women, some so stooped and wizened in the face that they must have seen at least forty summers, each carrying their few possessions in bundled blankets and each bearing or dragging by the hand a small child or two.

Warned of their impending arrival by his disapproving sacrist, Abbot Thurstan met the refugees from Theoford in the courtyard of the abbey, having had the gates opened wide and a table put out bearing the last of the fruit the monks had garnered from their gardens, some pickled vegetables from last year's crop and a cauldron of thin oat gruel flavoured with a few drops of rose water, for the Danes had made sure there was no honey left in Ely.

As was the custom within the Benedictine order on returning from any journey, Brother Godric prostrated himself before Thurstan and asked that prayers be said for any faults which may have overtaken him or sins he may have committed while away from the abbey. Thurstan blessed him and bade him rise, showing concern on his noble face for the long-haired and stinking, soot-grimed monk before him.

'You have been away from us for too long, Godric,' the abbot reproved him gently. 'Your appearance is gaunt and dirty. We have little food to fatten you on, but the apothecary can at least cut your hair, for it is moving with lice, then you can tell us your tale.'

'My Lord Abbot, these women are good folk from the village of Theoford,' Godric began, unable to contain his story.

'I know, my son, I know. I have visited among them and baptised their sons and daughters, even their grandsons.'

The old women of Theoford kept their heads bowed and their eyes averted even as the abbot ushered them towards the table of food and bade them eat. Whilst all were loyal enough to Ely Abbey, they were in awe of a figure such as Thurstan even when he displayed nothing but pious charity.

'Is this all there is?'

'The men of the village fight with Hereward. Young boys and girls act as scouts and runners for him, watching the river banks. The wives work their husbands' fields and nets for what they can find to eat now or save for winter. Only the very old and the very young have I brought to safety, for their village is under threat.'

'Have the Normans crossed the causeway?'

The voice startled Godric, for he had not heard the abbey's sacrist approach.

'No they have not. Aldreth is still defended, but the Normans are building siege engines there and at Stuntney too, from where they can rain fire and destruction down on Theoford. If they can force a landing there, they could march on Ely itself within the hour.'

'Does the King lead his armies in person?' Thurstan demanded.

'We do not know, my Lord Abbot. We have seen no royal banners or heard any trumpets from the Norman camps across the river.'

'King William will not announce himself with banners and trumpets,' said the sacrist. 'We will

288

know he is in Ely when he smashes in the abbey gates.'

'Such talk makes me sad, old friend, and will frighten these women and children who seek the sanctity of the abbey as their protection.'

Thurstan reached out and clasped the sacrist's good left hand.

'We must show charity, that is God's will. See that these good people share what food and shelter we have. Let God protect them here whilst Hereward protects their homes.'

'And how exactly,' the sacrist asked Brother Godric, 'does Hereward propose to defend Theoford against the Normans?'

'Hereward defends nothing,' said Godric proudly. 'He intends to attack.'

[viii]

At a point four miles downstream from Aldreth but still nearly two miles short of Theoford, Hereward and forty men crossed the River Ouse on two large rafts propelled by men wielding poles longer than the stilts of the legendary Hraga the Heron.

Using men who knew the Southern Fens as scouts, Hereward's forces pulled the rafts out of the Ouse and carried them shoulder-high across the half-mile of marshy ground which separated the Ouse from the River Cam at that point. Making sure they were unobserved by Norman eyes, they relaunched their rafts into the still waters of the Cam and crossed that river also. All this was done by moonlit night and went unseen by enemy eyes.

By dawn, their rafts were concealed in the reed-beds on the east bank of the Cam and Rufus and four men were left to guard them with their lives. Then Hereward and his company marched almost due south on firm ground, with Wicken Fen to their left and Burwell Fen to their right, until they came to the village of Reach, which they promptly surrounded.

The Fenland pirates closed a noose around the village and moved in, herding the inhabitants into the middle. Not that the villagers of Reach resisted their invaders, at least not at first. They were all women and children, the men of the village work-ing the fields, and many recognized some of the Fenmen, even claiming ties of kinship with them.

When they declared themselves to be men sworn to Hereward the defender of Ely against King William, the villagers stared at them as if they had spoken in a foreign tongue, though they under-stood the accent of the Fenlands well enough.

Hereward too was lost for words.

'We are less than a morning's walk from Ely and yet these serfs have no knowledge of the war we fight. How can that be?' he asked his com-panion Martin.

'There are no monks here in Reach and so no news reaches them. I doubt they see any travel-lers here from one year to the next,' replied Lightfoot.

But on that particular day he was wrong.

'Why are all you wives here in the village in the middle of the day rather than out in the fields helping your menfolk?' Hereward asked the assembled women of Reach, who had shown no particular fear at the sudden appearance of these dirty and heavily armed men.

One woman, holding a child with one hand and nursing a baby at her breast spoke out.

'We are no serfs here. Our husbands are sokemen or cottars and, yes, they are tending their fields without us, for we women await the arrival of Fenchel. Who comes this way each year at this time.'

'And who, in the name of God, is this Fenchel you know so well, yet you have never heard of Hereward?' roared Hereward and the wives of Reach shook with fright.

'Fenchel comes to us along the path to Burwell but he travels far and wide. He tells us tales of places far away such as Lincoln and even London, which he claims to have seen,' said the woman in a voice which suggested that Hereward himself was at fault for not having heard of this famous Fenchel.

Hereward's anger seemed to leave him at once and he stared down into the woman's face, capturing her eyes with his and allowing himself his broadest and most enchanting smile. The women of Reach began to feel more at ease and many smiled among themselves, following the blond warrior's lead. Only Martin Lightfoot knew that his master was laying a false trail of pleasantry.

'Dear mother,' Hereward said gently, reaching out to stroke the head of the infant at the woman's breast, 'I too have travelled far and seen Lincoln and London. I have seen Cornwall and even

Wales, albeit from a safe distance. I have crossed the oceans and seen Flanders and Friesia and even Normandy, and France once, by mistake, for I was lost. But in all my travels and among all the knights and noble ladies I have met, even the counts and barons and kings I have dined with, not to mention abbots and priors and even bishops, not one had ever heard of this *fucking* Fenchel you boast of! So tell me, good wife, if your children wish to still have a mother by sunset, who is this Fenchel and why is he coming here?'

Although both her children began to bawl at that exact moment, the woman remained calm and stood her ground. Such fortitude has long been noted among women of the Fens, though in other places it is called sheer stubbornness.

'Fenchel,' said the woman, drawing herself up to her full height, her eyes still locked with Hereward's, 'as everyone knows, is a master potter of Ipswich, a town famed for its pottery, and today is the day Fenchel brings his finest wares for us to buy.'

Then Hereward did something which surprised the women of Reach and his own men equally. He took the woman's face in both his hands and planted a chaste kiss on her forehead.

'But that is wonderful news, mother!' he exclaimed with an even bigger smile. 'Is it not, Martin?'

'Why should it be, Hereward?' asked Lightfoot, genuinely puzzled.

'Because this is the day Fenchel the master potter comes to sell his wares,' said Hereward, patting the woman's cheeks, 'and these good women have turned out to buy them, but they will not pay with money or jewels, for they have none. So what will they trade for Fenchel's pots? The fruits of their harvest I'll be bound and if we search their hovels I think we'll find some tasty morsels. Search the village. If you can eat it and we can lift it, it's ours.'

With a cheer, the hungry defenders of the Isle of Ely set to their task of plundering the poor village of Reach and they found the stores which the women had been harbouring for this one day in the year when Fenchel the potter visited, for it was widely known that the quality of Ipswich pottery was unsurpassed in all England and women, even in the backwaters of Reach, all have a strange urge to possess the latest jug, dish, jar, bowl, pipkin or platter, whatever the cost and however humble the table it adorned.

The plunderers of Reach found much to please their stomachs, for the women had prepared many delicacies for use in trade with Fenchel; smoked eels by the hundred, salted fish and pork joints, ducks preserved in their own fat, cabbages, beans and eggs pickled in brine, honey in abundance and blackberries and raspberries preserved in honey and even freshly brewed ale, though weak and flavourless compared to monastic brews, which had been prepared in honour of the annual visit of the noble Fenchel.

In addition to the goods which the villagers had set aside for trade, the plunderers also helped themselves to numerous sacks of grain and twenty chickens and six pigs had their necks wrung or their throats cut.

293

Only Brother Godric, who was with the expedition, raised a concern at this.

'Lord Hereward, hear my protest,' he said as the men of Ely tore the village of Reach apart. 'What this poor village has in surplus for trade is one matter, but what they have put aside to see them through the winter is another. Are we to let Englishmen and women starve? Is that not why we fight the Normans?'

Hereward gripped the scabbard of his firesteel sword until his knuckles bled white, but his voice remained calm.

'Brother monk, you speak true when you say we fight the Normans. The men of Ely do the fighting, not these villagers here. They have food here for the stealing because they have not joined our cause; they have stayed fat and happy under the Normans while others have fought for their freedom. There is more food here in this tiny village than there is on the whole Isle of Ely, therefore our need is the greater and we will take what we find. I will be generous, these women will still have husbands and the children will have fathers, for I will not make war on their menfolk or press them to our cause. Let these serfs of Reach run to their new Norman lords for protection if they reject the protection of Ely!'

Hereward's men cheered this speech, as they were beginning to cheer his every utterance, but men always cheer at the prospect of a full belly.

The women of Reach did not cheer. They cowered and huddled together in a group in the middle of the village around a now empty pigsty.

Hereward approached the woman with the

suckling babe.

'You, mother, tell me. Who is the lord of this village?'

'It was a Norman knight,' the woman told him, not afraid to look him in the eye, 'called Sir Frederick, though we never knew his family name. When he was cruelly murdered, his lands were given to Sir William de Warenne, a noble of high birth or so we are told, for none here have ever seen him.'

'You will find Sir William a most generous lord and master,' laughed Hereward, 'and charitable too. You should run to him for shelter; he will see you through the winter!'

At that he laughed even louder, but the laughter was in his throat and not his eyes.

He was not to know that the men of Reach, hiding in the fields beyond the village, had already decided to run to Sir William for help.

[ix]

They heard Fenchel the potter coming down the track from Burwell long before they saw him, for a potter on his yearly sales round carries more than mere pots.

His cart, pulled by a broken-winded, hollow-chested nag which looked as if it had seen as many summers as Fenchel himself, rattled and jangled to overflowing with all types of goods for the home and hearth. He carried iron flesh hooks of different lengths, for roasting meat, trowel heads and axe heads of all shapes, big sturdy buckets with iron handles, shears and knives as well as the pottery for which he was supposedly famed, offering a range of Ipswich ware from the smallest lamp and candlestick to cooking pots and cauldrons which a woman could not lift with one hand. For his richer customers, his cart also contained a range of jugs, cruets, bowls, ladles and even fancy handled cups.

For his special customers, that is to say, women, Fenchel also carried numerous combs of finely worked antler and a goodly stock of bone awls and pins, of which women are said to say they can never have too many. These small items were not displayed on Fenchel's cart, but hidden in a leather bag hung around his neck beneath his woollen shirt and their presence was only discovered after Hereward had jumped from the straw roof of one of the houses of Reach on to the unsuspecting potter, tumbling him from his cart, which left him winded and defenceless in the dirt.

The women of Reach, skulking in the shadows of their cottages, let out a collective moan of despair, for they surely thought that having had their larders and storerooms plundered, they were now going to see the new pots and cookware they had dreamed of all year be carried off by these Fenland pirates.

But Hereward surprised all by climbing into Fenchel's cart and selecting a large jar, held it above his head and began to shout.

'Pots! Pots! Good pots and jars! Earthen vessels and all first class!'

The women of Reach, although suspicious, could not help but congregate around the cart.

'And how do we pay you, now you have all our trade goods?' asked one fearlessly.

'Were I not of noble birth, I would demand a kiss!' said Hereward with a laugh. 'I am also married to a witch who will know if I betray her, so I will settle for a blessing. If you want a fine Ipswich pot then grant me your blessing and know my name, for I am Hereward, Defender of Ely.'

Hesitantly, one of the old crones of the village – a woman of forty years with not a tooth in her head – knelt swiftly before the cart and made the sign of the cross, muttering: 'Blessings on the Defender of Ely.'

'Why, thank you, mother, I am truly blessed, now what would you like from my fine collection of pots?'

When they saw this was no trick and that the long haired warrior who had robbed them that very morning was now showering them with gifts, the village women surrounded the cart, falling over themselves to give their blessings and stake their claims.

Hereward thought the pushing and jostling for position by the women a great joke and as his laughter increased, so did his generosity with Fenchel's goods. His men shouted encouragement to the women as if it were a sport and only Brother Godric remained aloof for he realized that the women's actions could be both blasphemous and high treason.

Dazed and bloodied about the nose, where Hereward had planted his forehead on him, Fenchel the potter had staggered to his feet only to see his worldly goods being freely dispensed in front of him. Enraged, he had railed against Hereward, shaking his pudgy fist and denouncing him as thief, robber, and outlaw, although under his breath. Even when a man may have the law on his side, when he is unarmed and outnumbered twenty-to-one it is best to curse quietly.

It was only when Hereward boasted to the village women that the price of a fine pot was a blessing on his name, and his name was said out loud, did Fenchel – who had noted the loss of his satchel of combs and pins which he reserved for 'special' customers and the purse of coins he kept down the front of his breeches – speak out loud and was heard to say, as if questioning the heavens: 'Hereward the Firestarter?'

On hearing this, Hereward, standing on the potter's cart dispensing his wares to left and right, rose erect and clapped his hands as if calling for silence and then shouted to all who could hear.

'Well, at least they've heard of me in Ipswich!'

In an instant Hereward lost interest in distributing Fenchel's pots, preferring to question the unfortunate potter, who was already regretting his outburst.

'So what do they say of me in Ipswich, Master Potter?' he asked with a smile, drawing a dagger and placing the tip of the blade into the left nostril of poor Fenchel's nose.

'They say that Hereward is a mighty warrior and his favourite weapon is fire,' said Fenchel thinking quickly, for he had some education.

'What else?' asked Hereward.

'That Hereward can walk over water and at

night can appear as a man ten feet tall and that he consorts with giants and witches.'

Hereward threw back his head and laughed, but his knife-point remained where it had been placed.

'Anything else? Tell the truth, Master Potter, do not spare my blushes.'

'They say – forgive me – that Hereward only strikes from the shadows and dare not face a Norman knight in combat.'

Brother Gothic tensed himself for he felt sure a storm was about to break over Hereward and Martin Lightfoot moved to stand at his master's shoulder.

But there was no storm. Hereward's voice was calm and gentle as he spoke.

'Do they say that about me in the streets of Ipswich? Do they really?'

'Perhaps not in Ipswich, my Lord, for I fear your fame has not yet reached there.'

'Then where did you hear these things, Master Potter?'

'In the village of Burwell, but two miles from here.'

'So the villagers of Burwell have heard of me, but not those of Reach. Do they not talk to each other? Do they feud?'

'It is not the villagers of Burwell who speak of you, my Lord. It is the garrison.'

'*Garrison?* There is a Norman garrison in Burwell?'

Now Hereward's voice did rise as a tempest off the sea.

'It is only five men. They collect taxes for the

estate and guard the road from Cambridge to the Abbey of St Edmunds,' said Fenchel, his brow now wet with sweated fear and his eyes tight closed, for he was expecting to have his nose slit in a heartbeat.

But Hereward's knife withdrew and instead of pain, Fenchel felt a comforting arm clasped around his shoulder. When he opened his eyes it was to find his face close to that of his tormentor and Hereward's staring eyes fixed him more firmly than any knife-point.

'You are sure there are only five Normans in Burwell?' asked Hereward and received a vigorous nod from Fenchel. 'Then we must pay them a visit as we are so close by. It is the only courteous thing to do.'

[x]

Every man who had accompanied Hereward to Reach expressed a desire to go with him to Burwell, such was their thirst for violence now, but Hereward took with him only Martin Lightfoot and Brother Godric. He gave orders for his men to begin to carry the plunder of Reach back to the rafts, for at least two trips would be necessary, and he gave instructions to be passed to Rufus telling him to arrange for the plunder to be rafted across both the Cam and the Ouse and guarded while the rafts were to return for the men alone.

His orders given, he then, with a flourish, begged the permission of Fenchel for the loan of his horse and cart, which of course the potter did not refuse.

300

With Brother Godric and Martin crouched in the cart among the few remaining pots and irons which the women of Reach had not yet claimed, Hereward took the reins, placed his sword at his feet, and turned the horse towards Burwell.

The journey was a short but slow one, for the potter's ancient horse was not used to pulling the weight of three men and in truth, the three could have walked the two miles faster, but Hereward insisted that the sight of Fenchel's cart approaching with one hooded man at the reins, would not cause any Norman sentry to raise an alarm.

It proved a wise precaution, for there was indeed a sentry posted on the edge of Burwell; a lone Norman trooper armed with a long spear, who put a hand to his eyes to shield against the western sun. When he recognized the cart as that of the potter who had left Burwell that very morning, he raised his hand in greeting. Hereward immediately waved back, although still some distance from the poor wattle huts of Burwell, and even began to sing 'Pots! Fine pots! All earth-fired and finest quality!' tunelessly at the top of his voice, as though in an alehouse late at night.

Hereward was still singing as the cart drew level with the sentry, and the sentry was still smiling at his terrible singing when the heavy scabbard of Hereward's sword smashed down on to the middle of his iron helmet.

Almost before the sentry, who was quite dead, had slumped to the ground, Hereward had jumped down from the cart and was shouting at the seemingly deserted village.

'Pots! Fine pots! Will no one buy my fine pots?'

His shouts were matched by a roar of rage as two more Norman soldiers sprang from the nearest hut to aid their fallen comrade, drawing their swords as they ran.

If they thought two on one would swing the fight in their favour, they were mistaken. Before Lightfoot and Godric had even climbed out of the potter's cart, Hereward had unsheathed his fire-steel blade and caught first the one in the throat and the other with a downswing across the hamstrings, leaving the second writhing in the dust howling and the first flat on his back, quickly bleeding to death as his lifeblood spurted through the fingers he held to his neck.

Hereward ordered Martin to search one side of the village while he searched the other and Brother Godric was left to tend to one dying man and one crippled man who was convinced he was about to die. There was little he could do for either.

'The village is empty!' Godric heard Martin shout. 'Their cooking fires are damped down but not cold, so they have not been gone long. There is bread here.'

'And meat,' said Hereward emerging from the soldiers' hut, chewing on a steaming leg of mutton. 'Find their horses.'

Still eating, Hereward walked over to the three Normans lying in the dirt of Burwell, looking down at each prone man as if seeing them for the first time: one dead, one dying and one crying in agony and clutching his leg. It was over this poor wretch that Hereward stood and looked down, juice from the mutton dripping on to the Norman's face.

'Where are the good folk of Burwell?' he asked the man, placing his boot on his chest.

'They have run into the fields or are hiding in Wicken Fen, may God rot them,' said the soldier through gritted teeth.

'And what do they fear so much that they hide?'

'They fear an outlaw they call a *berserker*, who fights with fire and robs their churches and holy places,' said the wounded solider bravely.

'What sort of people are they in Burwell that fear their own heroes?'

'Only the English would make heroes of their outlaws,' said the soldier, wincing in pain as Hereward pressed down on him with his boot.

'And does this outlaw or this hero have a name?'

'Hereward the Firestarter they call him, and then they spit to cleanse their mouth of that name.'

Brother Godric closed his eyes, expecting Hereward to do his worst, but instead he took a large bite of mutton and looked down at his captive as he chewed.

'What if I were to tell you, my young warrior, that my name was Hereward?'

'I know it to be so already,' answered the Norman.

'And if you said that name, would you spit also?'

'If it was with my last dying breath,' said the wounded trooper, staring up into Hereward's eyes which, in Brother Godric's estimation, was a braver thing to do than to speak the words he did.

'By God, but this Norman has balls!' exclaimed

Hereward. 'Pray that he keeps them, Brother Godric, and see to his wound. Try and staunch the bleeding, though I fear he may never walk straight again.'

'Help me stand, monk, and put a sword in my hand and we'll see who walks away from here.'

'I told you he had spirit!' said Hereward with a laugh, offering his left hand to the Norman to help him rise, whilst still gnawing at his mutton bone. 'But I will not take advantage of you, my young friend, for have you not seen how I have bested all three of you by myself alone? Next time perhaps you should have more men at your side—'

'Hereward,' Godric cried.

'What is it, Brother Monk?'

'Three – you bested three – but the potter said the garrison here was five.'

Hereward stared at him, uncomprehending, and was then distracted by a shout from Lightfoot at the other end of the village where he stood holding the bridles of three saddled horses.

'Three horses, Hereward! There were only three horses in the pasture, not five. Two are missing.'

Hereward turned on the surviving Norman and pushed him in the chest with his mutton bone until the soldier, who was in truth little more than a boy, had his back against the thatched hut he had emerged from.

'Where are they? Where are the other two?'

'You will see them soon enough, outlaw,' said the Norman proudly. 'As soon as the men of Reach ran here and told us that their village was being plundered and their women raped, I sent word to my father who patrols the Cambridge road. His cavalry will be here before the sun starts to set and his hunting dogs will track your stench across these marshes.'

'Brave words, young man. How old are you and what is your name?'

'I am fourteen years old and I am Richard, son of the Viscomte Osbert,' he answered (in the fashion of the French), 'who is a sworn and true knight of Sir William de Warennes.'

Hereward professed surprise.

'Then I am in distinguished company! But do you know my name?'

'It is Hereward the Outlaw, soon to be Hereward the Dead!' answered the young noble.

'You are right, Richard, son of Viscount Osbert,' said Hereward, and then he let the mutton leg drop from his right hand and threw his clenched fist into the boy's jaw. 'But you forgot to spit when you said it.'

It was with tenderness that Hereward caught the boy as he fell, and laid him back on the ground from which he had helped him stand only moments before.

'Godric, I was serious about his wound; see if you can bind it. Martin, put one of those horses between the shafts of the potter's cart and turn his old nag free,' Hereward ordered. 'Then load up all the food and weapons we can find here and let us get back to Reach where we have a score to settle.'

'Lord Hereward, they are poor and ignorant people,' pleaded Godric, having some knowledge by now of how Hereward's mind worked.

'You heard what he said!' stormed Hereward, 'He said the men of Reach came running to warn them. I did not make war on the men of Reach, I left them to their work in the fields, and we did not rape their women. I was generous to them. Generosity – that was my first mistake.'

[xi]

The Norman patrol which arrived in Burwell to find Richard, son of Osbert, tied and gagged (though his gashed and bleeding leg had been bound with sage leaves and a linen bandage), did not have to seek out the attackers of the garrison there. The pyre of smoke rising from the burning village of Reach was clearly visible from two miles away and pointed the trail they should follow.

The patrol rode in to Reach at the gallop, their horses shying and snorting at the smoke and smell of burning thatch and the wailing of the women bemoaning the loss of their houses, but firmly intent on rescuing their new pots despite the protests of a distraught Fenchel. It was the potter, furious with anger but impotent when it came to recovering his stolen property, who pointed to the Norman cavalry the path which Hereward and his pirates had taken towards the Fens and the River Cam.

The Normans needed little help from Fenchel, for the tracks of Hereward's force – footprints, hoof-prints and the tracks of the cart they had stolen from poor Fenchel – were plain for all to see. But the Norman troop commander (whose name is not known) was wise enough not to take cavalry horses blindly on to the narrow paths of the Fens and he called for the dogs which travelled with the patrol to be brought forward and let off their long leashes. The dogs were large wolfhounds, each as big as a small Welsh pony, which is the sort much favoured by the Norman aristocracy for hunting both deer and men and the cavalry captain's plan was clear: let the hounds find the English and then his men would ride them down before they could cross the Cam and before dusk fell.

That plan almost came to fruition more perfectly than the Norman captain could have dreamt, for just as dusk was falling, their dogs found the English raiders still waiting to cross the river.

In fact, most of the English had already been transferred across the Cam and were hauling one raft and their plunder to where they could cross the Ouse on to Ely. Hereward and five or six companions were loading the second raft with sacks of grain and weapons from Burwell, transferring them from Fenchel's cart. Martin Lightfoot had already crossed the Cam, swimming over with the three stolen horses, as had Brother Godric. And it was Godric, from the far bank who shouted a warning that they were about to be attacked by dogs.

One Fenman had barely time to scream as the leading wolfhound pounced and locked its jaws around his arm, the speed of the attack taking both man and dog into the dark river, locked in a deathly embrace from which neither surfaced.

Hereward let out a curse and then a roar of anger and drew his sword, wielding it in his right hand whilst in his left he brandished the wooden scabbard. Without a thought for his own safety, he ran towards the second hound swinging blade and club and the dog, more used to being the hunter than the hunted, slowed in its charge. It was the last thing it did as Hereward's iron and wood scabbard came down and knocked it senseless and then Hereward's blade removed its head in one swipe.

'Go!' he shouted, his face covered in blood sprayed from the wolfhound, 'Get on the raft and cross the river now! These dogs are not out hunting alone.'

The Fenmen worked as if the devil himself was after them, loading the raft until it lay dangerously low in the water and there was hardly room on it for the men themselves.

'Go, go, go,' Hereward urged his men.

'Hurry! They're coming!' shouted Godric from the far bank; for the Cam was not wide at this point and the monk could now clearly see the vanguard of the Norman cavalry coming down the path towards the raft.

'Poles!' Hereward shouted at his men. 'Get your poles and push off from the bank!'

Hereward knew that without the long willow poles to propel it across, the heavy raft would sit sluggishly in the slow current of the Cam and leave all on board an easy target for Norman arrows or spears. As his men pulled the poles from where they had hidden them in the reeds, Hereward grabbed one of the longest himself and made to push the rim of the raft away from the bank.

'Behind you!' screamed one of his loyal men on the raft and Hereward turned to see two Norman knights bearing down on him at full gallop.

He used the weapon he held in his hands, the long willow pole twice as long as a Norman lance, holding it as a knight would hold a lance and aiming at the breast of the rider hurtling towards him. The rider, unable to slow his horse or raise his shield in time, ran on to upraised pole and the force knocked him backwards out of his saddle.

The second Norman knight, seeing the fate of his comrade, did attempt to slow his charge but not before Hereward had changed his grip on the pole and swung it viciously at the front legs of his horse with a crack which was heard across the river.

The terrified horse collapsed on to its knees, skidding into the body of the dead wolfhound, snorting in fear as it smelled the dog's blood. Its rider was flung over its neck and pitched head-first into the Cam where the weight of his chain mail and weapons dragged him to its muddy bottom.

'Hereward, beware!' came the warning shout from the far bank, but Hereward had already seen more horsemen coming down the path from Reach; more than he cared to pause and count.

Yet it seemed to the Fenmen on the other bank, and those on the raft now in mid-stream, that Hereward was determined to attack them. They were mistaken, for although he ran towards the

309

oncoming cavalry, it was only to collect his sword, which he promptly sheathed and jammed into his belt. Then he waved to the Normans, shouted an insult for which there is no suitable word in English or Latin, turned and ran back to where he had dropped the raft pole and picked it up again.

But he used it not as a weapon this time, but as a means of crossing the river Cam, employing a trick he had been taught by Hraga the Heron on the Isle of Littleport.

Holding the pole at one end with both hands, pointing towards the river, he ran directly for the river's edge. To the amazement of all on the far bank, on the raft, and the Normans rapidly approaching, Hereward plunged the pole into the river and seemed to ride it, high into the air, through an arc until it was upright, his legs flailing as if he were still running on dry land. At the top of the arc, Hereward released his hold on the pole and seemed to fly towards the far bank, a distance no mortal man could possibly jump.

The Norman cavalry had a vision of their enemy flying high, feet-first through the air against the westerly setting sun, to be greeted by the roar of Fenmen cheering as their captain splashed safely into the mud and reeds on the far bank and then emerged rank with the stink of marsh gas, arms aloft and grinning like a madman.

[xii]

'We have a problem,' said the sacrist, kneeling in prayer to join his abbot.

'Really?' replied Thurstan, his head bowed. 'The Isle of Ely is besieged, our abbey is friendless and isolated, our people go hungry, winter is almost upon us and we have the King of England against us, who has probably declared us all traitors. Is this the problem you refer to, my brother?'

'All those things have indeed been sent to try us, Father Abbot, but I feel in my heart that our biggest problem is Hereward.'

'Is this revelation new to you, dear brother? What has Hereward done now?'

'His raids across the rivers will have angered the Norman nobles even further.'

'It is not, my sacrist, as if they felt peaceful and generous to us before,' observed Thurstan.

'It is true that he has brought back much-needed food for the people of the Isle from these raids...'

'*Stolen* food, which will not be eaten by those in Holy Orders in this abbey. The rules of the sainted Benedict are quite clear on that.'

'Nor by many others, for the spoils of Reach and Burwell will not go far among so many hungry mouths. If Hereward was trying to emulate our Lord by feeding the crowd with a few loaves and some smoked eels, then he is truly misguided.'

'Thoughts of Hereward seem to turn towards blasphemy these days. Are they not also saying in the streets that Hereward can walk on water?'

'The foolish do say so, but the truth is Hereward uses the tricks of the Fenmen to jump over dyke and stream or to walk through deep water on stilts. Such stratagems may be startling to the Normans and may make them wary or even afraid,' said the

311

sacrist as though debating a point of law.

'King William does not believe that mortal man can walk on water,' said Thurstan firmly.

'No, my Lord Abbot, he does not. That is why his men are building a bridge at Theoford.'

The abbot closed his eyes tightly in prayer.

'Can Hereward stop them?'

'No, but he will try. His best hope is to delay them until the winter rains and tides make the river rise, but his men are few and they are hungry and they will see their families starve, if not this year, then next. I fear this war will be over by Christmas.'

Thurstan opened his eyes and stared at his faithful companion.

'I am sure that is being said in every Norman castle in England. But, tell me brother, will the men of the Fens stay loyal to Hereward despite the tribulations ahead?'

'They will, good Abbot, and that is our problem. They love him.'

Seventeen

Giraldus

Oh dear. Hereward's noble purpose seems to have disappeared, for he has gone from a wandering knight questing for his birthright to a common robber of his own people, at least according to Brother Thomas. (Who still remains a mystery to

312

me for all the letters I have sent to Ely remain unanswered, which leads me to think they have lost the skill of writing there.) His account contains the seeds of the many stories and songs about Hereward – and just about every other outlaw the common folk of England adopt as a hero – in that he rode out to rob the rich in order to give to the poor.

But the account of Hereward's raids on Burwell and Reach were clearly a case of robbing the poor to feed the even poorer, at least if one discounts the loss of poor Fenchel's pottery. It must be assumed that being a potter of Ipswich, where pottery was an important industry and a much-respected trade, Fenchel was an Englishman and an honest one. The distribution of his wares by Hereward was straightforward robbery of a man of property, but what Hereward did to the people of Reach was much worse.

Not only did he steal their trade goods, but also their food stocks and then burned their houses, all on the eve of winter. No man who does that to his own people deserves to be called a hero.

I have never been to Reach, nor do I know anyone who ever has, but I can only imagine it to be a small place which suffered mightily that winter as the lord of the manor, Sir William de Warenne, was unlikely to feel in charitable mood that year.

I have, however, been to Burwell and it is a place of little consequence, the rents being in the gift of the Abbot of Ramsey at the time of Hereward, which was not unusual for over a quarter of the land of England was then owned by a bishop or an abbot, whilst less than one-fifth was owned by the

King who had come across the Channel to steal it all. Hereward seems to have had no compunction in raiding lands owned by English abbeys, although he claims to have been a sworn man of at least two and no doubt styled himself a defender of the Church in England.

It is thus that the legends and tavern talk would have it: Hereward unjustly dispossessed of his inheritance; Hereward unjustly outlawed; Hereward, the man who prevented the treasure of Peterborough from falling to the Normans; Hereward the lone defender of Ely and its abbey. Such is the danger of allowing history to be written (or in this case sung in the alehouses) by the losing side.

The truth is rarely so simple and the historian is honourbound to include at least some portion of the truth in his chronicle.

Is it not true that Hereward had no legitimate claim on the estate of Bourne? Is it not true that he was justly outlawed (at least once) for his violent conduct, when he cut off the hand of that country priest? Was he the lone defender of Ely? Possibly that is so, but if he had not defended it so aggressively, would it have been besieged in the first place?

And as to protecting the treasure of Peterborough from the Normans, the more I examine Brother Thomas's book, the more I suspect that the treasure was not being protected, but robbed and there are enough hints in his text to suggest that this robbery was suggested by none other than a woman – Hereward's wife Turfrida, who remained safe in Flanders – and the real object of it was not the relics, books, silks and church treasures but the private treasure deposited in Peterborough by Turfrida. It was this part of the treasure which was sliced off from the main haul and buried at Littleport, along with, no doubt, the two innocent boatmen Winter and Liveret.

Such an idea would be fanciful were it not for the fact that Hereward allowed King Svein to appropriate the bulk of the treasure without even an argument let alone a fight.

It is almost as if this whole rebellion of the east of England – which was started by Hereward's raid on Peterborough – was designed as a diversion to mask the main purpose, which was that of robbery. And all this with the tacit co-operation of the monks of some of the most important abbeys in England?

This must be surely nonsense, but there is no denying that in Brother Thomas's book, monks played their part as spies for both sides. Sir William de Warenne says as much, and there must have been a spy in his camp, otherwise how would Brother Thomas have known he did?

And Thomas makes no secret of the role played by Brother Godric who almost certainly helped in the robbery of Peterborough, forsook his prior and stayed in England when all the other monks of Peterborough went, however unwillingly, to Denmark. Even more, Godric clearly sided with Hereward's rebels at Aldreth and then again at Reach and Burwell and while he did not carry arms and did indeed plead for the villagers of Reach, there is little doubt where his sympathies lay.

It must be assumed that Godric's heart was pure, for certainly God looked kindly on him and protected him. Not only did Godric survive the war of the Fenmen and the wrath of King William, but he is known to have dedicated his life in the service of the church and some twenty-five or more years later was elected as Abbot of Peterborough, so highly was he thought of by his fellow brothers in Christ.

He did not enjoy a long tenure as abbot, for the Norman bishops of the day preferred one of their own in such a distinguished position and soon had him removed.

The memories of men are usually, and mercifully, short, but when it came to Hereward, the memories of the Normans were long indeed.

Eighteen

Thomas

Hereward the Witch-Killer

[i]

King William's engineers, under the direction of Sir William de Warenne, built their *ballistae* opposite Aldreth and Theoford along with a watchtower to guard them. The Fenmen of Ely had never encountered such machines before, nor indeed had they seen structures made by man which were as tall as those watchtowers; the guards on the top platform standing higher than even Hraga the Heron had on his unnaturally long stilts, just before he died.

They were blissfully unaware that the Norman guards in the watchtowers, high above the reeds and marsh grass, had a view over the flat landscape of Ely which only a hawk or an eagle could match.

Nor did the innocent Fenmen have any notion of what a Norman engine of war could do to their puny defences and fortifications. In truth, the engines built for Sir William were not the *ballistae* of ancient times, which fired large arrows or rounded stones as big as a man's fist, just as a crossbow fired a bolt. These were catapults or *mangonels* as they were more properly called, from the Greek, which could propel large stones or pots of Greek fire through the air over great distances and with great force. It was said that when quelling rebellious towns and walled cities in Normandy and Brittany, Duke William had used *mangonels* with great effect to launch the carcasses of dead and diseased animals and even whole beehives into the heart of his enemy's positions.

Most of the defenders of Ely watched the building of these catapults with interest and in a feeling of complete safety, for the machines were hundreds of paces away, more than twice the range of normal bowshot, along the causeway at Aldreth or across the river on the far bank at Theoford. And when the first missiles – blocks of stone brought from the building of Cambridge Castle for this

317

very purpose fell short of the earthworks at Aldreth and actually splashed into the river at Theoford – the ignorant Fenmen laughed and crowed
and made gestures at their enemies. They were not
to know that these were only ranging shots by the
Norman artillerymen and that the second and
third volleys, directed by the guards high atop the
watchtowers, would land with deadly accuracy.

At Aldreth the Normans used precious stone to
smash down the earthworks Siward had built and
defended, but at Theoford they relied on fire,
hurling large pots of burning pitch and oil across
the river to burst among the poor hovels with
roofs as dry as tinder.

So terrible was this sudden firestorm from the
skies that the defenders of Theoford fled into the
edges of Grunty Fen and from the shelter of the
reeds they watched the village burn to the ground.

[ii]

'Well, it's a start,' said Sir William watching the
funeral pyre of Theoford from the Norman camp
on Stuntney, 'and the wind is carrying the smoke
to the north so they will soon smell defeat in Ely.'

'Will it bring them to their senses?' asked Baron
Ivo. 'Will they plead for terms?'

'I think the monks would, for they know they
are isolated from the rest of their Church. The
Fenmen would, if they had the wit, though it
would do them no good, for their fate is sealed.
But both are frightened of Hereward. He is now
too powerful.'

'How can that be? He has few men and they have no cavalry and few weapons. Their only allies have deserted them and no others will come to their aid.'

'We have given him too many easy victories,' observed Sir William. 'Hereward has held us at the causeway and has even crossed the river to bring the fight to us.'

'Pah!' scoffed the Baron. 'Those raids were no more than flea bites. He has not bested us in open war.'

'Nor will he. He has more cunning than that. He will strike when and where he can, aiming for small victories and using tricks like stilt-walking which will make the simple folk of the Fens love him. These people, Ivo, have not harvested this year nor sown crops for next and now they see their homes burn.'

'So if we do nothing, they will starve to death.'

'Yes they will, my dear Ivo, but unfortunately not before the King gets here.'

'Then we'd better get a move on.'

[iii]

'What the fuck are they doing now?' asked Rufus, chewing on the remains of a smoked and dried eel from the previous summer's catch.

'I think they're building a bridge,' said Hereward, shielding his eyes against the rising sun which burned with an orange glare through the October morning mists.

'There's a chill in the air these days,' said Rufus,

319

concentrating on his eel rather than the Normans. 'Winter is a-coming.'

'The sooner the better,' said Hereward. 'We need the waters to rise.'

'Why do they need a bridge?' asked the monk Godric, who had joined the two captains as they had crawled on their bellies through the reeds to the very edge of where the river ford which gave Theoford its name, even though the village itself was a still-smoking ruin.

'The ford is passable here,' said Hereward, 'for the river is not deep, but to cross through the water in single file is a slow business. They know we could pick them off and one dead horse in the water will frighten all the others. So they are building a floating bridge. I have seen this in Flanders. Sometimes they tie boats together sideways on and lay planks across them. Here, they seem to be using barrels and logs and sheep hides which they have sewn up and inflated with bellows. They will string two ropes across the river and build their bridge between them.'

Godric the innocent monk still could not comprehend this.

'Are you saying they will ride horses and men across floating wood and skins?'

'Oh yes. The bridge will not last. If the wind blows or the river rises and runs fast, the bridge will break. But if they are lucky and we are not, it will last long enough for them to get across.'

'And what do you give for the chances of our army of farmers and fishermen, up against Norman cavalry?' asked Rufus.

'Not much,' said Hereward.

'Then we are truly doomed,' said Godric, making the sign of the cross, 'as soon as the Normans cross the bridge.'

'The bridge isn't finished yet,' said Hereward with a smile.

'So what can we do?' asked the young monk with desperation in his throat.

'We let them finish their bridge,' answered Hereward.

Which is exactly what they did.

Hereward ordered his army, such as it was, back into the safety of Grunty Fen where they could conceal themselves even from the Norman look-outs high atop the watchtower. This suited the Fenmen well, for they were not only out of range but also out of sight of the Normans' infernal machine which continued to bombard the Ely bank of the river even though there was little left to burn of Theoford. An additional blessing was that Grunty Fen was the last place left on the Isle where it was possible to find fish, lampreys and eels still swimming and even the few birds and fowls which had not yet left for winter. Compared to a normal year, the hunting was sparse indeed, but to the hungry Fenmen, Grunty was a richly stocked larder.

Hereward was happy for his men to hide and busy themselves in trapping and fishing, for there was little they could do against the enemy artillery. Had they themselves tried to get within bow shot of the Normans working the machine or building their floating bridge, they would have been easy prey for the crossbowmen positioned all along the watchtower.

He established a line of young boys to act as runners between the river and Grunty Fen and kept only Martin Lightfoot, Rufus and Godric with him on the riverbank, where they observed the Norman bridge builders for two days, lying on their bellies in the reeds. To get to the river-bank they had to crawl like snakes through the ashes of Theoford and their clothing and skin became so deeply begrimed with black soot that even lying in the reedy water margins of the river failed to cleanse them.

They watched the floating bridge advance out into and across the river and even saw two brave and naked Normans swim to the Ely bank to attach two thick ropes to tree stumps. These ropes would eventually anchor the bridge when complete.

Hereward could easily have cut those ropes, or the throats of the pair who had swum them across from Stuntney, but he resisted the temptation for he had noticed a weakness in the bridge which better served his purpose, but it was a weakness he could exploit when the bridge was anchored on both banks.

In their camp in Grunty Fen, Hereward called his men together before dusk and instructed them to go to the riverbank in the hour before dawn and to conceal themselves in a place where they could see the floating bridge, but not be seen themselves. When he was asked by his men what would be the signal to attack, Hereward told them there would be no attack. They were there to watch, not fight.

Then he asked Rufus to find him daggers with

long and thin blades and a decent whetstone on which to sharpen them and when he had personally done this task to his satisfaction, he and Lightfoot left the camp without farewells save for a blessing from Brother Godric.

During the night the pair entered the Ouse and, using the long hollow stems of rushes to breathe through, swam underwater until they fetched up against the bridge.

Convinced that the defenders of Ely had forsaken the Theoford bank near the bridge (which they had), the Normans were lax in their vigilance, relying on their crossbowmen in the watchtower from above and a few patrolling sentries with torches on the Stuntney shore.

Sir William de Warenne had judged, wrongly, that an attack on the bridge would come from fire-rafts floated downstream and had stationed men at points along the southern bank of the Ouse to give early warning of such a threat. He had even had his men cut long poles so they could fend off a burning raft before it could spread fire to the planks and timbers of the bridge. Such was the slowness of the current it was felt that any such threat would be seen early and easily dealt with. None in the Norman camp had foreseen that the real danger would come from *under* the bridge.

In the darkness and the black water, Hereward and Lightfoot found their way by touch alone and each time they felt a rope, they used their blades to cut it, although they were careful not to damage the guide ropes at each side which anchored the bridge between the two shores. With each inflated

323

sheepskin, they slid their blades in carefully where the skins protruded above the surface, for they did not wish to leave a trail of bubbles in the water to make the Normans suspicious.

Wriggling like eels, the two men traversed the span of the bridge under the surface of the water, breathing through their reeds (an old wildfowlers' trick) and only letting their faces out of the river when sure that they were hidden by the planks and ropes of the bridge, their knives causing pinpricks of destruction as they went. Near the Ely shore, they swam downstream a safe distance before climbing out on to the bank, where they embraced but said not a word, for the sound of voices carries far across the Fens at night.

They slept the rest of the night in the burned-out circle of a cottage in Theoford and just before dawn were wakened by the sounds and smells of the Norman camp stirring across the river.

Shivering in his wet clothing, Hereward nudged his companion awake and instructed him to start for Ely where he was to tell Abbot Thurstan that the Normans had been defeated at Theoford.

Such was his devotion to Hereward by now that Lightfoot never thought to question his master but did as he had been ordered. Then Hereward crawled on his belly once more through the ashes of Theoford, rubbing the black ash into his arms, face, hair and beard until he looked like a creature of the night. At the spot where they had watched the Norman bridge builders, he retrieved his sword from its hiding place under an old heron's nest and he waited for dawn.

The Normans also waited for dawn.

[iv]

A troop of cavalry riding the most docile and surest-footed ponies formed up in a column of two riders abreast on the Stuntney bank as Sir William de Warenne, seated on a stool outside his tent, eating roast chicken, supervised the crossing of the bridge.

As was only prudent, the Normans sent three of their strongest knights across first on foot, before committing their horses, and only then after the sentries on high in the watchtower had shouted down that there was no sign of movement on the Ely bank.

The three knights tested the bridge as they walked, with their boots and the shafts of their spears. So subtle was the damage done by Martin and Hereward that the bridge continued to float with the weight of these men as if they were but feathers, although a sharper eye in the Norman camp would have noticed that the bridge was floating lower in the water by the span of a hand than the day before. But Norman eyes were not sharp that day.

The three knights acting as scouts or bridge testers reached the Ely shore and once on solid ground (of which there is little enough in the Fens), they shouted to their comrades that they had walked to Ely without getting their boots wet. This gave the Norman cavalry great heart and the vanguard nudged their horses forward.

When the first Norman horse stepped on to the

325

bridge, Hereward drew his sword and burst from his hiding place.

It was the cavalry troop which shouted the first warning, for Hereward himself made no sound, but it was too late for their scouts.

Hereward slew the first before the Norman even knew he was in danger, with a downward blow which sliced his helmet, and the head inside it, in half.

The second scout turned to see a pitch-black monster advancing on him, the morning light reflecting off the firesteel blade already smeared with blood and other matter best left unmentioned.

That Norman knight moved as if his limbs had turned to stone as what appeared to him as the very devil himself closed with him. The devil, though, as all good Christian men do know, can move faster than the eye can see and the knight made no move at all to defend himself as Hereward's blade swung under his long shield and caught his legs under the hem of his mail coat. As his knees buckled under him, the black demon towered above him and thrust the point of his sword into his throat.

The third knight, acting more from fear than in bravery, hooked his spear under his arm and, raising his shield to protect his left side, advanced on the slayer of his comrades.

Hereward easily parried the first jab of the spear with his blade and as his opponent staggered, off balance, he made a delicate thrust downwards and skewered the knight's right foot through his leather boot.

The knight dropped his spear and shield and howled in agony as Hereward withdrew his blade and smashed the lobed pommel of his sword into the doomed man's face.

Hereward moved behind his enemy, forcing him to his knees and knocking off his helmet, turning him so that the unfortunate knight's body would act as a shield against the bolts of the Norman crossbowmen in the watchtower, though few shots were made as the sentries in the tower had taken great fright at the black demon who seemed to be slaughtering their knights with ease.

The cavalry troop, being made of sterner stuff, was enraged by what they had seen and the natural instinct to charge into the attack was tempered only by the fear that they would be exposed to attack whilst on the bridge. Hereward knew this and determined to put their minds at ease.

Holding his sword across the throat of his prisoner, he shouted his taunts loudly across the creaking bridge.

'How many Normans does it take to best one Englishman? I have killed two and taken one prisoner this morning with not a cut or a bruise in return. And all this poor fellow here under my blade can think of is why do his friends not ride to his rescue? Are they afraid of one Fenman who stands alone to defy them? Well this answer must be "Yes" when your friends are Norman and the Fenman is Hereward!'

At this, the mounted knights shouted back a volley of curses and spurred their horses on to the planks of the bridge. Such was their outrage that five or six jostled for position in order to get over the bridge and attack their taunter, and more followed until eight men and horses were clattering across, the beating of their hooves on wood echoing across the water.

Hereward continued to shout insults at the cavalry, goading them into even more haste and he also wished to keep their eyes on him and not on the bouncing, creaking bridge beneath them. And so with a shout, he drew his firesteel blade across the throat of his poor prisoner, leaning back to avoid the fountain of blood which looked to the horsemen as if he were laughing at the plight of his victim.

Heedless of their own safety, they urged their horses on and whereas the bridge might have carried one or perhaps two horses, the weight of thirteen mounted troopers was too much for its solidity had been fatally weakened by the knives of Hereward and Lightfoot.

Even Hereward was shocked as the bridge collapsed, sinking in the middle, plunging men and horses into the water before they could even offer up a prayer and then he did laugh at the surprised looks on the faces of the riders.

But Hereward was not finished, for he wanted the Normans to remember this victory. Pushing aside the corpse of the knight whose throat he had slit, he ran to the Ely end of the bridge and after saluting the Stuntney shore with his sword, he slashed at the ropes which anchored the bridge and kicked the cut ends into the river. The bridge itself was already destroyed before he did this, but his defiant gesture, as crossbow bolts whistled over his head, showed his contempt for his enemy.

Many a Norman heart sank, as well as horses and men, that day at Theoford, but it was said that the cheering and singing of the Fenmen, who had watched the battle from the reeds, could be heard in Ely itself that morning.

[v]

'Now I am angry,' said Sir William de Warenne. 'I will give a hundred marks of silver to the man who brings me that madman's head in a sack.'

For once, Baron Ivo was proving the more composed of the two commanders.

'That ought to do it, but if I get my hands on the little bastard, I'll make you a present of his head only after I've made him watch me cut off all his other bits and feed them to my hounds.'

'We have to catch him first, my dear Ivo.'

'Which means getting on to that cursed island and preferably before the King arrives. Does he not expect this war to be over by winter and it is now November?'

'I know what the King expects,' snapped De Warenne, and then his face broke into a smile, 'but I think you may, have hit on something, Ivo.'

'I have?'

'You said that this Isle of Ely is cursed to us as we have no luck in storming it, and that is true enough. Yet what if those on the Isle believed themselves cursed? What if we can show them that following Hereward curses them to fire and death and pestilence?'

'And how do we do that?'

'Move the catapult as close to Ely as we can and build more watchtowers to defend it. Then tell the artillerymen to send over fire by night and burn everything in range.'

'Even the fields and property of the abbey?'

'Even those. I will answer for it. Then send to Cambridge to root out an apothecary and buy as much poison and purgatives as there are in that town, along with as much rotting meat as you can find. By daylight I want the catapult to send a bounty of disease and filth into Ely. Let us see how hungry they are over there.'

'There is talk of a witch in Cambridge,' said Ivo keenly, warming to the task ahead.

'That does not surprise me at all,' answered Sir William. 'I'm sure there are more than one in that place.'

'What if we paid a witch to curse them properly? That would give those treacherous monks something to think about.'

'They say Hereward's wife Turfrida is a witch. I met her in St Omer, you know, several years ago. True, she is plain and she speaks her thoughts aloud far more than a normal woman should, but I cannot see her frightening anyone.'

'Perhaps she frightened Hereward, which is why he is here and she is not.'

'You may be right, old friend, and your plan does have merit for these Fen people are a superstitious lot. Go and find us a true sorceress who can give a good curse. It will cheer our own men for their minds will be much troubled after seeing their comrades drowned in the river this morning.'

'There was one who did not drown,' said Ivo. 'He was seen washed up on the Ely bank half a mile downstream.'

'Does he live?'

'Probably. It was my wife's cousin Deda. He was always a lucky little sod.'

[vi]

News that a Norman knight had survived the disaster of the bridge over the River Ouse had also reached Hereward. Brother Godric begged Hereward to allow him to visit with this prisoner to see if he could supply any information.

'What information?' Hereward had asked him.

'On the disposition of the Norman forces opposing us,' Godric had answered.

'There are more of them than there are of us and they are on that side of the river and we are on this,' said Hereward. 'What more can a half-drowned Norman rat tell us? Slit his belly and roll him back into the water.'

'Then let me see him in the name of Christian charity,' pleaded Godric. 'Or at least let me find out if there could be a ransom for his safe return.'

'Ransom?' Hereward's eyes sparkled like stars in winter. 'Go to, Brother Monk, and see to our prisoner's comfort.'

His eyes grew even wider when he learned the identity of their waterlogged prisoner, for he knew from Brother Godric that Sir Deda had been the knight who had negotiated the departure of the Danes from Ely, and who therefore had the ear of the Norman generals if not the King himself.

Several in Hereward's company, including Godric and Martin Lightfoot, felt sure that Hereward would give the order to hang the prisoner or at least put him to torture in view of the Normans on the Isle of Stuntney. But instead Hereward gave orders which none expected, telling Godric to see that the prisoner was taken to the infirmary in Ely for the treatment of his wounds and to inform Abbot Thurstan that the abbey's refectory was to be cleared for a feast when their Norman guest was sufficiently recovered.

That said, Hereward then told Lightfoot and Rufus to organize all their men in a scouring of Grunty Fen for every animal that could be trapped that day, with runners to be sent to every hamlet on the Isle to demand a contribution, however small, of grain from each hungry family. Such grain as they harvested this way was to be delivered to the abbey brew-house and bakery to make fresh ale and new bread and a boy was sent running to tell the monks to prepare fires, for the brewery and bake-house at Ely had been cold for several weeks.

He also instructed two of his Fenmen to watch the river for a night and a day, in case the bloated bodies of Norman cavalry horses should begin to appear, for it was not often that men could go fishing for fresh meat.

For three days, as the air turned damp and the morning mists turned to chilly fog, the inhabitants of the Isle of Ely were lulled into a false sense of well-being. Despite their hunger, a feast was being prepared, which naturally gave rise to rumours that the guest of honour was not a prisoner pulled half-dead from the river at all, but a noble emissary sent by King William to treat with Hereward, the fearless defender of Ely. Some versions of the story said that this emissary had been sent to negotiate an honourable peace treaty with Hereward. Some went further and claimed that Hereward was to be recognized as a valiant foe and knighted into the ranks of Norman nobility, to be given the title of Baron of Ely and the fiefdom of the Isle and also his beloved estate of Bourne.

But such is the way the minds of simple folk wander when they are drunk or hungry and know that death is not far away.

On the fourth day of his restful captivity, Sir Deda was summoned to the refectory to partake of a feast in his honour to which he readily agreed for if he was to be killed, he at least wanted it done on a full stomach. He found himself seated on the right hand of Hereward who in turn sat at the right hand of Abbot Thurstan. Also present were the sacrist, the infirmarian and the almoner of the abbey sitting with some twenty monks, who were invited because they did not eat meat. Brother Godric was there, as were Rufus and Lightfoot. Even Siward the White was released from his duties at Aldreth for one night to attend, along with twenty of the defenders of the Fens who had been selected by the drawing of lots. If any of them had doubts about dining with the enemy, those doubts were dispersed when they saw and smelled the feast tables piled high before them.

Not only was there fresh ale and warm bread

(albeit somewhat gritty due to the sweepings in the flour grist), but the roast or boiled meat of roe deer, goat, otter and horse, roast ducks and herons and fresh perch, pike, roach as well as lampreys and eels split and smoked.

If it was possible to get drunk on food alone, then many of the Fenmen did so that night and all admitted that Hereward proved a most genial host, for his behaviour towards the prisoner Sir Deda was never less than courteous and generous. He conversed intimately with the Norman knight often speaking close to his ear so that no other could overhear and this drew worried looks from Brother Godric and Abbot Thurstan and severe stares from Thurstan's sacrist.

However the feast concluded without incident other than the announcement by Hereward that Sir Deda, although a foe, was a true and noble knight and if a boat could be found to ferry him across the river, he was free to go. This was news which surprised everyone in the abbey that day, especially Sir Deda, but Hereward made good his word.

When no spare boat could be found (for the few that had not been stolen by the Danes were hidden from both the Normans and Hereward in Grunty Fen), a small raft was made by lashing saplings and firewood to two small barrels. Sir Deda was given a small plank with which to row himself to the Stuntney shore and did so kneeling on his makeshift square platform of wood.

As he rowed away from Ely, already on his knees, he gave thanks to a merciful God.

'So they eat well in Ely, do they?'

'They have all manner of meats and many types of fish from the freshwater, not the sea, which they eat in place of the herring they like so much. They have bread and ale which is fresh but has no strength, but no wine or cider. The monks of Ely seem devout and devoted to their Abbot Thurstan, a charitable man who is much troubled by this war. The men of Ely are devoted to Hereward, who is far from troubled by the war, rather he thrives on it.'

'You tell us little that we did not know, Sir Deda,' said Sir William, 'but our prayers have been answered that you have returned to us. Now go and rest and get yourself fitted with weapons and a horse, for you are of more use to us as a sword than as a spy.'

If Sir Deda realized he had been slighted by his commander, he did not show it. Rather he smiled proudly at the thought that Sir William valued his skill at arms.

'That boy is an idiot,' said Sir William as the tent flaps closed behind Deda.

'It was interesting what he said about the food situation over there,' said Baron Ivo, 'but yes, he always was a stupid boy.'

'That feast was put on solely for Deda's benefit. Do you think he was aware he was eating his own horse? It was a show to fool a simple mind, a deception. Let us not give them time to plan any more tricks. Has the catapult been moved to within range of Ely?'

'The artillerymen have placed it on what little firm ground there is on this damned island. They think they will be in range of the outlying cottages and some of the poorer hovels of Ely but they do not think they can reach the abbey itself,' Ivo reported.

'Perhaps that is for the best,' mused Sir William. 'I want those people on the Isle pounded hard and I want them frightened. If they see their homes burn while the abbey remains safe, they may lose their faith in the monks of Ely.'

'But what of their faith in Hereward?'

'That we will only dislodge by defeating him, which is why we must keep their eyes on us here on Stuntney. Have the other catapult brought from Aldreth and give orders for the men to busy themselves cutting timber and building more watchtowers all along the river making as much noise as they can. Whilst their spies are watching us, send all the engineers back to Aldreth in secret and have them make preparations for bridging the gaps in the causeway, so that it can be done quickly and with great surprise when the time comes.'

'Before the King arrives?'

'If it be the will of God,' Sir William said demurely, 'I am sure the King would be pleased to hear Christmas Mass said in Ely.'

'Where is the King?'

'In London, where there is much to keep him busy, but you should send a patrol to Bromdun (now Brandan in Suffolk) where they should tell the manor to make ready to receive the King and his bodyguard within the week.'

'The King will be at Bromdun?' asked a surprised Baron Ivo.

'Of course not, but the manor at Bromdun is in the gift of Ely Abbey and you can be sure that word will reach Ely of this news. It may help keep the eyes of the Fenmen looking east and north rather than south, at Aldreth.'

'We could give those rebels something else to look at,' Ivo offered.

'What did you have in mind, my friend?'

'My men have located a powerful witch in Cambridge. It is said that for a few pennies she will curse your enemies. For a piece of silver she will curse an entire island for us. She is called The Pythoness, for she works best with snakes and lizards.'

'Then let us put her to work,' said Sir William.

[viii]

On Ely they watched and prayed.

They saw the Norman camp over on the Isle of Stuntney become a hive of activity. They heard axes biting into trees and nails being hammered and they smelled the Norman cooking fires which reminded them of the feast prepared for the prisoner Deda while so many went hungry, and they saw the watchtowers building towards the sky in a line along the eastern bank of the Ouse. From the platforms of those towers, the crossbowmen could ensure that no Fenman would safely show himself during daylight on the

337

Ely bank.

And they prayed for deliverance from their enemies, even for a pestilence to strike down the Normans; but above all they prayed for the winter rains to come and swell the rivers or for the winter tides to come and flood the Fens, for in the Fens, water flows both to and from the sea.

The defenders of Ely thought their prayers had been answered when the first hard frost struck in the last week of November, but that also reminded many that their families hiding in makeshift shelters in Grunty Fen were cold and hungry and winter was upon them.

Those who had fled into the marshes of Grunty from Theoford were soon joined by many from Ely as the Normans began to bombard them from Stuntney. By night they would send over large pots of burning oil, which smashed on impact spreading fire and terror and consuming the poorer dwellings of the town. By day, the catapults would throw the rotting carcasses of horses which had spent the summer ripening in the dank waters at Aldreth, which terrified the inhabitants of Ely less than fire, for they had seen rotting meat before, but it did remind them of their hunger.

Abbot Thurstan instructed the brothers of Ely to remain vigilant throughout the nights to help quell the fires in the town and gave a dispensation from mid-day prayers for any monk who had experience of trapping animals or birds in their lives before Holy Orders.

Thurstan himself devoted himself to constant prayer, for the smell of Ely burning and the cries of the old women and children were like a dagger to the good abbot's heart. His spirits fell further when his sacrist told him that flint-knappers had arrived from Bromdun (which was a famous source of quality flints) with the news that King William was expected there.

'How did they get through?'

'By boat down the Little Ouse,' the sacrist answered, 'and then down the Wellstream to Littleport where they waited for night before rowing to Ely. They claimed they had no difficulty for the fires burning in the town guided them here.'

'They saw no Normans?'

'Not after they left Bromdun. They say the Wellstream north of Littleport is empty of traffic.'

'Then there could still be a route off this Isle, should anyone wish to leave,' the abbot said thoughtfully. 'Perhaps calling at Littleport and then disappearing across the Fens to who knows where?'

'Hereward will not leave unless he is forced to,' said the sacrist sadly. 'He is enjoying himself too much.'

[ix]

The sacrist's words proved nothing but the truth when Baron Taillebois installed the Cambridge Pythoness on top of the watchtower nearest to Ely.

The sight of this old witch dressed in black rags, with her face painted white, and a long fat snake curled around her shoulders struck mortal fear into the simple people of Ely. When the witch began to scream curses across the river at them in their own language, they feared for their very souls. Yet few could avert their eyes from that distant figure high on her tower as she swayed and sang and screamed, interrupting her curses by playing on drum and flute and igniting small bowls of mysterious tinder which she would then hold above her head as blood-red smoke issued forth from them.

Such a hellish spectacle made many of the innocent folk of Ely flock to their abbey to seek solace and protection from their noble abbot and many of Hereward's men cowered in their hides in Grunty Fen. When word reached those men under the command of Siward at Aldreth, many ran from their posts to Theoford, some out of ignorant curiosity and some out of fear for their wives and children.

The hard man Rufus, who had not flinched when faced with Norman blade or arrow, sat in a ditch with his back to the river and his hands over his ears and refused to move as long as the witch continued to hurl her curses across the river, and even Martin Lightfoot, though he had travelled wider and seen more than a normal Fenman would in several lifetimes, was a superstitious Fenman at heart and he too shivered with fear.

Only Hereward seemed genuinely unafraid of the old hag's screeching and he would walk with his head high (though out of bow shot) along the banks of the Ouse opposite the witch's tower, his hands on his hips, shouting back across the water to engage her.

'You are too far away, Mother Crone, I cannot

340

hear you. Come down out of the branches and float across this river to me so you can whisper in my ear and I can put something in yours, though it won't be my tongue!'

But Baron Ivo had paid the Pythoness of Cambridge well and she had listened well to her instructions.

'You have no need to speak to me, Hereward of Bourne, for I know who you are. You are proud to be a hard man but you are also an outlaw and a thief and a fire-starter, a twisted firestarter. I would curse your soul to everlasting hell but surely it is already on its way there!'

'That is mighty bold talk for a painted old whore who has to take her pleasures with a snake as no man will look at her!'

'There is none on Ely who can match my python for length and girth,' cackled the witch, holding her snake above her head with both hands.

'Then get your pleasure where and when you can, old hag,' shouted Hereward, 'for you will be in hell before me and I spit on your curses.'

'But I do not curse you, Hereward, for you have cursed yourself. You have robbed the church and you have plotted treason against your lawful king. You placed the mark of the devil on yourself many years ago. It is the men of Ely that I curse, for in their blindness they have followed you into treason and rebellion.'

'Silence, crone!'

'And their blindness will be real for the King will come and put out their eyes–'

'I said be quiet or I will leap this river and climb

that tower and rip out your tongue!'

'And those who he leaves with sight, he will lop off a foot or a hand so that men will know them as traitors for ever more.'

'You do not frighten me, Sorceress!' shouted Hereward across the water. 'I know your tricks and your schemes. I know all the wiles of witches, for am I not married to one?'

'And she will be a widow soon enough, Hereward!' cried the Pythoness. 'A lonely widow across the sea in a foreign land.'

'But that is one witch,' answered Hereward boldly, 'who never had need of a soft, fat snake!'

As he rejoined them, his men clapped Hereward on the back, judging him to have got the better of the witch in their war of words; but Hereward knew that battles were not won by words alone.

'That hag cannot harm us if we have faith in our God and our cause, which is to defend the holy Abbey of Ely from those Norman bastards. Her curses are as nothing; do not listen to them.'

'It is difficult not to hear her, Hereward, and she must have power for she has a python as a familiar,' said Martin Lightfoot, who was only saying aloud the fears of all the Fenmen.

'Very well then, my dear comrade, if you feel so strongly about it, let us go and kill the bitch tonight, but if we're going to do it, we had better get going.'

Hereward's plan to kill the witch was bold and unexpected. For once he left his trusted captain Rufus behind, for he had seen the effect of the sorceress on him. He chose, as always, his faithful

342

Martin to accompany him and the brave Siward, who if truth were ever to be known had killed more Normans than any other Englishman in the battle for Ely, Hereward included.

Brother Godric too was left behind and therefore no accurate account of what happened, other than Hereward's, is known, but many in the abbey saw the flint-knappers of Bromdun dispossessed of their boat despite the protests of Abbot Thurstan, who held traditional views on the sanctity of private property among Englishmen.

As a compromise, Hereward agreed to take the flint merchants with him as guides and extra hands at the oars, thus ensuring that the boat would remain in their possession, for he had no intention of returning in it. With its cargo of flints off-loaded and replaced with more weapons than it seemed three warriors could wield, the boat made good progress down the Wellstream and glided by Littleport in the grey, chilly afternoon. They were aided by the current until the boat turned into the tributary known as the Little Ouse, or Bromdun River, which required all five of them to row in harmony. As dusk began to fall, the boat cut through the water with Hockold Fen on the left and Lakingheath Fen to the right.

In truth Hereward was thankful for the presence of the flintknappers of Bromdun, for without them and their homing instincts, the boat would for sure have become entangled in the byways and streams of the wetlands which surrounded them.

It is also true to say that their reluctant guides gave thanks themselves when they landed the boat on the slopes of the higher ground which led

343

to Bromdun, for they were then free to hide in the reeds until Hereward's work was done.

The manor at Bromdun was a long house with many stables and barns by it. If anything it was a richer house, its wealth based on the trade in flints, than the manor of Bourne which Hereward had so long coveted and, like Bourne, it was occupied by Normans.

It was not difficult to find even in the dark of night for the patrol Baron Ivo had sent there thought themselves safe from attack and had lit lamps which could be seen from great distances, as well as cooking fires and the smell of roasting meat acted as a lure to the hungry heroes of Ely.

Martin Lightfoot, because of his skill with horses, volunteered to scout the manor and its outbuildings and returned to Hereward's side to report that there were ten cavalry ponies stabled there and only one sleepy sentry warming his boots by a glowing brazier near the corner of the house.

'Take him first,' Hereward ordered his companions, 'then the rest but remember to leave one alive.'

'Let Martin keep one alive,' said Siward, 'for I will not remember to be merciful.'

'And it is not in my nature to be kind to Normans,' said Hereward, grinning in the dark, 'so it must be Martin the Merciful this night.'

In the boat from Ely they had brought all manner of weapons, among them a sack of torches prepared with the last oil and pitch available on the Isle. Hereward took charge of these and selected his firesteel blade and a short-

344

handled axe as his weapons. Siward likewise took up sword and axe, while Martin chose a length of stout rope fashioned into a noose and a pair of daggers with bone handles and long, finely honed blades.

In the dark, Siward said: 'I have never murdered men asleep in their beds before.'

To which Hereward replied: 'Then we had better wake the bastards up! It's the least we can do before we send them to eternal sleep.'

The massacre at Bromdun Manor began with the strangling of the lone sentry with Martin Lightfoot's noose. Then Hereward lit his torches from the dead man's brazier and gave two to each of his companions. They had no need of further instructions, their faces glowed red and wild in the light as the three warriors ran around the house setting fire to the thatch eaves.

The roof caught quickly, for thatch will burn however damp the air, and then Siward used his axe to smash in the front door and the Englishmen threw their torches into the house.

'Awake! Awake!' shouted Hereward. 'For Death comes to you from Ely this night!'

Without waiting for a reply to his challenge, Hereward charged into the house with Siward hot on his heels, swinging their blades and laying about them as their torches set alight the Normans' straw bedding. Into this soon blazing inferno of flames and blood and screams, ran Martin Lightfoot, who skewered one dazed and choking trooper with a dagger before slipping the noose he carried over the head of a second who was struggling from his blankets. That one he

345

dragged outside like a dog and held a blade to his eye whilst his companions completed the slaughter.

The Norman garrison of Bromdun were dead before the main frame timbers of the manor caught alight, though as Hereward and Siward escaped they were showered with burning thatch which fell from the collapsing roof.

His chest heaving, his face grimed with soot and his beard smoking from still burning embers of thatch, Hereward stood astride their single prisoner and allowed fresh blood from the blade of his sword to drip on the man's face.

'We came all the way from Ely to see your king,' he said, speaking in Flemish which the Norman seemed to understand better than English, 'but he is not here, so you will have to take my challenge to him.'

'Challenge?' asked the terrified prisoner.

'Take a horse and fly to your master. Is it Warenne or Cut-Bush?'

'We ... are ... men of Baron Taillebois,' stammered that helpless man who did not know that Taillebois's name in English had a cruder meaning.

'Then get back to your baron and tell him you have been spared only to deliver this challenge: that Hereward, rightful Lord of Bourne in Lincolnshire and sworn defender of Ely Abbey, challenges William of Normandy to meet him in single combat at any place of his choosing, so that this war may be settled once and for all.'

The trooper rose unsteadily to his feet, mouth agape as if he had witnessed a miracle; then he turned and ran for the stables without looking back.

Hereward wiped the blade of his sword against his leather breeches and looked at the burning manor house now well ablaze.

'Shit! We've got to get the tunics and mail off those dead Normans before they burn. Come on, let's do it. I hate it when they crisp up like pork crackling.'

[x]

Later, the crossbowmen on the watchtowers on Stuntney claimed they had seen the flames of Bromdun Manor across some fifteen miles of fenland, as it burned that night, though they could not know the source of the fire.

It was in the hour before noon that the sole survivor of the Bromdun patrol rode wildly into the Norman camp at Stuntney and craved an audience with his liege lord Taillebois; On his knees in the Baron's tent, with Sir William looking on, the poor wretch begged forgiveness for deserting his post and abandoning his fellow troopers, but mostly for repeating the message given to him by Hereward.

'You are sure it was Hereward the Outlaw?' demanded the Baron.

'He was a giant of a man with long golden hair and he carried a decorated blade and his eyes shone like an animal's even in the night, and he had a guard of thirty or more battle-trained warriors.'

'You lie, soldier. Until you said that last, I was prepared to believe you,' said Sir William slowly, his hand moving to the dagger in his belt, 'but there are not thirty battle-trained warriors on the entire Isle of Ely. That's what makes this pathetic little war rather embarrassing. Now tell the truth or by God I'll relieve you of that which you had always thought a woman would want some day. How many men did Hereward have with him?'

'Two, my Lord, that I saw.'

'And so how did they best ten of you?' snarled Ivo.

'They fired the manor while we slept.'

'That sounds like Hereward,' said the baron nodding in agreement with himself. 'And he told you to deliver this ... challenge.. . of his?'

'Yes, my Lord. Hereward challenges King William to single combat.'

'That *definitely* sounds like Hereward,' agreed Sir William.

The two commanders whipped their men into action and within the hour a company of some eighty men were armed and mounted. They were despatched for Bromdun accompanied by three of Sir William's favourite wolfhounds and four local men from Stuntney pressed into service as guides because they knew the safe paths through the Fens and had wives and children who could be left behind as hostages.

As soon as the company had departed, Sir William took Baron Ivo on one side.

'A word, old friend, concerning this challenge thrown down by Hereward.'

'Will the King accept?'

'Don't be ridiculous! There are enough men of noble birth waiting in line to fight William without him having to bother himself with mad, landless English outlaws. It was not the challenge itself, but his delivery of it which could play to our advantage.'

'It could?'

'Think, my dear Baron. If Hereward is at Bromdun killing your men and delivering his challenge, *then he is not* on Ely. The rebels there will have seen our cavalry assemble and depart so they may suspect that Hereward has struck some sort of blow, but will not know the outcome. All they know is that Hereward has not yet returned. And that is what we play to our advantage. We spread the rumour that Hereward is dead, killed by King William himself if you like, and our men have ridden to Bromdun today to collect his head, which we will send over on the catapult tomorrow. That ought to get them shitting themselves.'

'A worthy plan,' said Ivo, rubbing his hands together, 'but how do we spread that rumour over on the Isle?'

'God's face, Ivo, you have a witch, don't you? Let's use her!'

[xi]

But Hereward and his companions were not in Bromdun. In fact they were closer to Stuntney than Bromdun, which they had left while the embers of the manor house still lit the night.

They had dressed themselves as best they could

in the chain mail, tunics and helmets of the dead and singed Normans and then helped themselves to whatever provisions they could find unburned, for men at war eat whenever and whatever they can. Then they selected two Norman ponies each and, guided by Lightfoot, who knew the land (and more importantly, the water) they rode hard through the remainder of the night and into the dawn.

On high, dry ground not far from Soeham, they hid in a copse of trees from which they could overlook the track from Stuntney which looped around the fenland to Bromdun, tethered the horses, lay down on their cloaks and slept the morning away.

Around midday they were woken by the pangs of hunger but dare not risk a cooking fire even though Siward offered to kill and butcher one of the horses they had ridden and were now abandoning for a fresher mount. Lightfoot climbed the tallest tree in the copse, from where he could see the wooden watchtowers on the banks of the Ouse and also the frenzied activity in the Norman camp at Stuntney.

When the company of cavalry rode out for Bromdun, as Hereward had predicted they would to his friends, they passed within half a mile of their quarry's hiding place.

As dusk began to fall, the three companions, armed and helmeted like Norman troopers, rode down from Soeham Moor and across the track on to Stuntney, riding through the outskirts of the Norman camp. They went unchallenged by sentries who felt secure in the knowledge that

Hereward was elsewhere being hunted by a company of their own knights.

Leaving their horses hobbled on the bank of the Ouse near the remains of the wrecked bridge to Theoford, they marched with heads high under first one watchtower and then a second. The third tower not only protected the two Norman catapults ranged on Ely but was also home to Baron Ivo's witch, and as full darkness came, torches and lamps were lit up the height of its outer frame. Thus the people of Ely could not forget her malicious presence no matter how familiar her screeching had become.

At the foot of the witch's tower, Norman artillerymen were loading their catapults with pots of pitch which they ignited before firing on to the Isle. These pots of liquid fire were smaller than the ones used in the bombardment of Theoford, for the distance to Ely was greater, and could be carried by one man alone. Hereward's roving eye located a pile of these earthenware pots and with impunity, he and his companions began to move the pile closer to the base of the watchtower.

The men working the *mangonels* were too intent on sending fire pots to burn Ely and the guards on the other tower strained their eyes watching the far bank of the river. None realized that their biggest enemy was at that very moment among them.

Baron Ivo's witch, high atop her torch-lit tower with a snake as long as a Norman lance and twice as thick draped around her shoulders, would have seen nothing untoward had she looked down. But she did not, so intent was she on chanting her

351

curses into the night towards Ely.

'Are there any men left on the Island of Eels?' she cackled, holding the python above her head. 'If there are, they will go hungry this winter for this wise old serpent who is my familiar tells me he has cursed these swamps and streams so that eels will never more breed there.'

To the eel fishermen of Ely this was indeed a curse which carried much fear, but the witch had not finished with them.

'There again, I say to my serpent: "Are there any men left on Ely?" and he tells me that with his snake's eyes he can see not a single one! All the real men that there were on Ely went to their deaths in a place called Bromdun yesterday. They were the brave men of Ely, who went out to challenge King William and valiantly they went to the fight, but I had put a curse on their sword-arms and a charm to watch over King William, though he was protected by God and the right of kings and made short work of those foolish men who opposed him.

'I saw the King strike them down one after the other in a vision as clear as day and by tomorrow you will see proof for yourselves, for the heads of those foolish men will dangle from this tower as playthings for my python. I have seen these things and my curses brought them about, for none should doubt the power of Fion, the Sorceress of Cambridge.'

As the witch began to sing in a high-pitched whine whilst plucking at a small harp, turning her body in a circular dance on the platform of the watchtower, Hereward, many feet directly below her, was planning her death.

The artillerymen, busy firing the catapult, had not noticed that most of their pots of pitch and oil were now stacked around the witch's tower, so intent were they on cranking back the catapult for another shot.

As they loaded a pot into the cup of the catapult and put a torch to the rags at the neck of the pot, Hereward struck the first blow, but he struck not at a man but at that pot with its smouldering fuse still on the arm of the catapult. The jar smashed into a thousand pieces under Hereward's blade and the contents poured out, igniting on the fuse of rags.

Suddenly night became day and liquid fire flew into the faces of those nearest the catapult save for Hereward who had turned away even as he struck and though he felt a scorching on the back of his neck as he walked away, his back to the flames, he had once again shown that fire was his friend and favourite weapon of choice.

It was the signal for Siward to use his axe to smash the pots they had stacked against the tower and for Martin to remove one of the torches from the tower frame.

Having seen the catapult set on fire below her and observing the confusion and panic of running men, the witch had halted her cursing ritual and had thrown one leg over the platform to begin to climb to earth.

It was only then that she saw the three men dressed in soldiers' garb standing at the base of the tower looking up at her. And she saw one hand a lit torch to another and then the one holding the torch removed his Norman helmet and shook his head.

In the light of the burning catapult she saw that the man had long golden hair and that he smiled at her as he dropped the torch at his feet.

[xii]

'God had stretched his arm over the men of Ely that night for the Normans did not challenge them,' reported Brother Godric, 'though it is true they were more concerned to quell the fire consuming their infernal engine of war rather than save the witch of Cambridge. As the fire spread up her tower, Hereward and Siward laid into the wood with their axes and when the structure fell, God guided it to fall on the Norman catapult.'

'God works in all ways, some of them mysteries to us,' said Abbot Thurstan quietly, then indicated that Godric should continue.

'As the tower cracked and swayed, Hereward was heard to shout to the witch that it was he, Hereward, who was not dead, who had come to show the Pythoness the value of a true curse applied with fire and sword.'

'Hereward cursed *her?*' asked Thurstan with an air of disapproval.

'I heard it with my own ears, my Lord, for by now the fire in the Norman camp had drawn all the men of Ely to the riverbank.'

'It must have been quite a spectacle,' said the sacrist, 'but then Hereward always did put on a good show for his men.'

'It was as if the very fires of hell were reaching up out the ground to grasp that sorceress. When the timbers gave way and the tower collapsed, Hereward and his kinsman Siward leapt in to the inferno and hacked that evil creature to pieces. Hereward emerged from the smoke carrying her head by her hair and in the light of the fire we saw him spit on it and throw it into the river. Captain Siward emerged with her python and it too had lost its head.

'It was only then that the Normans on the other watchtowers seemed to realize that their enemy was among them and began to fire their cross-bows and it seemed as if our warriors would surely be captured or killed. But then Martin Lightfoot appeared from the reeds almost as if by magic, with three ponies in tow.'

'There is nothing magical about Lightfoot and the sudden acquisition of horses,' interrupted the sacrist, but Godric was not chastened by this.

'Our warriors mounted and urged the ponies to plunge into the river, which they did for they feared the water less than they did the flames and confusion of the Norman camp. The ponies swam for our shore, bearing Hereward, Siward and Lightfoot as though they were guardian angels sent to guide them home.'

'Steady on, Brother Godric,' warned the sacrist.

'They reached the Isle safely although the air was thick with Norman arrows and iron bolts and our men rushed to pull them from the water with a great cheer, even with the body of the witch's great python!'

'God must be thanked that none of our defenders were hurt,' said the abbot solemnly.

'I am afraid we have three souls to pray for,' said Godric sadly, 'for two men and a boy were shot with crossbow bolts as they pulled men and horses from the river.'

'Why did they bring the witch's python with them?' asked the sacrist in honest wonderment.

'Hereward insists they make good eating. He says they taste like chicken.'

The defenders of Ely and their heroes had three days and nights to celebrate their victory over the Cambridge witch. On the edges of Grunty Fen, out of range of the Norman missiles, they lit fires and told stories throughout the cold nights, feasting on snake meat and horse flesh thanks to the Norman ponies Hereward had brought with him.

They felt themselves safe, for the witch was gone, their captains had returned, they had food and they took warmth from their fires against the chilly nights. During the days they welcomed the rains of winter, for they knew the waters of the Fens and the rivers would rise and make the Isle of Ely even more of a fortress.

But simple men forget and sometimes see only that which they want to.

Rising rivers and broadening Fens may well have made it more difficult for an invader on foot or horse to cross to Ely, but they only eased the way for an invader who came by boat.

[xiii]

In the first week of December, Sir William de

Warenne and Baron Taillebois were summoned from the camp at Stuntney and ordered to report to Cambridge Castle. The rider who delivered this message left them in no doubt that it was an order and not a request.

They found the frosty mud streets of Cambridge churning with horses and men wearing the liveries of the noblest houses of Normandy and the King's own standard draped from the main gate of the castle. The yards and halls of the castle itself teemed with monks, all versed in languages and the law and all chosen by the King's brother, Bishop Odo, who followed King William like crows dancing around carrion. It was said that William liked to record every piece of property he stole and that he demanded a lawyer's seal of approval on every death sentence he dispensed; but if it was said, it was said quietly.

Ivo and Sir William were received by a pair of monkish clerks in the company of six of the King's personal bodyguard, which comprised only the hardest men of Caen in Normandy, who relieved them of their swords (as was the custom when the king himself went unarmed).

They were shown in to a small hall with a fireplace in which a log fire blazed and a table on which beeswax candles burned. There was a jug there and goblets and the monk who ushered them in told them it was wine should they wish to partake, and he could have food brought from the kitchen by one of the gluttons if the two noble lords were hungry.

Baron Ivo poured himself wine from the jug and tasted it, smacking his lips in approval for although the wine was of poor quality, it was the first he had tasted in several months.

'I wonder what King William wants of us?' said Ivo, unaware that the doors of the hall had been opened for their host.

'The King requires nothing of you except your loyalty,' came a voice, the sound of which chilled both men. 'He has come to Cambridge for one reason only and that is to tell you, my noble lords, how he is going to get rid of this little fucker Hereward once and for all!'

'My King,' said the two lords together, bowing as was expected.

'I am glad you remember *me,* for *you* have been ever in my thoughts these past six – or is it seven? – months whilst you have been away from me fighting this terrible enemy in the east and I have been merely fighting enemies in the north, in the west and in the south of this country.'

De Warenne, who was said to fear no man save King William, bowed again, but lower this time.

'My Lord, this war of ours in the east should never have gone this far, for it is merely a pea-sants' revolt inspired by some foolish monks.'

'Then why has it lasted so long, this revolt as you call it?' demanded the King.

'Because of one man,' said De Warenne. 'A man called Hereward.'

'That name again. I have already heard songs in the street about this outlaw. I hear he even issued a challenge to me. For such impudence alone he deserves to die, though his other crimes are legion.'

'Ely is not an easy place to take, my King,' said

Baron Ivo nervously, 'nor Hereward an easy man
to kill.'

'Not so far, my dear Baron,' said the King, 'but
things have changed. I'm here now.'

[xiv]

King William's plan was simple: he intended to
attack the Isle of Ely simultaneously by land and
by water and he made it clear that he expected
his barons to make the plan work whatever the
cost to their estates and fortunes.

The barons, said the King, had tried assault with
cavalry, bombardment, besiegement and even
witchcraft. Now was the time to use the strategy
for which the Normans were famed – overwhelming force, showing mercy to none save the Holy
Church.

Sir William pleaded that he and Baron Ivo had
not been idle and their plan had been to distract
the defenders of Ely to the east while the engineers the King had sent had been working in
secret to the south and were now ready to repair
the causeway at Aldreth, having prepared sandbags to fill the smaller holes and planking to span
the widest breaches. Such preparations had been
made in secret and it would be possible, if the
right moment was chosen, to repair and cross the
causeway in a single rush.

'I have heard much of this causeway at Aldreth,
but I also hear that from Aldreth to Ely is a distance of seven miles through these flooded fields
they call Fens. To cross these with an army at

speed would require local guides for I believe there to be secret paths known only to those born on that damned island.'

'The King is remarkably well-informed,' observed Sir William.

'That's why I'm a king,' came the King's curt reply, 'whilst you have spent half a year paddling around these bloody swamps being humiliated by a bunch of cut-throat outlaws. I want this ended! Within a week!'

The two Norman commanders stared at each other in silence.

'My Lord, that is not possible,' said Baron Ivo, steeling himself for one of King William's famous outbursts of temper.

'Why so, my dear Baron? You have assured me the causeway at Aldreth can be bridged so that my army can cross. I have already sent a fleet around the coast to this place called Lynne. By now they will have entered the River Ouse and they have orders to lay off the island of Littleport. They should be in position in two days,' said the King calmly.

'They attack from the north?'

'They do not attack at all. They are there to be *seen* and we must make sure they are seen and that the defenders of Ely take note of my personal standards which will be flown from those ships, so they will *think* I intend to attack from the north.'

'But you will invade from the south,' said De Warenne, 'at Aldreth.'

'Quite so, Sir William,' said the King through a curled lip. 'With a grasp of strategy such as you show I am only amazed that this Hereward has outwitted you so long.'

'It is this damned Fenland, my Lord, which has confounded us as much as Hereward,' Sir William said in his defence. 'The Fens are treacherous and the water in them rises every day with the winter tides and the rains. You may get an army across to Aldreth but by the time it is in position to besiege the town of Ely, the rebels will have vanished into the mists.'

'I have no intention of besieging Ely itself, I will simply ride in there and I will do it before the rebels even know I have crossed on to the Isle.'

'That is not possible, my Lord,' said Ivo before thinking.

'I say it is and I am King.'

'The King intends to cross Grunty Fen,' said De Warenne, 'and enter Ely from the west, by land, while the rebels are watching for an attack from the east or from the water.'

'Can it be done?' Ivo blurted out.

'I will do it with speed and surprise!' announced King William proudly. 'Speed and surprise.'

'My Lord, it is not possible to cross Grunty Fen with an army at speed.'

'It is if you have guides who know the secret paths of the Fenmen!'

The King clasped his arms around his chest, which was something he was known to do in his rare moments of happiness.

'Where would we find such guides, my Lord?' asked De Warenne.

'Among the good monks of Ely itself,' said the King with a broad smile. 'That's the surprise.'

Unknown to his barons, King William had sent two monks as messengers to Ely. They had departed from Cambridge in a small rowing boat the night before with instructions to remain totally silent, keep their shallow-drafted punt in midstream and if challenged by either side, to speak only Latin. The monks were hard men, schooled at the Fecamp monastery in Normandy and were prepared to suffer any hardship; such was their devotion to their church and their duke. They had been recommended to the task by Bishop Odo, whom they feared more than King William, who in turn they feared far more than Hereward and the Fenland rebels.

The two messengers, whose names are known only to God, floated down the River Cam and then their tiny craft joined the stronger River Ouse. In darkness, they passed the Norman pickets on the Stuntney shore unchallenged. In truth, these sentries were reluctant to take up positions too close to the river bank after seeing what had happened to the Cambridge Sorceress, and the rain which now fell by day and night persuaded them further to remain close to their tents.

They were totally unseen from the Ely shore until they rounded the bend in the river beyond the Isle of Stuntney. There two brothers from the abbey, casting a fishing net into the river from the wooden docks in the misty dawn, just having come from the prayers which Benedictines call Lauds, saw them and recognizing their habits, waved for them to make a landing.

The messengers were taken to meet with the sacrist, who gave instructions that no other soul on the Isle be told of their presence and then in the abbey church, they delivered the King's message to Abbot Thurstan.

The good and gentle abbot listened in silence, but tears were pouring down his face when he asked: 'Is there no other way?'

And the sacrist said there was not.

[xvi]

As was expected, when the first Norman boats appeared in the Wellstream north of Littleport, they drew the defenders of Ely like flies to a carcase. So many craft had not been seen on the river for many months, since the Danes had deserted the Isle; indeed, many of the boats now used by King William were those stolen originally by King Svein of Denmark. Their rightful owners from the coast around Lynne and Wisbech got little use of them that year.

Though he could not have known it (but being the King he probably did), William's naval force positioned so close to Littleport ensured that Hereward's attention would be concentrated there. It took strong counsel from Martin Lightfoot to prevent him from going immediately to Littleport to recover his portion of the Peterborough treasure which he buried there six months before.

There was no doubt, argued Lightfoot, that it

was foolish to consider such an act in daylight in view of Norman ships and with all the defenders of Ely at their side – for the rebel Fenmen were looking to Hereward for leadership in dealing with the King's fleet, which they felt sure would dock at Ely itself. Eventually Hereward agreed with his loyal friend that it was wisest not to do anything to draw attention to Littleport, but to defend Ely instead.

'I will burn the hythes and landing places around their ears if they try to land at Ely, then I will burn their boats so William the Bastard will have to swim back to Normandy!'

The men of Ely loved Hereward even more for this defiance and began to build what defences they could, from whatever they could. As there was no oil or pitch left on the Isle, they constructed fire-traps from casks crammed with fine wood shavings and sawdust and every length of timber taller than a man was sharpened to a point and lodged in the frame of the docks so that if the Norman boats attempted to land, their soldiers would have to climb over the back of a man-made hedgehog.

The captains Siward and Rufus were overseers of this work, while Hereward strode along the shoreline at the northernmost tip of the Isle, his sword in its heavy sheath (now more famous than the firesteel blade itself for the number of Norman heads it had broken) across his shoulders. He made sure that all his men saw him walking there, unafraid, proud and defiant, and would from time to time shout a challenge, in the crudest of terms, to the Norman boats visible on the Wellstream beyond Littleport. It is unlikely that the invaders could hear such a challenge at such a distance, but the men of Ely reasoned that if they could see the enemy, then the enemy could see Hereward and it was as if his very presence, in open view, was keeping them at bay.

For the fleet did not move, instead its leading boats anchored themselves so they formed a line across the river halfway between Littleport and the junction with the Bromdun River and there they stayed all day. Had the men of Ely more skill with numbers, they would have noticed the next morning as the fog rising off the river slowly melted away, that the number of Norman boats had increased three-fold.

Siward, who could count, urged the defenders of Ely (for now they truly were defenders of the town) to greater efforts and made the abbey smithy work through day and night to put a cutting edge on every piece of metal they could find, whilst Rufus and Lightfoot roamed the abbey itself searching for weapons or food, though they found none of either.

At noon, Hereward bade his captains walk with him along the northern shoreline where they could talk in private but still be seen by their men, for Hereward knew their spirit and courage would shatter like glass if their heroes were not in plain sight.

'Ely has not seen so many boats in many months,' said Siward, pointing down river.

'But they have not tried to land any troops,' grunted Rufus. 'Perhaps they are sitting in those boats shitting themselves at the thought of fight-

365

ing us.'

'Why don't they land on Littleport?' said Hereward, betraying his thoughts.

'They would gain no advantage,' answered Lightfoot wisely, 'unless they had guides to take them across the fords from that Isle to this and no man of the Fens would betray us to the Normans that way.'

'We should pray that is so and so should the people of Littleport, for if any there betray us I swear I will burn their homes and slaughter them all.'

'We have nothing to fear from Littleport,' said Lightfoot so that only Hereward could hear him. 'Only Hraga the Heron who was with us when we buried the Lady Turfrida's treasure and he is dead. Most of the villagers of Littleport have already fled either into the Fens or into the abbey here, with the other women of the Isle.'

'Did you find anything useful in the abbey?' Hereward asked.

'Old women, babies and lots of prayer,' answered Rufus. 'Nothing useful in a fight.'

'This is not a fight we can win, is it, Hereward?' said Siward.

'Do not say that, old friend. The Normans are not on Ely and we are not dead yet, but we might get the monks to pray for us at vespers.' Hereward spoke with a smile and his eyes flashed. 'If King William comes we will crack his skull and put a skewer in his liver. If he bests us here on Ely, we fly into the Fens and fight on from there. You see how the Fenmen love us. They will hide us; they will feed us.'

'They have little enough to feed themselves this winter,' said Siward gloomily.

'Then we must ask our gracious Abbot Thurstan to pray for full bellies for the simple folk of these Fens, as well as for their souls. We must ask Brother Godric to speak to the abbot for us. Where is Godric? I have not seen him today.'

The four warriors stood in a circle and exchanged glances but only Martin Lightfoot answered:

'He is not in the abbey precincts, and neither is the abbot.'

[xvii]

Even as Lightfoot spoke, the first Norman horses were treading on to the firm ground of the Isle of Ely, being greeted at Aldreth by Abbot Thurstan, his sacrist and a distraught Brother Godric.

The defence of the causeway at Aldreth had been left in the trust of four young boys, who were not expected to fight but to run with a warning to Hereward and Siward in Ely should danger approach them from across the river. Wet, hungry and shivering behind their earthworks, they did not expect an enemy to approach them from behind and so were surprised and frightened by the three hooded figures which loomed out of the dusk and though they cried out in terror they were soon comforted by the familiar face of the kindly Thurstan.

They recognized Brother Godric too, for he had been with them at Aldreth before and they knew him to be a man trusted by Hereward, but the third monk they did not know and they sensed, as only children and animals can, that he wished to remain aloof from them. Thurstan had no reservations about offering his cloak to protect two of the boys from the cold evening rain and persuading all four to kneel in the mud with him in prayer. Their enthusiasm for such prayer was bolstered when Godric produced from his satchel a few strips of smoke-dried eel, which they devoured with relish.

Because he was their abbot, the spiritual leader of the Isle of Ely, and because they were young and of low birth, the boys did not dare question the presence of Thurstan and his monks that night on the causeway at Aldreth. When he told them he would stand guard that night and they could sleep, they did as they were told, but boys being boys, at least one was likely to have been awake when Brother Godric and the tall, un-smiling monk who kept his arms within his cloak, lit a small pottery cresset lamp and placed it on the highest part of the earthwork, its tiny flickering flame facing out across the dark, rain-swept causeway.

But in the flat Fens, a tiny light can be seen for miles even on the stormiest of nights and this one was soon answered by a dozen or more torches from the Cottenham side of the causeway.

By midday, just as Hereward and his captains were inspecting the defences of Ely seven miles away, Norman engineers completed their makeshift repairs to the damaged causeway. The first cavalry horses to cross the repaired breach did so blindfolded so they could not see the rotting corpses of men and horses which were still trapped in the brown water under the sandbags and timbers with which the engineers had plugged the gaps, though their riders saw them if they looked down, and they shuddered.

With a troop of cavalry on Ely and the Norman engineers already dismantling the earthworks thrown up by Siward, flags were waved to the far end of the causeway and King William, surrounded by his bodyguard, advanced on to the Isle which had defied him for so many months.

There was no army to oppose him, but likewise there were no crowds to cheer him, only three tired and downcast monks and four frightened boys and for such an audience the King would not even dismount and he left speech to Sir William de Warenne who rode to his left.

'You are Abbot Thurstan,' pronounced Sir William, pointing with his riding crop, 'who has defied the lawful King of England and harboured outlaws and rebels here on Ely.' It was not a question, more a judgement; then his crop flicked towards the other two robed and hooded figures.

'The crippled one is known to me, but the young one is not. Is he to be our guide?'

'I will be your guide across Grunty Fen,' said Thurstan proudly. 'I would not allow another to perform the task I have agreed to.'

'Well said, good Brother. Do you now acknowledge William of Normandy to be your rightful King?'

'I don't give a fuck whether he does or not,' growled the King himself, 'as long as he knows the way across this swamp. Lead on, old man. Let us get this over with.'

Thus it was Abbot Thurstan's penance, or so he thought, to lead the soldiers of the Conqueror to their last victory over honest Englishmen, for never again was William faced with rebellion from the lowest peasantry fighting to protect their church.

Over secret paths unknown to any save a handful of Fenmen, Thurstan safely led the Norman column who always had firm ground under their feet even though the slightest diversion from the path would have seen man and horse disappear to their doom under the matted weeds. Fearing ambush or treachery, King William had deployed a troop of crossbowmen to walk ten paces behind the three monks who led the way. In the deepest part of Grunty, where the reeds still stood tall as a man even in winter, these archers exchanged looks of curiosity when they heard the sobbing of the old abbot, for the nearer they got to Ely, the more inconsolable he became.

'You have done what had to be done, Father Abbot,' the sacrist said, throwing his left arm over Thurstan's heaving shoulders. 'For the good of the abbey, the Church and the people of Ely.'

'Were we not acting for the good of the abbey and the Church when we began this rebellion?' replied Thurstan through floods of tears.

'God will judge us,' said the sacrist.

'But William will judge Hereward,' said Godric who had remained silent until now.

'Hereward will not be taken alive,' answered the sacrist.

'And how many will die fighting for him?' sobbed the abbot. 'There has been enough kill-ing.'

'They will not fight for Hereward if he deserts them,' said the sacrist softly.

'The men love him and he loves their loyalty,' wailed Godric. 'Why would he desert them?'

'I know why,' said the sacrist, keeping his eyes to the ground as the three men walked and talked. 'There is something Hereward wants even more than a glorious death fighting the King of England in single combat, which everyone except Hereward knows is never going to be.'

'We will soon emerge from Grunty at the hamlet of Witchford. You must go ahead of us, Godric. We will tell the Normans you have gone to calm the villagers, if there are any left there, which I doubt. Once you are out of sight, you must run to the abbey and seek out the librarian. Tell him you are acting for me and you require a particular scroll which he will find in with the books and rolls brought here from Peterborough. It is a petition to the Assizes from many years ago, detailing the claims of Toki of Lincoln – your father, as well as Hereward's grandfather – to the manor and estates of Bourne in Lincolnshire. Take this scroll to Hereward with all speed and tell him the Normans will be on him before nightfall and if he is to claim Bourne Manor he must take these deeds and leave Ely immediately. With him gone, the King will be merciful.'

'But we do not know that to be true,' argued the young and innocent Godric.

'We can but pray that the King will be merciful,' said Thurstan, choking back yet more tears. 'You must do as my faithful sacrist commands.'

'No,' said Godric, 'we know that the scroll is a petition to the court drawn up by clerks under the old laws, it is not the deeds to the manor.'

'We know that,' said the sacrist, 'but Hereward cannot read.'

[xviii]

Thus did the siege of Ely end, not with the clash of mighty armies or the personal combat of champions, nor by the intervention of God, but with a frightened young monk running through the rain along the docks with a scroll of worthless parchment in his sleeve.

King William and his army emerged from Grunty Fen at Witchford, which was all but deserted save for a few old women and even fewer young children, and William ordered his baggage train to be brought up and his camp to be established there, for he refused to grace rebellious Ely with his presence that night.

Then, in the failing afternoon light, he charged on Ely with two hundred heavy cavalry and the very sound of their hooves pounding on the earth made many a Fen-dweller turn and run before they even saw them.

Unopposed, William entered Ely from the south and immediately sent signallers to the riverbank where they shot two fire arrows into the air to signal the Norman fleet anchored down the Well-stream.

Those fire arrows and the sight of the distant Norman ships beginning to move slowly towards them, were the first indications many of the defenders of Ely there on the northern bank of the Isle had that the enemy was upon them. When a Norman patrol was seen riding by the gates of the abbey itself, many a rebel fell to his knees and began to pray.

Many more looked to prayer rather than their weapons when they saw two files of Normans advancing upon their positions. On the one flank, Baron Taillebois commanded the archers, on the other Sir William de Warenne led the cavalry; and even as Baron Ivo gave the order for the first volley of bolts to be fired, Fenmen could be seen throwing down their weapons and plunging into the river, for on that northern tip of the Isle, there was nowhere else to go.

Sir William's cavalry advanced but at only a slow trot for there was no room for a charge at speed, nor any need, for most of the defenders of Ely allowed themselves to be squeezed into a circle of Norman spears as a sign of surrender.

Later, when reporting to the King, Baron Ivo said that the rebels had all seemed bewitched or dazed, as if they had been drunk the night before, and all were heard to say the same thing: 'Hereward. Where is Hereward?'

When King William demanded an answer to the very same question, none could be given, not even from the captains Siward and Rufus who had also, as if under some sort of spell, surrendered without a fight.

That night William's torturers worked hard and

373

late under his personal supervision. In the court-yard of the abbey they cut a hand off the first twenty Fenmen prisoners, a foot off the next twenty and they blinded a further twenty, for such was the penalty for treason. Recognizing fellow warriors in the characters of Siward and his cousin Rufus, William did not have them maimed, but hanged them from a crossbeam of the wooden dock of Ely so the lower half of the bodies provided food for the fish of the River Ouse.

Although this happened a week before Christmas, King William did not celebrate Mass in Ely Abbey.

He entered the abbey precincts just the once before retiring to his camp at Witchford, entering the abbey church accompanied by Sir William and Baron Ivo and watched by the brethren of Ely he threw a single gold mark on to the altar and proclaimed:

'I pay God for this desecration.'

In the days which followed the lifting of the siege of the Isle of Ely, many more tears were shed as more Fenmen were caught and maimed, their wives raped by the invaders, their children taken and given into slavery, though not a single monk of Ely was harmed. It proved to be the harshest of winters.

Sir William de Warenne was appointed the guarantor of the peace on Ely and his first duty was to fine Abbot Thurstan one thousand marks for not welcoming the King properly. Ely Abbey was also charged with the cost of supporting a permanent garrison of Norman cavalry who were to ensure that rebellion was indeed a thing of the past in the Fenlands.

But of Hereward and Martin Lightfoot – and Brother Godric – there was no sign.

Nineteen

Giraldus

Can Brother Thomas really leave his history like this? Can it be that Hereward the Hard Man, Hereward the Firestarter and Hereward the Witch-Killer is, at the end, merely Hereward the Coward who deserts his kinsmen, his army and the abbey he has sworn to defend?

For my patron, Baldwin le Wac, a small man fond only of the sound of his own voice, and his family tree, I need a hero. That was what I was holding out for. What Thomas's book has given me is less than that but also more in so many ways.

It is easy now for me to see how this Hereward of history became the stuff of legend, for all legends are planted in truth. Brother Thomas had no reason to lie, for his book was a true confession. He says himself he expects none to ever read it, which the professional historian may well think, but would never admit.

Once again, there is much in his account which is reflected in popular ballads and the folk tales of the common people. Anyone who has ever travelled in the east of England will have heard the story of how King William crossed to Ely stepping over the waterlogged bodies of dead horses and men, for it is a tale told to frighten small children and men in the alehouses of Cambridge, which is to say, the same thing.

But in his book, Thomas tells us how and when it happened for a fact and many other things of which he writes are justified by history or legal record.

It is certainly true that a garrison was imposed upon Ely and, later, under the first King Henry, a castle was built there, for Ely continued to pay for its rebellious nature long after Hereward had gone from that island sanctuary.

It is well-known that King William made his camp at Witchford, a place which is known for absolutely nothing else, rather than grace Ely with his own person. The story of his casting a single gold mark at the altar of the abbey church has also been told for generations, though whether this was a sign of piety or disdain depends on the teller of the tale.

It is recorded that Abbot Thurstan was fined one thousand marks by Sir William de Warenne for 'not welcoming the King properly'. It is also recorded – by Norman clerks in their great book of records – that more than three-quarters of the lands in the gift of Ely Abbey were transferred to (many would say stolen by) the very same William de Warenne at this time.

It is also a matter of fact that when Sir William eventually died quietly in his bed, his widow sent a gift of one hundred shillings to the monks of

Ely; a gift which was rejected and returned. It was even said that the monks there offered prayers not for the salvation, but for the damnation, of Sir William's soul, which they did willingly without payment or favour.

At the time Thomas was writing, more than thirty years after the events he clearly witnessed, Ely continued to be squeezed. During the building of the mighty cathedral there, Ely was charged to pay a rent no less than four thousand eels every Lent to Peterborough Abbey in exchange for stone from one of their quarries.

All this is documented elsewhere and known to historians, so I should have no reason to doubt the account this Thomas (whoever he was) gives of Hereward. Yet there is much to question in his account, for he seems to know more than any respectable historian should.

Could it be, could it possibly be that Thomas has told a story not of a heroic rebellion against an invader, but of an elaborate crime of some sort? A robbery perhaps? A robbery of one holy abbey, Peterborough, condoned by another, Ely, simply to restore the property of a wife of Flanders who knew she would be dispossessed under Norman law?

It cannot be so, for that is surely madness. Yet Thomas lays a trail which leads that way. But I do not have to follow that trail, even if it leads to the truth, for I am a renowned and respected historian.

Twenty

Thomas

The End of Hereward

[i]

What little is left to tell of Hereward is best told quickly and is known mostly from the witness of Brother Godric, for it was Godric who ran to Hereward with the news that the siege of Ely had been broken. And though he carried these tidings of Hereward's defeat, he also carried a parchment which held all Hereward's dreams.

Hereward and Lightfoot were patrolling the northern river bank together when Godric flew to their side and told them, breathlessly, that the Normans would be upon them before night and that they must flee.

'I do not fear the Normans!' Hereward growled. 'All I have is my life and they can have that – if they can take it!'

'But the people of Ely do fear them, Hereward, and they do not have your courage,' pleaded Godric and then he said a silent prayer before he continued. 'And you have more than your life to lose. I have been told to give you this scroll on which are the deeds to the Manor of Bourne.'

'Thurstan ordered you to give me this?'

378

'So they would not fall into King William's hands. Bourne is in your possession now but if you oppose the King openly – if you challenge him or fight his person here on Ely – then you will never have that estate, for he would have you hung for a traitor or a rebel.'

'And so we run? We leave our comrades here, who have suffered so much, to Norman mercy?' cried Lightfoot, for many on Ely were his kin.

'If you flee now, William takes the Isle without a fight, something his barons could not do in seven months. None will dispute his military genius and he will give thanks to God and show mercy to the Fenmen. If you draw your sword, the Fenmen will follow you to your death. You must leave this island now and never look back. Leave Ely and go back to Bourne.'

'So I am to be called Hereward the Coward? The Hard Man who ran away when his enemies got too close?' snarled Hereward.

'They cannot call you those things, for are you not a sworn man of Ely, just as you were once a sworn man of Peterborough?'

'I am; I am sworn before witnesses and before God.'

'Then no man will be able to slight you, for Thurstan the Abbot of Ely has ordered it so. You would only be doing your sworn duty.'

'What is to stop King William from hunting us down?'

The sacrist had warned Godric that Hereward would ask this.

'Why should he? He wants an end to this war before Christmas. Thurstan has surrendered the abbey and the Isle without bloodshed and William has promised not to punish those sworn to the abbey.'

Godric gave the answer he had been told to give even though in his own heart he was sure that William's clemency would apply only to the monks devoted to the abbey. The sacrist had said that Hereward would be satisfied with this answer, because it was the answer he wanted to hear. The sacrist had said that Hereward would not be able to take his eyes from the scroll purporting to be the deeds of Bourne and he had been right in that also, for though the writing on that scroll meant nothing to him, he believed it to mean everything.

In fact it meant his death.

[ii]

Without a glance back or shouted farewell, Hereward and Lightfoot left Ely by walking quickly to the one fordable place in the river which separated Ely from Littleport and plunging into the icy current. They took with them a reluctant Brother Godric despite his protestations, saying they had need of an honest man on Littleport.

Bemused, soaking wet and chilled to the bone, Godric trudged behind the two warriors as they strode towards the middle of the small isle to a cottage which they told the young monk had been the home of Hraga the stilt-walker.

There they met with Hraga's widow and told her she was a widow and that Hraga had died bravely and was buried at Aldreth. As there had been no traffic on the river for many months, little news had reached Littleport since the summer. Godric advised her to take her two painfully thin daughters and go to Ely to throw herself on the charity of Abbot Thurstan, a plan which Hereward supported with enthusiasm as he and Martin intended to take Hraga's boat, which would leave the widow without any means of feeding her children. Godric thought that this must be the reason Hereward had asked him to accompany them but there was another task for him to perform and that was to act as a witness.

In a small coppice behind Hraga's cottage, under the roots of the largest tree, Hereward and Martin dug away the light sandy soil with their hands until they revealed three large leather bags tied at the neck with stout rope. From one of them Hereward took a smaller purse of coins and then retied the bag and replaced it.

'Is this the treasure from Peterborough?' breathed Godric.

'It is from Peterborough, but it is not the treasure of the abbey there. The coins and precious stones and jewellery in these bags are all the property of my wife Turfrida under Old English law and under the laws of Flanders,' said Hereward. 'They were deposits made by her family in the years before the Normans came and blighted this land.'

'And a Norman abbot like Turold was not likely to recognize her rights of property, for under Norman law a woman's property belongs to her husband.'

'Who was declared outlaw by that very abbey in

381

Peterborough,' Hereward said, a smile returning to his face. 'So when Abbot Thurstan felt the need to protect all the treasures of Peterborough from the Normans, I offered to serve Ely and my wife at the same time.'

Hereward took six pennies and four half-pennies from the jangling purse he had recovered and handed them to Godric.

'These are for Hraga's widow. When there is food again on Ely, buy some for her. Tell her and anyone who asks that the money is for Hraga's boat, which is hidden in a creek to the west of here. I will not have it said that I stole from honest Englishmen.'

'Is this why you brought me here?'

'In part, good monk, in part. You have proved yourself both loyal and brave and you are not only a holy man but you are a kinsman – my uncle no less!' Now Hereward's smile was broad; a smile of genuine love, but also of sadness.

'This is why I chose you to see this hiding place. We cannot take Turfrida's treasure with us, so it will remain here until I return or my wife comes to England. You are now its guardian, dear uncle. Take care of it, for if you have ever had cause to fear me, believe me you will have more cause to fear my wife!'

'Your wife?' the monk said unsure of what he was hearing. 'Your wife will come to Ely?'

'If I do not return to St Omer, she will come here, you can be sure of that. She will know what happened here, for the monks of Ely and those of the Abbey of St Bertin are closer than real brothers and they gossip like old women. My wife hears all they say, for she is a witch and has the power to see into men's minds, though she lacks the power to see the future for I cannot think she saw my fate.'

'Only God knows what lies in the future for us,' said Godric.

'Of course that is so, my young and wise uncle,' said Hereward putting an arm around Godric's shoulders. 'And I know you will pray for me, because you are the only monk who has never played me false. I have been a sworn man of two holy abbeys. One of them outlawed me and one has now abandoned me. In Flanders I gave my allegiance to a wife, not an abbey. She has never played me wrong and never asked for anything save the return of her property.'

'But why not take it to her, Hereward? Go to Flanders with her treasure and live there as man and wife.'

'What sort of man would I be with no estates or position to offer her? She is a rich woman in her own right and will be a rich widow.'

'Do not speak of such things, Hereward,' chided Lightfoot gently. 'It can only bring us bad luck. We must get Hraga's boat into the water and take our bearings before dark.'

'Yes, we must go. Thank God you are still here to guide me, Martin.' Hereward spoke softly as if the life had gone out of him and he put his fingers to his forehead as though wounded.

'Are you hurt, Hereward?' Godric asked with tenderness.

'Hereward has a malady which is cured by the root of the Christmas Rose,' Lightfoot answered

383

for him, 'but we have none left. Some times he has nightmares during the day and his head aches, and at such times, the black seeds of the peony can help to soothe him.'

'Is this due to some poison or enchantment put upon him?' Godric spoke to Lightfoot, for it was as if Hereward's curiously mismatched eyes were open but did not see.

'He has suffered since we were boys. At times, his temper is the best medicine, which is why he likes to fight so much. It makes him forget his pain and any wounds to his body are slight when compared to the pain in his head. Only the Lady Turfrida knew how to soothe that pain, but even she could not cure it.'

'We must pray for him,' said Godric urgently. 'At Ely, we will have all the monks pray for him.'

'I do not think that would be allowed,' said Hereward, 'and besides, it is too late to pray for Hereward.'

Then Martin Lightfoot, groom, bodyguard and faithful attendant, took his master by the arm and led him away into the Fenland mists.

[iii]

'The mad bastard just walked away? After all we've been through, all the expense, all the humiliation, *we let* that fucker walk off into the marshes?'

'Calm yourself, Ivo,' said De Warenne. 'It is to our advantage.'

'How in God's name can it be to our advantage?' stormed the Baron, red in the face with rage and not a little drunk on the wine that he had purchased (at inflated prices) from stewards of King William's baggage train.

King William had kept good his promise not to grace Ely with his favour and had formed his camp at Witchford, leaving Taillebois and De Warenne to make their quarters in the abbey's chapter house. Their baggage and comforts had been carried there across the courtyard where Ivo's torturers were still busy imposing the penalty for rebellion on the limbs of the Fenmen.

Whilst Baron Ivo had taken charge of public punishments and the provision of victuals for the invading army, Sir William had installed a score of monks, all skilled in writing and accounting, to take an inventory of whatever remained of value on Ely and to hear (and mostly dismiss) the numerous petitions for clemency or the King's mercy which had begun almost before the Norman knights had tethered their horses.

'My dear Ivo, it must be to our advantage that Hereward is not to be found. We have avoided bloodshed, at least the blood of our own men and we have deprived our enemy of a martyr's death. We must make sure that everyone knows, not just here on Ely but far and wide, that Hereward ran rather than face King William. Let the legend of Hereward be a sour one. Let it say that he scuttled away into the swamps, leaving his captains and his men to torture and death.'

Baron Ivo allowed himself a smile and called for more wine.

'Good; I like that,' Taillebois nodded in agreement. 'But I would have liked to see that madman's head on a pole for all the trouble he has caused.'

'On a pole would be too public,' said Sir William, 'but I would sleep more soundly if I was sure his head was no longer on his body.'

'Then the King must hunt him down!'

'He will not. The war here is over and he sees no reason to boost Hereward's reputation with a manhunt. Of course, he would have no objection if the expense of such a hunt was carried by his loyal barons, and if it were done quietly.'

'But where would we start? The man has vanished into the wetlands. We could not take him when we knew he was on Ely, what chance do we have when he could be anywhere? He might even have...'

The baron stopped talking as a hooded figure shrouded in monk's robes approached them.

'I know where he is,' said the figure.

'Brother sacrist,' said Sir William, 'I was expecting it to be you.'

[iv]

With January, the first deep snows of the winter came to Lincolnshire, silencing the flat fields and woods with a white blanket. There had been no visitors to the village of Bourne for a month before Christmas and none were expected now until the snows had melted. Yet strangers came.

First, two thin and haggard men wrapped in blankets against the wind and riding lame horses, good only for their meat, passed through the village and if any villagers saw them, they did so though cracks in their doors or tears in their walls as they huddled in their hovels with their animals and waited for the riders to pass.

Neither man nor beast, save perhaps a winter hare, saw the riders approach Bourne Manor and force open the door. There was none there to stop them for the house had been deserted for over a year; its Norman lord, Ogier, having returned to Brittany a cripple unable to walk unaided and his Breton servants having decided to spend the winter in Lincoln.

For a week the two strangers carried firewood from one of the barns into the cold house and lit fires which burned all day, taking the edge off the winter. They also carried inside load after load of straw to serve as bedding, and in an earth-dug cellar they found a small amount of mouldy grain, strips of dried goat meat, a dozen jars of turnips pickled in brine and even a small cask of sour apple wine.

With one of the horses slaughtered and large joints of it roasting in the hall's fireplace, the two new residents of Bourne Manor were as comfortable as men could be as the snow fell even thicker outside.

Then came the others, the riders who came quietly and almost invisibly and with a single purpose.

Sir William de Warenne had selected twenty of his most trusted men from his personal bodyguard and Baron Taillebois did likewise. At his own expense, Sir William equipped them with the best horses, the best weapons and the warmest clothing, including fur-lined cloaks, seal-skin boots and white tunics which went over their chain mail and helped them blend with the snowy land.

On the edge of Bourne they dismounted and tethered their horses in the woods away from the main track from Peterborough. Leaving six men to guard their string of mounts, Sir William, Baron Ivo and over thirty men, many of whom had lost comrades and kin at Aldreth, Bromdun, Burwell or Stuntney, circled the village on foot until they came to the manor house.

They were guided without error by a monk who had been there before.

The soldiers could smell their prey long before they saw the outline of the long manor house, from the scent of wood smoke and roasting meat, but as they walked nearer silently they could see chinks of orange light glowing around the edges of the front door.

On the advice of the monk, Sir William deployed most of his men in an arc around this door, but sent six around to the kitchens at the rear of the house.

'They are eating their horses,' said Baron Ivo sniffing the air. 'We will find them with stuffed bellies and asleep in front of a banked-up fire, for they think themselves snug and safe.'

'Then it's time to wake them up,' said Sir William. 'Tell the axe men to knock on their door.'

Baron Ivo drew his own sword as the signal for his men to advance and shouted: 'Awake the house! Wake up in there! Awake to your fate!'

His battle cry was quickly taken up by his men

who rushed through the swirling snow to land their axe-heads on the door of the house. Their shouts of 'Awake! Awake!' rang out even above the splintering of timber and few, if any, heard the monk who had guided them say: 'You will never take Hereward asleep.'

With the door down, Sir William's soldiers poured into the hall of the house one after the other, weapons raised, almost falling over each other, but still shouting 'Wake up! Wake up!' to a seemingly empty house.

Outside in the snow, Sir William, Baron Ivo and the hooded monk saw their men enter the hall as if it was devouring them, save for the last two attempting to squeeze through the shattered doorway. They could even feel the heat and see the orange flames of a roaring fire in the fireplace. But only when it was too late did they see their quarry.

Above the broken door, from the trimmed eaves of the thatched roof, the carpet of snow – which lay thick and even across all the roof except for where the chimney hole smoked – began to slide to earth and slide in the shape of a man, for Hereward had carved himself a bed in the thick thatch and covered himself with a cloak and had then been concealed by the morning's snow.

As he landed on his feet, he shook himself free of cloak and his white skin of snow, his sword in its sheath clutched to his chest. Even though only an arm's length from them, the two soldiers in the doorway were not aware of his presence until he had clubbed first the one and then the other to the ground with his faithful iron-bound scabbard.

'Hereward is always awake when he has enemies to greet!' shouted the hard man of the Fens as he drew his blade and plunged into the house.

'Watch your backs!' cried out Sir William. 'For God's sake get out of there!'

'He is one against twenty,' cursed Baron Ivo. 'This is witchcraft'

'No witchcraft, just Hereward,' said the monk, but his words were lost to the others, drowned by the screams already coming from Bourne Manor.

On that day, if on no other, did Hereward earn the name Berserker, for he fought wildly against great odds in a confined space from which there was no escape. Yet it was not he who was caught but his enemies, for Hereward had turned Bourne Manor into a trap – a fire trap. In every corner of the main hall was piled firewood and kindling, underfoot a thick layer of straw and in the fireplace a banked log fire bursting with flame.

Hereward hacked and swung his firesteel blade, forcing his enemies back on to each other until they were so tightly packed they could not use their own swords and some stumbled and fell into the fireplace, dislodging the logs there, which rolled, still burning, into the straw.

In a heartbeat it seemed as if the whole floor of the hall was afire, and then the piles of kindling began to catch, and smoke and flames began to take the whole house.

Swords in hand, but powerless, Sir William and Baron Ivo looked on with open mouths as the manor house burned and their men began to burn with it or at least those whom Hereward did not kill first.

Through the smoke billowing out of the doorway staggered one Norman trooper, without sword or helmet, his hair alight and blood spurting on to the snow from where his left shoulder had once held his arm in place. Screaming and coughing in equal measure, the man staggered towards his commanders who flinched in fear as they saw a figure loom out of the smoke behind him and with a downward stroke, split the man's skull with his blade.

Sir William and Baron Ivo stared across the dead man's body to his killer and realized that no more than ten feet separated them from the mad eyes of a blood-spattered Hereward.

Both knights raised their swords to the guard position, for they were no cowards, but Hereward had eyes only for the figure in monk's robes who stood with them.

'You!' he shouted, pointing the tip of his sword at the monk. 'Now I remember you; and I curse you!'

Then, with a howl of pure rage, Hereward turned his back on the barons and monk alike and ran back into the blazing house.

[v]

It was said afterwards that twenty-four Norman knights had entered the manor house at Bourne that day and that none had emerged alive, for the roof beams had caught fire and the whole house collapsed.

To that toll must be added the trooper with the

cut throat found later by Baron Ivo's men as they returned to their horses. Not only had one of the guards been killed so silently that his comrades nearby were unaware of his death, but one of their finest mounts was found to be missing.

Sir William de Warenne and Baron Ivo Taillebois never drew their swords in anger again and both died rich old men in their beds. The monk who had betrayed Ely to King William and Hereward in the flames of Bourne returned to his abbey to resign his position as sacrist and to do what penance God allowed for the next thirty years.

Of Martin Lightfoot, there was no sign at Bourne.

In the week after Easter that year, after the snow and ice had melted and the wildfowl had begun to return to the Fenlands, a boat arrived in Ely from Lynne carrying monks from the Abbey of St Bertin in Flanders, escorting the Lady Turfrida.

Brother Godric, who was now dedicated to supporting the sad and chastened Abbot Thurstan in all things, met with Turfrida and showed her the hospitality of the abbey, poor as it now was. With the help of some orphaned boys, for there were few able-bodied men left on Ely, he had her rowed to the Isle of Littleport. It is said that they dug for a whole day in the roots of trees behind the cottage which had once been the home of a famous stilt-walker but found nothing except turned earth.

Godric returned to a life dedicated to God, a life which Turfrida also adopted for she threw herself on the charity of the nunnery at Crowland Abbey, devoting herself to a chaste and pious life until the ripe old age of fifty-three.

The nuns who buried her there at Crowland proclaimed her to have been the finest herbalist known to the abbey.

Of Hereward, little was written which was true but much was whispered and then sung or told in heroic ballads as his legend grew. I am an old man now and all I can do is tell his story as it was, even if no one will read it, or choose to believe it if they did.

That is my penance.

Twenty-One

Giraldus

Brother Thomas needs to work on his endings. He writes of a ferocious battle and the heroic death of Hereward in a manner which would certainly have appealed to the composers of the old Viking sagas and yet he tells the story with overwhelming sadness.

Once again, his book has the ring of truth to it, as if Thomas himself was a part of these events. There are many legends of how Hereward met his end. Some say he was reconciled with his enemy, King William, who granted him the manor of Bourne and even made him a knight! Such a thing is fanciful and there are no records which I can find (and so therefore they do not exist) which mention any 'Sir Hereward, Lord of Bourne'.

393

Others say he returned to Flanders and his wife and became a knight there, but that is unlikely as Flanders would not have succoured an enemy of Normandy in those days. Still others maintain that he and Martin Lightfoot fled to France seeking fame and fortune and were never heard of again, which would not be an unnatural fate for anyone who fled to that sorry country.

Certainly none seem to have heard of Martin Lightfoot again.

There are stories and songs of Hereward sending for Turfrida from Flanders and the two of them living out their lives in Norfolk as farmers, a profession which would seem to suit neither of them. There again, there are stories of Hereward taking a second bride, a Saxon widow, and their producing many children – all daughters – at least one of which was named Turfrida.

But I will stay with Brother Thomas's story of Hereward's end, for there have long been tales of how he met his death in an ambush by twenty-four Norman knights, the very number mentioned in Thomas's book.

I have also confirmed another part of his book, for I have written to Crowland Abbey and, praise be to God, received a prompt reply. The librarian there assures me that there is a grave in the abbey churchyard bearing the mortal remains of a nun known as Turfrida, who served Crowland piously and in all chastity.

Best of all, Thomas has given me inspiration for my own work, my family tree for the officious Baldwin le Wac who now owns Bourne Manor, which is the only work available today for a poor, forgotten historian.

'Hereward is always awake!' he is said to have cried as he attacked his attackers proving, even at the end, the Normans never caught him unaware.

To call him Hereward the Always-Awake is surely a far nobler name for a family tree than Hereward the Outlaw, or Plunderer or Witch-Killer, or any of his other justly deserved titles.

It will not take much skill to persuade Baldwin, who is a man of little learning but much wealth, that 'le Wac' is a Norman derivation of what in Old English would have been "the Wake". I will even show him how it can be written in the Old English; though he cannot even read Latin such is his ignorance.

Thomas's book will need considerable recension and shortening. I will retain much of his work and make great play of Hereward's bravery in the face of large odds, his skill as a commander of men and how he struggled to regain his family property which had been claimed by the Normans, who were once so heroic but now, such are the times, are deeply unfashionable.

I think I will refrain from including his exploits as a plunderer of the holy church, his exploits as a mercenary for foreign kings, his desertion of his men at Ely and the suspicion of his involvement in the murder of Sir William de Warenne's brother-in-law, which surely gave that noble Earl the cause for a blood feud.

Thus I will utilize only a small amount of Thomas's book and conform more to the legend of Hereward than the truth.

I must add a postscript here, for I have *finally* received an answer to all my letters to Ely Abbey.

It comes from the prior there, who tells me in a preamble of the extensive amount of time and effort he has had to expend in the abbey library to answer my simple questions.

Eventually, he gets to the point and tells me that although they have no copy of Brother Thomas's book, their library does have a record that such a book once existed almost one hundred years ago.

Among the scholars and copyists of Ely, it has indeed some fame, for the way in which it was written rather than its content.

The author, Thomas, had entered the brotherhood of Ely from humble origins and with disadvantage of having lost his right hand in some random act of violence in his past. To overcome this disfigurement, Brother Thomas taught himself to write with his left hand and became a skilled copyist and writer of letters for the abbey and in particular for its beloved Abbot Thurstan, conducting abbey business abroad and corresponding with other Benedictine houses throughout the world.

In such high esteem was Thomas held that he was appointed sacrist to Ely Abbey and held such office at the time Ely was infested with Danes and then besieged and sorely taxed by the Normans. Later, he abjured all titles and offices in the abbey and devoted himself to working among the sick and maimed of Ely, or in the distressed fields such as were left in the abbey's possession. From that moment on he was known only as Brother Thomas, though some called him

Sinister because he wrote with his left hand, until he was taken peacefully to Christ in the reign of the first King Henry.

No one at the abbey today can remember ever knowing what Thomas's name was when he entered the monastery but it was thought he had once been a country priest, perhaps in Lincolnshire.

Were my brothers in Ely the slightest bit interested, I could give them the answer: *Oswulf.*

For was it not Oswulf who was so cruelly maimed by Hereward? And could it be that Oswulf, or Thomas as he became, pursued Hereward throughout his time as the Sacrist of Ely? Their fates seemed to have been intertwined at every stage, even if Hereward did not realize it until the end. But to what purpose?

Could it be that Oswulf/Thomas followed Hereward's career with a view to vengeance for the affront to his own person?

If guilty of such a sin of Pride, then writing the book that none would read may indeed have been Brother Thomas's penance.

I shall do my work and re-write his for a stipend paid by a fool.

That will be my penance.

The publishers hope that this book has given you enjoyable reading. Large Print Books are especially designed to be as easy to see and hold as possible. If you wish a complete list of our books please ask at your local library or write directly to:

Magna Large Print Books
Magna House, Long Preston,
Skipton, North Yorkshire.
BD23 4ND

This Large Print Book for the partially sighted, who cannot read normal print, is published under the auspices of

THE ULVERSCROFT FOUNDATION

THE ULVERSCROFT FOUNDATION

... we hope that you have enjoyed this Large Print Book. Please think for a moment about those people who have worse eyesight problems than you ... and are unable to even read or enjoy Large Print, without great difficulty.

You can help them by sending a donation, large or small to:

**The Ulverscroft Foundation,
1, The Green, Bradgate Road,
Anstey, Leicestershire, LE7 7FU,
England.**
or request a copy of our brochure for more details.

The Foundation will use all your help to assist those people who are handicapped by various sight problems and need special attention.

Thank you very much for your help.